minutemeals
20-minute gourmet menus

Edited by Evie Righter

Hungry Minds, Inc.

New York, NY · Cleveland, OH · Indianapolis, IN

Published by

Hungry Minds™

909 Third Avenue
New York, NY 10022

www.hungryminds.com

For general information on Hungry Minds' products and services please contact our Customer Care Department within the U.S. at 800-762-2974, outside the U.S. at 317-572-3993 or fax 317-572-4002.

For sales inquiries and reseller information, including discounts, premium and bulk quantity sales, and foreign-language translations, please contact our Customer Care Department at 800-434-3422, fax 317-572-4002, or write to Hungry Minds, Inc., Attn: Customer Care Department, 10475 Crosspoint Boulevard, Indianapolis, IN 46256.

ISBN: 0-7645-6596-6

Cataloging-in-Publication Data is available upon request from the Library of Congress.

minutemeals

Joe Langhan, President, minutemeals.com Inc.

Miriam Garron, Managing Editor

Miriam Rubin, Consulting Food Editor

Cover design by Amy Trombat

Interior design by Edwin Kuo

Cover photograph © Jonelle Weaver/FPG International/Getty Images

Cover food photography by Carmine Filloramo

Manufactured in the United States of America

10   9   8   7   6   5   4   3   2   1

welcome to our first book!

Many of you may know us from our web site, minutemeals.com, as a source of quick, inspired home cooking with gourmet results. For those new to minutemeals, we'd like to introduce ourselves.

minutemeals.com was created for busy people who still want great food. Of course, you can always order pizza, or open a few cans and heat up dinner, but we suspected that many people wanted more than that—and so, minutemeals was born. In 20 minutes you will have a complete home-cooked meal on the table, including dessert.

how is it possible? We have a talented group of culinary professionals who develop these appealing menus. Their 75 years of combined expertise are brought together to create the very best in a flash. Each chef brings his or her own ideas, tips, and techniques to get it all done in just 20 minutes. With this wealth of talent, dinner becomes a highlight of the day, not a headache.

with each menu, you get personal input from the culinary expert who created it. Sometimes that may mean an insight into how that chef likes to vary the dish, how to serve it, or why the developer decided to make it in the first place. The minutemeals chefs are all listed on page vi.

key to each menu is its gameplan. Don't start cooking until you have read it because it is there to assist you as an organizational tool. How you go about making a minutemeal, the sequence of how you do, affects how long it will take you. The gameplan takes the guesswork out of cooking the meal.

today, everyone is looking for great taste, as well as health-conscious meals. We have an entire chapter of healthy menus that are delectable as well as good for you. Each one has 30% or fewer calories from fat, and follows the guidelines set by the American Heart Association and the American Cancer Association.

it was our dream to give people really good food every night of the week, no matter how busy they may be. As we know from our web site, people are thrilled with minutemeals. Try a few of our menus and see for yourself; 20 minutes is a small investment for a wonderful home-cooked meal.

Evie Righter, *Editor*

minutemeals

20-minute gourmet menus

meet the minutemeals chefs

We'd like you to meet the chefs behind minutemeals, the people whose creativity and ingenuity created the delicious menus in this book. Their combined expertise is our ace in the hole—the secret that keeps our menus fresh, interesting, and full of great ideas. You'll find their helpful comments throughout the book, paired with the menus they created.

Nancy Allen

Carolyn Black

Sharon Bowers

Amanda Cushman

Hillary Davis

Ruth Fisher

Miriam Garron

Joanne Hayes

Connie McCole

Linda Pelaccio

Marge Perry

Paul Picuitto

Katell Plevan

Anne de Ravel

Kyle Shadix

how to use this book

minutemeals is designed to be as efficient as possible. Twenty minutes, after all, is a short amount of time to cook a full meal and place it on the table. For you to be able to do the cooking with as few setbacks as possible, we took care of as many of the time-consuming details as we could to ensure your success. Rely on our system and you will have a delicious dinner on the table in 20 minutes.

Each menu includes a shopping list of the major ingredients needed, as well as a complete list of ingredients we consider standard pantry items. No more hunting through multiple recipes to glean what you need to buy on the way home—we've done that for you. Our "menu gameplan" then shows the sequence of just how to go about cooking the meal—what dish needs to be started first, what should follow, and so on. We've also noted when to preheat the oven or broiler so that it will be sufficiently heated for maximum cooking results. The double-page format of each menu guarantees that when you refer to the cooking directions of any given dish you are always on the "same page."

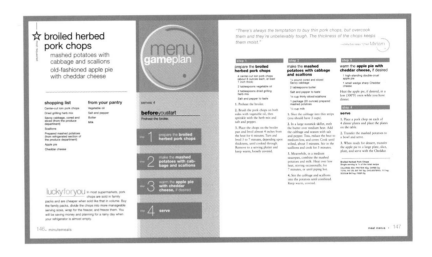

This book offers 150 menus, divided among 6 chapters. We've highlighted which of the menus have scored as "☆ most requested" on our web site. These menus are a great place to start. Then pick and choose from the rest. The menus have remarkable variety, including 20 healthy menus, where the nutrient analysis per serving is for the entire menu, dessert as well.

The minutemeals clock starts ticking when you put the ingredients for a menu on the kitchen counter. The first several times you make a menu expect it to take a few minutes more than you had anticipated: the system itself and the recipes are new to you and, as the saying goes, practice makes perfect. Once you've had the practice, we know that you will find the results delicious . . . and quick.

quick tips from the pros

jacques pépin

plan ahead and save time

when I am able to cook some things ahead of time, I try not to dirty more than one pan. Instead, I rinse my sauté pan immediately and use it to cook the next dish—so I don't end up with a sink full of dirty pots and pans.

i love to put my microwave to use for reheating dishes that I make ahead. Then I can transfer the finished dish right to a serving bowl, and reheat it just before serving. And I also hold finished dishes in a 170- to 180-degree oven; at that temperature, the foods stay warm but don't continue to cook.

i really take advantage of my local supermarket to create a pantry well-stocked with items that have a long shelf-life and require little preparation: Canned beans and high-quality canned tomatoes are obvious examples, but I also use lesser known items like smoked oysters in many dishes.

i also keep my refrigerator well stocked with ingredients that add flavor to dishes without much preparation: Fresh oranges and lemons for zest and juice, scallions, and fresh ginger are just a few of the common supermarket ingredients that I always have on hand.

Master Chef Jacques Pépin, the celebrated host of numerous award-winning cooking shows on national public television—his most recent is *Jacques Pépin Celebrates*—is also a food columnist, cooking teacher, and author of 21 cookbooks, including the classics *La Technique* and *La Methode* (now available as *Jacques Pépin's Complete Techniques*). Jacques is currently the Dean of Special Programs at New York's French Culinary Institute.

graham kerr

healthy food can be fast

don't let food lie around before freezing. It will continue to cook, perhaps ruin a crisp texture. Put the ingredients in a reclosable bag, seal it, and then cool it in very cold water or over ice cubes before freezing.

steaming is swift and so allows only minor leaching of water-soluble nutrients. At the same time it preserves color. I like to use the steamer for fresh fish. I place the fillets (no larger than 6 ounces each) on a plate with appropriate seasonings and steam for 6 to 8 minutes. The trick is to provide easy access to the plate, especially when it's hot and running with precious juices. Be sure your steamer has enough room for an 8-inch pie plate—making a 10-inch diameter optimal.

i believe blenders belong in the swift kitchen. A modern blender really can crush ice, make bread crumbs, reconstitute juice in a flash, "cream" soups, puree vegetables and fruits smooth enough for babies, make dips and batters . . . and on and on.

the blender works especially well for making smooth vegetable sauces. Begin with 1 pound of a raw, unpeeled vegetable like parsnip, carrot, sweet potato, winter squash or peas, new lima beans. Peel, cut roughly and steam it until quite tender, almost overcooked. Now combine approximately $1^1/2$ cups of the cooked vegetable with a 12-ounce can of evaporated skim milk in a blender, cover, and start to process at the lowest speed and build to puree. A good blender will whip through this in only 2 to 3 minutes. Now add $^1/2$ cup of yogurt cheese (yogurt drained in a fine-mesh strainer, or one lined with a coffee filter, overnight in the refrigerator) if you want a creamier puree.

Graham Kerr, who first gained fame as television's *Galloping Gourmet*, has spent the last 23 years refining a healthy cuisine based on sound nutrition and creative cooking. He is the author of many books, including the two-volume *Graham Kerr's Gathering Place*, with recipes from his new PBS series of the same name, *Graham Kerr's Swiftly Seasoned*, *Graham Kerr's Minimax Cookbook*, and *Graham Kerr's Creative Choices Cookbook*. Graham has shared his recipes and philosophy on numerous television series on PBS and The Discovery Channel.

nick malgieri

fast ways to enjoy great desserts

utilize the freezer. Any cake can be frozen before frosting. All you have to do when you want to serve is defrost, fill, and finish.

drier cookies such as biscotti keep well in a tightly closed container at room temperature. You can put a great assortment of cookies together if you start a couple of weeks in advance.

on a Saturday or Sunday, bake a pie or tart; wrap and chill. When ready to serve, reheat for 10 minutes in a 350-degree oven, and cool to room temperature.

Nick Malgieri's cookbooks include the award-winning *Chocolate: From Simple Cookies to Extravagant Showstoppers* and *How to Bake*, as well as *Cookies Unlimited*, *Nick Malgieri's Perfect Pastry*, and *Great Italian Desserts*. The founder of many renowned professional pastry programs, Nick is currently the director of the baking program at New York's Institute of Culinary Education.

minute

20-minute gourmet

main-course soup and salad menus

meals

menus

microwave
black bean soup
with smoked ham

vegetable sticks

corn bread

applesauce with heavy cream and gingersnaps

serves 4

step 1 make the **microwave black bean soup**

step 2 heat the **corn bread**

step 3 plate the **vegetable sticks and garnishes**

step 4 serve

shopping list

Lean reduced-sodium smoked ham or turkey

Black beans

No-salt-added tomato sauce

Corn bread or muffins

Salsa

Sour cream or nonfat plain yogurt

Applesauce

Heavy cream

Gingersnaps

from the salad bar

Vegetable sticks (or from the produce department)

Chopped scallions

from your pantry

Onion

Olive oil

Dried oregano

Cayenne pepper (optional)

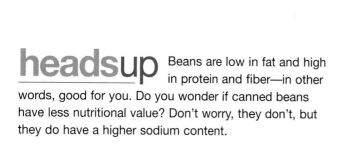 Beans are low in fat and high in protein and fiber—in other words, good for you. Do you wonder if canned beans have less nutritional value? Don't worry, they don't, but they do have a higher sodium content.

"I always used to cook dried beans from scratch. Now I used canned—and the soup still tastes great!"

—minutemeals' Chef Miriam

step 1

make the **microwave black bean soup**

2 ounces lean reduced-sodium smoked ham

1 cup chopped onion (about 1 large onion)

1 teaspoon olive oil

2 cans (16 ounces each) black beans, undrained

1 can (8 ounces) no-salt-added tomato sauce

1/2 teaspoon dried oregano leaves

1/8 teaspoon cayenne pepper (optional)

1. Cube the smoked ham to measure 1/2 cup. Chop enough onion to measure 1 cup.

2. In a 1-quart microwave-safe dish with lid, combine the olive oil and onion. Microwave on High for 1 minute.

3. Stir in the black beans, with their liquid, the tomato sauce, oregano, and cayenne, if using. Cover and microwave on High for 8 to 10 minutes, or until heated through. Remove the dish from the microwave and stir in the ham or turkey.

step 2

heat the **corn bread**

1 package store-bought premade corn bread or muffins

While the soup is cooking, heat the corn bread in a toaster oven until warm.

step 3

plate the **vegetable sticks and garnishes**

Precut vegetable sticks, such as carrots and celery

Fresh or jarred salsa

Sour cream or nonfat plain yogurt

Chopped scallions

1. Place the vegetable sticks in a bowl and put the bowl on the table.

2. Place the soup garnishes in separate bowls and arrange on the table.

step 4

serve

1. Ladle the soup into 4 large bowls and place on the table with the warm corn bread. Top the soup with one or all of the garnishes.

2. When ready for dessert, spoon the applesauce into bowls. Pass the heavy cream separately along with the gingersnaps. Or, crumble some of the gingersnaps over the applesauce before serving, then add the cream.

Microwave Black Bean Soup with Smoked Ham
Single serving is 1/4 of the total recipe

CALORIES 198; PROTEIN 18g; CARBS 42g; TOTAL FAT 4g; SAT FAT 0g; CHOLESTEROL 7mg; SODIUM 156mg; FIBER 13g

pasta e fagioli
(white bean and pasta soup)

caesar salad

oranges and apples with honey

shopping list

Sweet Italian sausage
(optional)

Onion slices
(from the salad bar)

Canned diced tomatoes

Dry white wine

Cannellini beans

Small shaped pasta,
such as elbows

Prewashed romaine lettuce

Caesar salad dressing

Croutons

Oranges

Apples

from your pantry

Garlic

Olive oil or garlic-flavored oil

Dried rosemary

Dried thyme

Fat-free reduced-sodium
chicken broth

Salt and pepper

Honey

Grated Parmesan cheese

menu
gameplan

serves 4

step 1 make the
pasta e fagioli

step 2 assemble the **caesar salad**

step 3 **serve**

headsup

Flavored oil, as in the garlic-flavored oil we suggest for the soup, livens up a dish in a hurry. There are now a host of flavored oils on the market to choose from: rosemary, basil, roasted pepper, and many more. You can use them in any number of ways, on pasta, in salad dressings, for cooking. You could even drizzle some over a bowl of this soup for last-minute flavoring.

"When I tasted this soup, I could not believe it had cooked for only 20 minutes. Fresh herbs and cheese make a big difference."

—minutemeals' Chef Anne

make the *pasta e fagioli*

1 garlic clove (omit if using garlic-flavored oil)

2 tablespoons olive oil or garlic-flavored oil

1/4 pound sweet Italian sausage (optional)

1/4 cup onion slices

1/2 teaspoon dried rosemary, crumbled, or 1 small fresh rosemary sprig

1/2 teaspoon dried thyme or 1 small fresh thyme sprig

1/2 cup canned diced tomatoes

1 cup dry white wine

2 cans (16 ounces each) cannellini beans

2 cans (14 1/2 ounces each) fat-free reduced-sodium chicken broth

Salt and pepper to taste

1/2 cup small shaped pasta, such as elbows

Grated Parmesan cheese, for serving (optional)

1. Finely chop the garlic to measure 1 teaspoon.

2. In a 3-quart saucepan, heat the oil over medium-high heat until hot. Add the sausage, if using, minced garlic (omit if using garlic oil), onions, rosemary, and thyme. Cook, stirring and breaking up the sausage, for 2 minutes. Add the diced tomatoes and cook for 2 minutes.

3. Add the wine and boil for 2 minutes, until reduced by half.

4. Rinse and drain the beans. Add them with the chicken broth to the pan, stir to combine, and season with salt and pepper. Cover and bring to a boil.

5. Stir in the pasta, reduce the heat to medium-low, and partially cover. Simmer gently for 10 to 12 minutes, or until the pasta is tender.

step 2

assemble the **caesar salad**

1 bag (10 ounces) prewashed romaine lettuce

Store-bought Caesar salad dressing to taste

Croutons to taste

Tear the romaine into bite-sized pieces and put in a large salad bowl. Add dressing to taste and toss to coat. Sprinkle croutons generously over the top. Put the bowl on the table, with 4 salad plates for serving.

step 3

serve

1. Ladle the soup into bowls and garnish with grated Parmesan for sprinkling over the top, if desired.

2. When ready for dessert, cut the oranges and apples into wedges and place on a platter. Pour honey into 2 small bowls and place on the table for dipping with the fruit.

Pasta e Fagioli
Single serving is 1/4 of the total recipe
CALORIES 408; PROTEIN 22g; CARBS 44g;
TOTAL FAT 10g; SAT FAT 1g; CHOLESTEROL 18mg;
SODIUM 1621mg; FIBER 11g

gazpacho
baby lettuce and black olive salads
country-style bread
mixed melon chunks with shredded coconut

serves 4

shopping list

Mixed vegetable juice

Salsa

Assorted ripe olives
(from the deli counter)

Prewashed baby lettuces

Precut melon for 4
(from the produce
department)

Shredded coconut

Lime

Country-style bread

from the salad bar

Cucumber slices

Olive oil and garlic croutons
(or packaged)

Green pepper strips

Celery slices

from your pantry

Red wine or cider vinegar

Olive oil

Salad dressing of choice,
store-bought or homemade

beforeyoustart

Place the soup bowls, a large pitcher
or serving bowl for the soup, and salad
plates in the freezer to chill.

| step | 1 | make the **gazpacho;** prepare the **toppings** |

| step | 2 | make the **baby lettuce and black olive salads** |

| step | 3 | prepare the **mixed melon chunks with shredded coconut** |

| step | 4 | **serve** |

 Gazpacho is the perfect
make-ahead recipe,
because it is meant to be served really cold, including the
bowls and pitcher in which it is served. Make the soup
earlier in the day, chill it, and relax. You've just finished
the major part of the menu.

"Don't skimp on the toppings for this refreshing soup—they add wonderful texture and contrast. Have fun with them!"

—minutemeals' Chef Joanne

step 1

make the **gazpacho**; prepare the **toppings**

4 cups (32 ounces) canned mixed vegetable juice, well chilled

3/4 cup salsa, well chilled

1 1/2 cups cucumber slices

1 1/2 cups olive oil and garlic croutons

2 tablespoons red wine or cider vinegar

2 tablespoons olive oil

1/2 cup green pepper strips

1/2 cup celery slices

1. In a blender, combine 2 cups of the vegetable juice, the salsa, 1 cup of the cucumber slices, 1 cup of the croutons, the vinegar, and the olive oil. Blend until smooth.

2. Transfer the soup to the chilled pitcher or serving bowl and stir in the remaining 2 cups of vegetable juice.

3. Prepare the toppings: Finely chop the remaining 1/2 cup cucumber slices, the pepper strips, and the celery slices and put each in a separate bowl. Crumble the remaining 1/2 cup croutons and put in another small bowl. Place all on the table.

step 2

make the **baby lettuce and black olive salads**

1 bag (5 ounces) prewashed baby lettuces

3/4 cup assorted ripe olives

Salad dressing of choice, for drizzling

Divide the lettuce among 4 chilled salad plates. Top each salad with some of the olives, then drizzle with dressing. Place the salads on the table.

step 3

prepare the **mixed melon chunks with shredded coconut**

Precut melon chunks, such as cantaloupe and honeydew, for 4

1/4 cup shredded coconut

1 fresh lime

1. Divide the melon chunks among 4 dessert bowls and place in the refrigerator until serving time.

2. Put the shredded coconut in a bowl.

3. Quarter the lime and reserve.

step 4

serve

1. Place the bread on a bread board, cut it in wedges for serving, and place on the table.

2. Pour or ladle the gazpacho into the chilled bowls and serve at once with any or all of the toppings.

3. When ready for dessert, squeeze the juice of 1 lime wedge over each serving of melon. Serve, with the shredded coconut to be added at the table.

Gazpacho
Single serving is 1/4 of the total recipe
CALORIES 171; PROTEIN 5g; CARBS 20g; TOTAL FAT 9g; SAT FAT 1g; CHOLESTEROL 0mg; SODIUM 1045mg; FIBER 1g

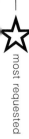
☆ microwave chunky potato soup

marinated vegetable salad
buttermilk biscuits
raspberries and lemon cookies

menu
gameplan

shopping list

Onion

Ready-to-use diced red or other thin-skinned potatoes (in airtight bags in the produce department)

Low-fat sour cream or plain nonfat yogurt

Buttermilk biscuits

Prewashed salad greens of choice for 4

Lemon (for juice)

Raspberries

Lemon cookies

from the salad bar

Chopped scallions or chives

Marinated vegetables of choice (or jarred)

from your pantry

Fat-free reduced-sodium chicken broth

Low-fat (1%) milk

All-purpose flour

Cayenne pepper

Salt and pepper

serves 4

beforeyoustart

Preheat the oven to 350°F to heat the biscuits.

step 1 make the **microwave chunky potato soup**

step 2 heat the **buttermilk biscuits**

step 3 plate the **marinated vegetable salad**

step 4 **serve**

luckyforyou Even the shopping for this menu is easy. Ready-to-use potatoes save an incredible amount of prep time.

"I look forward to this soup almost any time of the year. It's comforting but low-calorie and amazingly quick, thanks to the microwave."

—minutemeals' Chef Miriam

step 1

make the **microwave chunky potato soup**

1 medium onion

1 pound diced red or other thin-skinned potatoes (in airtight bags in the produce department)

1 can (14 1/2 ounces) fat-free reduced-sodium chicken broth

1 1/2 cups low-fat (1%) milk

3 tablespoons all-purpose flour

1/8 teaspoon cayenne pepper

1/4 teaspoon salt

1/4 teaspoon pepper

1/2 cup low-fat sour cream or plain nonfat yogurt

Chopped scallions or snipped chives

1. Chop the onion.

2. In a 2-quart microwave-safe dish or large measuring cup, combine the potatoes and onion. Pour in the chicken broth. Cover and microwave on High for 5 minutes. Stir, cover, and microwave on High for 5 to 8 minutes, until the potatoes are fork-tender.

3. In a bowl, whisk the milk into the flour until smooth.

4. Pour the milk mixture into the soup and add the cayenne. Cover and microwave on High for 3 to 5 minutes, until the soup just starts to bubble and is lightly thickened. Stir in the salt and pepper.

step 2

heat the **buttermilk biscuits**

1 package buttermilk biscuits

Preheat the oven to 350°F. Place the biscuits on a baking sheet and heat until warmed through, about 8 to 10 minutes. Transfer to a bread basket and cover with a napkin to keep warm. Place the basket on the table.

step 3

plate the **marinated vegetable salad**

Prewashed salad greens of choice for 4

1/2 cup each of marinated vegetables of choice (if using jarred, drain and reserve some of the oil)

Juice of 1/2 lemon

Line a platter with the greens and arrange the marinated vegetables on top. Drizzle with a bit of the oil from the vegetables, then squeeze fresh lemon juice over all. Place the platter on the table, with 4 salad plates for serving.

step 4

serve

1. Serve the soup in bowls with a spoonful of sour cream or yogurt and a sprinkling of scallions or chopped chives.

2. When ready for dessert, rinse the berries, shake dry, and serve in bowls. Pass the cookies separately.

Microwave Chunky Potato Soup
Single serving is 1/4 of the total recipe

CALORIES 231; PROTEIN 8g; CARBS 41g; TOTAL FAT 4g; SAT FAT 0g; CHOLESTEROL 10 mg; SODIUM 283 mg; FIBER 4g

ramen noodle soup
with fresh vegetables
california rolls
orange ice with mandarin oranges

shopping list

California rolls or other vegetable sushi (from the refrigerated prepared foods section)

Ramen noodle soup

Canned sliced mushrooms

Mandarin oranges

Orange ice

from the salad bar

Snow peas

Broccoli florets (or from the produce department)

Grated carrots (or from the produce department)

Chopped scallions

from your pantry

Lite soy sauce

Pepper

Toasted sesame oil

serves 4

beforeyoustart

Place the mandarin oranges in the freezer to chill. Bring the water to a boil in a large saucepan, covered, over medium-high heat for the soup.

step **1** plate the **california rolls**

step **2** make the **ramen noodle soup with fresh vegetables**

step **3** **serve**

 There is almost always a variety of egg rolls in the frozen foods section of most supermarkets. Keep some in your freezer and serve them in place of the California rolls in this menu.

"I love Chinese soups and this one is a great meal-in-a-bowl. We have a name for it: 'the slurp supper.'"

—minutemeals' Chef Miriam

step 1

plate the **california rolls**

2 packages (6 rolls per package) California rolls or other vegetable sushi

Lite soy sauce

1. Arrange the California rolls or sushi on a plate and place on the table.

2. Pour soy sauce into a shallow bowl and place on the table for serving with California rolls or sushi.

step 2

make the **ramen noodle soup with fresh vegetables**

4 cups water

1 cup stringed snow peas

1 cup trimmed broccoli florets

1 cup grated carrots

2 packages (3 ounces each) ramen noodle soup, your favorite flavor

1 can (4 ounces) sliced mushrooms

Pepper to taste (optional)

About 1/4 cup chopped scallions

Toasted sesame oil (optional)

1. In a large saucepan, bring the water to a boil, covered, over medium-high heat. Rinse the snow peas.

2. When the water boils, add the broccoli and cook, stirring, for 1 minute. Add the carrots and ramen noodles and cook, stirring, for 2 minutes. Drain the mushrooms and add them with the snow peas to the pan and bring back to a boil. Simmer, stirring, for 1 minute, or until the noodles are just tender. (This will vary depending upon the brand of soup used.)

3. Remove the pan from the heat and stir in the flavor packets and pepper, if desired.

step 3

serve

1. Ladle the soup into 4 wide bowls and sprinkle each with chopped scallions. If desired, add a drop or two of toasted sesame oil to each bowl before serving.

2. When ready for dessert, drain the mandarin oranges. Scoop the orange ice into small bowls and garnish with the orange sections. Serve.

Ramen Noodle Soup with Fresh Vegetables
Single serving is 1/4 of the total recipe
CALORIES 201; PROTEIN 6g; CARBS 28g;
TOTAL FAT 7g; SAT FAT 3g; CHOLESTEROL 0mg;
SODIUM 849mg; FIBER 4g

tortellini in broth
with baby spinach and beans

roasted red pepper and smoked mozzarella salads

seeded italian bread

poached dried fruit compote

shopping list

Cheese tortellini, frozen or fresh

Apple juice

Mixed dried fruits

Small white beans

Prewashed baby spinach leaves or escarole, kale, or beet greens

Jarred roasted red or yellow peppers

Smoked or fresh mozzarella

Seeded Italian bread

from your pantry

Salt and pepper

Olive oil

Brown sugar

Ground cinnamon

Ground cloves

Garlic

Fat-free reduced-sodium chicken broth

Dried sage

Vinaigrette dressing, store-bought or homemade

serves 4

beforeyoustart

Bring the water to a boil in a large pot, covered, over high heat.

step 1   cook the **tortellini**

step 2   poach the **dried fruits**

step 3   make the **broth with baby spinach and beans**

step 4   assemble the **salads**

step 5   **serve**

headsup
Remember that after the tortellini are initially cooked, they cook again—it's only a mini cook, we know, but it counts. Be careful not to overcook them the first time or they'll be soft and maybe even fall apart when the soup is done.

"This menu is simple, but good, with lots of bright flavors and textures. There's always room for simple, when it's good."

—minutemeals' Chef Hillary

step 1
cook the **tortellini**

4 quarts water

Salt to taste

1 package (9 ounces) frozen or fresh cheese tortellini

2 teaspoons olive oil

1. Pour the water into a pasta pot. Add salt to taste, cover, and bring to a boil over high heat. Add the tortellini, stir, reduce the heat to a simmer, and cook until the tortellini float to the top, about 5 to 7 minutes for frozen tortellini, 2 to 5 minutes for fresh.

2. Drain the tortellini, rinse under cold water to stop the cooking, and return to the pot. Toss with the olive oil to prevent sticking. Cover loosely with plastic wrap and let stand at room temperature.

step 2
poach the **dried fruits**

1/2 cup apple juice

1/2 cup water

1 tablespoon brown sugar

1/4 teaspoon ground cinnamon

Pinch of ground cloves

8 ounces mixed dried fruits

In a medium saucepan, bring the apple juice, water, brown sugar, and spices to a boil over medium heat. Add the dried fruits. Simmer until softened, about 10 minutes. Let stand until serving time.

step 3
make the **broth with baby spinach and beans**

1 can (16 ounces) small white beans

4 garlic cloves

2 cans (14 1/2 ounces each) fat-free reduced-sodium chicken broth

1 cup water

1 teaspoon dried sage, crumbled

3 cups prewashed baby spinach leaves or escarole, kale, or beet greens, washed and chopped

1. Rinse and drain the white beans. Finely chop the garlic.

2. In a large saucepan, combine the garlic, chicken broth, water, and sage, cover, and bring to a boil over high heat.

3. Add the spinach and beans, reduce the heat to medium-low, and cover partially. Simmer until the spinach is tender, about 3 to 5 minutes.

step 4
assemble the **salads**

1 jar (12 ounces) roasted red or yellow peppers

1/2 pound smoked or fresh mozzarella

1/4 cup vinaigrette dressing

Salt and pepper to taste

1. Drain the roasted peppers and slice 1/2 inch thick. Thinly slice the mozzarella.

2. Divide the peppers and mozzarella among 4 salad plates, alternating the slices. Drizzle vinaigrette over each and season with the salt and pepper. Place on the table.

step 5
serve

1. Stir the tortellini into the seasoned broth and simmer for 1 minute, or until heated through.

2. Put the Italian bread on a cutting board with a serrated knife and place on the table.

3. Ladle the soup into 4 large bowls and serve immediately.

4. When ready for dessert, serve the poached fruit in small bowls, with some of the poaching liquid spooned on top.

Tortellini in Broth with Baby Spinach and Beans
Single serving is 1/4 of the total recipe
CALORIES 226; PROTEIN 10g; CARBS 38g; TOTAL FAT 4g; SAT FAT 0g; CHOLESTEROL 4mg; SODIUM 495mg; FIBER 6g

☆ fresh vegetable soup

apple berry salad
sesame cheese toasts
chocolate cherry ice cream

shopping list

Zucchini
Ripe tomatoes
Fresh thyme
Prepared pesto
Small loaf Italian bread
Jarlsberg cheese
Sesame seeds
Fresh berries
Golden Delicious apple
Chocolate cherry ice cream

from the salad bar

Mushroom slices (or from the produce department)
Carrot slices
Celery slices
Chopped scallions
Boston lettuce leaves

from your pantry

Olive oil
Vegetable or fat-free reduced-sodium chicken broth
Ground cumin
Salt and pepper
Vinaigrette dressing, store-bought or homemade

luckyforyou

There's an easy solution if the prospect of making individual sesame toasts is more than you can manage: Make Parmesan bread. Halve the Italian bread horizontally, brush both sides with olive oil, sprinkle with grated Parmesan, and toast until golden.

menu gameplan

serves 4 to 6

step 1 make the **fresh vegetable soup**

step 2 make the **sesame cheese toasts**

step 3 make the **apple berry salad**

step 4 **serve**

"I can spend days developing recipes and on those nights dinner just has to be simple. This soup menu really is. Plus, I love all the fresh vegetables."

—minutemeals' Chef Joanne

step 1
make the **fresh vegetable soup**

- 1 medium zucchini
- 2 large ripe tomatoes
- 1 tablespoon olive oil
- 1/2 cup mushroom slices
- 1/2 cup carrot slices
- 1/2 cup celery slices
- 1/2 cup chopped scallions
- 2 cans (14 1/2 ounces each) vegetable or fat-free reduced-sodium chicken broth
- 1 teaspoon ground cumin
- 3/4 teaspoon fresh thyme leaves or 1/4 teaspoon dried
- Salt and pepper to taste
- 2 tablespoons prepared pesto

1. Halve the zucchini lengthwise and slice into 1/4-inch-thick pieces. Coarsely chop the tomatoes.

2. In a large heavy saucepan or Dutch oven, heat the oil over medium-high heat until hot. Add the mushrooms, carrots, celery, and scallions, and cook for 3 to 4 minutes, stirring constantly, until the vegetables start to brown.

3. Add the zucchini slices, chopped tomatoes, broth, cumin, thyme, and salt and pepper. Cover the pot and bring the mixture to a boil; cook for 5 minutes, or until the vegetables are tender. (If desired, add water to the soup to restore any liquid that has cooked off.)

step 2
make the **sesame cheese toasts**

- 1 small loaf Italian bread
- 1/2 cup shredded Jarlsberg cheese
- 1 tablespoon olive oil
- 2 teaspoons sesame seeds

1. Cut the loaf of Italian bread into 10 slices. Wrap and reserve end slices for another use. Shred enough cheese to measure 1/2 cup.

2. Brush one side of each piece of bread with some of the olive oil. Sprinkle the shredded cheese and sesame seeds over the slices. Toast in a toaster oven, in batches if necessary, just until the cheese bubbles and the seeds begin to brown, about 5 minutes. Transfer to a serving plate and place on the table.

step 3
make the **apple berry salad**

- 1 cup mixed fresh berries, such as raspberries and blueberries
- 1 Golden Delicious apple
- 1/4 cup vinaigrette dressing
- 3 cups Boston lettuce leaves

1. Rinse and drain the berries. Rinse and core the apple and coarsely chop it. Combine the berries, apple, and vinaigrette in a medium bowl.

2. Divide the lettuce among 4 salad plates. Top with the fruit mixture. Place on the table.

step 4
serve

1. Swirl the pesto into the soup just before serving. Ladle the soup into 4 large soup bowls, and serve at once with the cheese toasts and accompanying salads.

2. When ready for dessert, scoop the ice cream into small bowls. Serve.

Fresh Vegetable Soup
Single serving is 1/4 of the total recipe
CALORIES 150; PROTEIN 5g; CARBS 9g;
TOTAL FAT 11g; SAT FAT 1g; CHOLESTEROL 4mg;
SODIUM 131mg; FIBER 3g

beef and vegetable soup

green salad with pears
warm sourdough rolls
hot fudge sundaes

shopping list

Chopped onion
(frozen or from the salad bar)

Presliced mushrooms
(from the produce department)

Frozen mixed vegetables

Rare roast beef, sliced
(from the deli counter)

Walnut pieces

Ripe Bartlett or Bosc pear

Prewashed mixed spring or
baby greens

Sourdough rolls

Vanilla ice cream

Hot fudge sauce

Whipped cream

from your pantry

Butter

Reduced-sodium beef broth

Dried thyme

Salt and pepper

Low-fat (2%) milk

Cornstarch

Dry sherry (optional)

Vinaigrette dressing,
store-bought or homemade

Freshly ground black pepper

serves 4

beforeyoustart

Preheat the oven to 350°F to toast the walnuts and heat the rolls. Place the jar of fudge sauce in a pan of very hot water and let stand while you have dinner.

step **1** make the **beef and vegetable soup**

step **2** while the soup is simmering, assemble the **green salad with peas**

step **3** heat the **sourdough rolls**

step **4** **serve**

luckyforyou Prewashed salad greens are available in all kinds of different combinations. If the baby greens don't look fresh to you, choose a European or Italian blend. Don't buy a head of lettuce—you won't have the time to prepare it.

"Not inclined to buy rare roast beef? This soup will be better if you do—the beef cooks when it's added to the soup."

—minutemeals' Chef Miriam

step 1

make the **beef and vegetable soup**

2 tablespoons butter

1 cup chopped onion

1 box (8 ounces) presliced mushrooms

1 can (14 1/2 ounces) reduced-sodium beef broth

1/2 teaspoon dried thyme

Salt and pepper to taste

1 cup low-fat (2%) milk

1 tablespoon cornstarch

1 package (10 ounces) frozen mixed vegetables

6 ounces rare roast beef, cut into 1/4-inch thick strips

1 tablespoon dry sherry (optional)

1. In a 3-quart saucepan, melt the butter over medium-high heat. Add the onion and mushrooms and cook, stirring occasionally, for 2 minutes. Stir in the beef broth, thyme, and salt and pepper and bring to a boil over high heat. Reduce the heat and simmer, stirring occasionally, for 10 minutes.

2. Meanwhile, stir the milk into the cornstarch until well blended.

3. Stir the milk mixture into the soup and simmer, stirring, for 3 minutes. Add the mixed vegetables and cook another 3 minutes.

4. Stir in the roast beef and cook until heated through. Stir in the sherry, if desired, and season with salt and pepper. Remove the pan from the heat.

step 2

while the soup is simmering, assemble the **green salad with pears**

1/2 cup walnut pieces

1 ripe large pear, such as Bartlett or Bosc

1 bag (5 ounces) mixed spring or baby greens

1/4 cup vinaigrette dressing

Freshly ground black pepper to taste

1. Preheat the oven to 350°F. Spread the walnuts on a small baking sheet. Toast until lightly colored and fragrant, 6 to 8 minutes. Remove and let cool.

2. Rinse the pear, halve, and core it. Cut into 1/2-inch pieces.

3. In a large salad bowl, combine the salad greens with the dressing. Add the walnuts and pear and toss. Divide the salad among 4 salad plates and grind fresh pepper over each. Place on the table.

step 3

heat the **sourdough rolls**

4 sourdough rolls

Place the rolls on a small baking sheet and heat in the already heated oven for 5 minutes, or until warmed through.

step 4

serve

1. Ladle the soup into 4 bowls and serve.

2. When ready for dessert, scoop vanilla ice cream into 4 sundae glasses. Spoon some of the hot fudge sauce over each and top with whipped cream. Serve, with additional fudge sauce, if desired.

Beef and Vegetable Soup
Single serving is 1/4 of the total recipe
CALORIES 314; PROTEIN 20g; CARBS 19g; TOTAL FAT 17g; SAT FAT 4g; CHOLESTEROL 67mg; SODIUM 252mg; FIBER 4g

gingery chicken vegetable soup
with tofu

mixed greens vinaigrette

french bread

orange wedges and fortune cookies

menu gameplan

serves 4

step	1	make the **gingery chicken vegetable soup with tofu**
step	2	make the **mixed greens vinaigrette**
step	3	**serve**

shopping list

Chinese cabbage

Watercress

Shiitake mushrooms

Gingerroot

Firm tofu

Boneless skinless chicken breast cut for stir-fry

Prewashed mixed salad greens

French bread

Oranges

Fortune cookies

from the salad bar

Chopped scallions

Thinly sliced red pepper strips

from your pantry

Fat-free reduced-sodium chicken broth

Rice vinegar

Lite soy sauce

Olive oil

Red wine vinegar

Salt and pepper

headsup In most supermarkets now, there is typically a selection of tofu that includes firm, soft, and spiced. They are not interchangeable; you want the firm for this soup. Remove the tofu from the package, dice it, and add it to the soup. If you have tofu left over, store it in water to cover in a bowl in the refrigerator or it will dry out. Be sure to change the water daily.

"I like tofu a lot, but for those who don't, add thin-cut fresh noodles instead. Capellini works, and so do Chinese-style noodles."

—minutemeals' Chef Amanda

step 1

make the **gingery chicken vegetable soup with tofu**

2 cans (14 1/2 ounces each) fat-free reduced-sodium chicken broth

1 large wedge Chinese cabbage

1 bunch watercress

1/4 pound shiitake mushrooms

2 tablespoons grated fresh ginger

1/4 cup chopped scallions

1 generous cup thinly sliced red pepper strips

3 to 4 ounces firm tofu

1/2 pound boneless skinless chicken breast cut for stir-fry

1 tablespoon rice vinegar

3 tablespoons lite soy sauce

1. Pour the chicken broth into a large saucepan, cover, and bring to a boil over high heat.

2. Meanwhile, shred the cabbage. Rinse and stem the watercress. Stem and thinly slice the shiitake mushrooms. Grate enough ginger to measure 2 tablespoons.

3. When the broth boils, add the cabbage, mushrooms, scallions, ginger, and pepper strips. Cover and simmer for 5 minutes.

4. Drain the tofu and cut it into small cubes.

5. Add the chicken to the soup, cover, and simmer for 5 minutes. Stir in the watercress, rice vinegar, soy sauce, and tofu. Simmer for 5 minutes, or until the tofu is heated through.

step 2

make the **mixed greens vinaigrette**

1 bag (5 ounces) prewashed mixed salad greens

3 tablespoons olive oil

1 1/2 tablespoons red wine vinegar

Salt and pepper to taste

Put the greens in a salad bowl, add the olive oil, vinegar, and salt and pepper, and toss. Place the bowl on the table, with 4 salad plates for serving.

step 3

serve

1. Ladle the soup into 4 large soup bowls and serve.

2. Slice the bread, place in a bread basket, and serve.

3. When ready for dessert, cut the oranges into wedges and serve on a platter with the fortune cookies alongside.

Gingery Chicken Vegetable Soup with Tofu
Single serving is 1/4 of the total recipe
CALORIES 158; PROTEIN 21g; CARBS 11g; TOTAL FAT 4g; SAT FAT 0g; CHOLESTEROL 35mg; SODIUM 438mg; FIBER 1g

stacked mexican chicken soup
cheese and chile quesadillas
chocolate ice cream roll

serves 4 to 6 generously

shopping list

Ripe tomato

Lime

Kidney or pinto beans

Skinless boneless chicken breast halves

Frozen corn

Ripe avocado

Salsa

Cilantro sprigs

Flour tortillas (7-inch diameter)

Pre-grated Monterey Jack or Cheddar cheese

Chocolate ice cream roll

from the salad bar

Prewashed romaine leaves

Sliced green olives

Sliced black olives

from your pantry

Fat-free reduced-sodium chicken broth

Olive oil spray

Canned diced green chiles or green tomatillo salsa

beforeyoustart

Preheat the oven to 450°F to bake the quesadillas.

step 1 make the **stacked mexican chicken soup**

step 2 make the **cheese and chile quesadillas**

step 3 serve

 With the exception of only a few fresh ingredients, the makings of this soup are almost all standard pantry or freezer staples, which makes this a fantastic last-minute meal.

"This is a versatile fiesta! You can make this soup with chicken breast, skinless turkey breast, and even lean ground turkey."

—minutemeals' Chef Nancy

make the **stacked mexican chicken soup**

1 large ripe tomato

1 lime

1 can (16 ounces) kidney or pinto beans

1 pound skinless boneless chicken breast halves

6 cups fat-free reduced-sodium chicken broth

1 cup frozen corn

4 to 6 prewashed romaine leaves

1/2 to 3/4 cup sliced green olives

1/2 to 3/4 cup sliced black olives

1 ripe avocado

1 cup store-bought salsa

1/2 cup loosely packed cilantro sprigs

1. Core the tomato and cut into 1/2-inch cubes. Cut the lime into 4 or 6 wedges. Rinse and drain the beans. Cut the chicken breasts into 1/2-inch cubes.

2. Pour the chicken broth into a large saucepan, cover, and bring to a boil over high heat. Add the chicken, tomato, and beans and bring to a boil. Lower the heat and simmer the soup until the chicken is cooked through, about 4 to 6 minutes. Add the corn and remove the pan from the heat.

3. Finely shred the romaine leaves and pile on a platter. Peel, pit, and chop the avocado. Add the green and black olives, avocado, and lime wedges to the platter. Place the salsa in a bowl. Place the platter and salsa on the table.

4. Coarsely chop the cilantro sprigs to measure 1/2 cup.

step 2

make the **cheese and chile quesadillas**

Olive oil spray

4 to 6 flour tortillas (7-inch diameter)

6 to 8 ounces pre-grated Monterey Jack or Cheddar cheese

1 can (4 ounces) diced green chiles or green tomatillo salsa

1. Preheat the oven to 450°F. Coat 1 or 2 cookie sheets with olive oil spray.

2. One at a time, sprinkle some of the cheese and chiles or a spoonful of the salsa over one side of each tortilla. Fold the other side over to cover the topping; mist the top of the tortilla lightly with spray and transfer to the prepared cookie sheets. Bake for about 5 minutes, or until the cheese is melted. Transfer the quesadillas to a warm platter and place on the table.

step 3

serve

1. Reheat the soup mixture to boiling, if necessary, and stir in the chopped cilantro. Ladle the soup into 4 large soup bowls.

2. Invite each diner to add their favorite ingredients on the platter to their soup, stacking them, if desired. Season with a squeeze of fresh lime juice.

3. When ready for dessert, cut the ice cream roll into slices and serve on dessert plates.

Stacked Mexican Chicken Soup
Single serving is 1/4 of the total recipe
CALORIES 477; PROTEIN 38g; CARBS 44g; TOTAL FAT 18g; SAT FAT 2g; CHOLESTEROL 66mg; SODIUM 1772mg; FIBER 7g

turkey chowder

beets vinaigrette on mixed greens
corn bread
pumpkin pie with ice cream sauce

serves 4

shopping list

Roasted turkey breast

Red or white thin-skinned potatoes (available in airtight bags in the produce department)

Frozen corn

Light or heavy cream

Corn bread

Prewashed mixed spring or baby greens

Pumpkin pie

Vanilla ice cream

from the salad bar

Onion slices

Celery sticks (or from the produce department)

Sliced beets (or jarred)

from your pantry

Fat-free reduced-sodium chicken broth

Butter

Dried thyme or dried herb seasoning blend

Salt and pepper

Cornstarch

Vinaigrette dressing, store-bought or homemade

beforeyoustart

Preheat the oven to 300°F. Remove the vanilla ice cream from the freezer to melt.

step 1 make the **turkey chowder**

step 2 heat the **corn bread**

step 3 prepare the **beets vinaigrette on mixed greens**

step 4 **serve**

headsup

If you let the chowder boil after you've added the cream, it will curdle, which is not something you want to happen. Cook the chowder only until the turkey is heated through, then, to be on the safe side, remove the pan from the heat.

"Many people are scared off at the thought of making chowder, but it's not complicated at all, and it feels 'special'—informal but grand."

—minutemeals' Chef Anne

make the **turkey chowder**

1 pound roasted turkey breast

1 cup onion slices

1 cup celery sticks

2 cans (14 1/2 ounces each) fat-free reduced-sodium chicken broth

2 tablespoons butter

2 to 2 1/2 cups diced red or white thin-skinned potatoes

1/2 teaspoon dried thyme or dried herb seasoning blend

Salt and pepper to taste

1 package (10 ounces) frozen corn

2 tablespoons cornstarch

1 cup light or heavy cream

1. Remove the skin from the turkey breast and cut enough of the meat into 1/2-inch chunks to measure 2 1/2 cups. Roughly chop the sliced onions and celery.

2. Pour the chicken broth into a 4-cup microwave-safe glass measure. Microwave on High for 3 minutes, until hot.

3. In a large heavy saucepan, melt the butter over medium heat. Add the chopped onions and celery and cook, stirring, for 3 minutes.

4. Add the hot broth, potatoes, thyme, and salt and pepper and bring to a boil over high heat. Stir in the frozen corn and cover. Bring to a boil, reduce the heat to medium-high, and simmer for 5 minutes.

5. Meanwhile, in a bowl, stir the cornstarch into the cream until blended. Add to the pan and stir until lightly thickened. Add the turkey and season with salt and pepper. Simmer, stirring frequently, until the turkey is heated through, about 2 minutes. Do not let the chowder boil.

step 2

heat the **corn bread**

1 package premade corn bread

Preheat the oven to 300°F. Place the corn bread on a baking sheet and place in the oven until heated through.

step 3

prepare the **beets vinaigrette on mixed greens**

1 bag (5 ounces) prewashed mixed spring or baby greens

1 cup sliced beets, drained

1/4 cup vinaigrette dressing

Divide the greens among 4 salad plates. Arrange some of the beets on top and drizzle with dressing.

step 4

serve

1. Ladle the chowder into 4 large soup bowls and serve with the warm corn bread.

2. When ready for dessert, cut the pie into slices and pour some of the melted ice cream over the top. Or spoon a pool of the ice cream sauce on each plate and set a slice of the pie down in it.

Turkey Chowder
Single serving is 1/4 of the total recipe
CALORIES: 566; PROTEIN 34g; CARBS 46g;
TOTAL FAT 31g; SAT FAT 12g; CHOLESTEROL 123mg;
SODIUM 1133mg; FIBER 5g

new england seafood chowder

tossed salad with cherry tomatoes

strawberries with balsamic vinegar

menu gameplan

shopping list

Red potatoes

Carrots

Celery

Lemon (for zest)

Fresh flat-leaf parsley

Cod or scrod fillets

Bay scallops

Oyster crackers

Prewashed salad greens

Strawberries

from the salad bar

Chopped scallions

Cherry tomatoes

from your pantry

Low-fat (2%) milk

All-purpose flour

Canola oil

Fat-free reduced-sodium chicken broth

Salt and pepper

Tabasco sauce

Vinaigrette dressing, store-bought or homemade

Balsamic vinegar

Dark brown sugar

serves 4 to 6

step 1 make the **new england seafood chowder**

step 2 assemble the **tossed salad with cherry tomatoes**

step 3 prepare the **strawberries with balsamic vinegar**

step 4 **serve**

luckyforyou

Bay scallops are almost always available and are substantially less expensive than sea scallops. If sea scallops are all that is available when you want to make this, consider doubling the amount of cod and omitting the scallops altogether.

"I set out to develop a chowder that made good sense nutritionally. This chowder isn't loaded with fat, and it still tastes delicious."

—minutemeals' Chef Tina

step 1

make the **new england seafood chowder**

- 3 small red potatoes
- 2 medium carrots
- 1 large celery stalk
- 1 tablespoon lemon zest (1 large lemon)
- 2 tablespoons finely chopped flat-leaf parsley
- 1/2 pound cod or scrod fillets
- 3 1/4 cups low-fat (2%) milk
- 3 tablespoons all-purpose flour
- 2 tablespoons canola oil
- 1 can (14 1/2 ounces) fat-free reduced-sodium chicken broth
- 1/2 pound bay scallops
- 1/3 cup chopped scallions
- Salt and pepper to taste
- Tabasco sauce to taste
- Oyster crackers, for serving

1. Scrub and dice the potatoes. Finely chop the carrots and celery. Grate enough of the lemon zest to measure 1 tablespoon. Finely chop enough parsley to measure 2 tablespoons.

2. Cut the fish fillets into 1/2-inch pieces.

3. In a 4-cup microwave-safe container, microwave the milk on High until hot.

4. In a 4-quart saucepan, mix the flour and canola oil over medium heat, stirring, until a smooth paste forms. Add the hot milk and chicken broth and whisk until smooth. Add the potatoes, carrots, and celery. Bring to a boil, stirring often, and cover. Simmer about 10 minutes, until the vegetables are tender.

5. Add the cod, scallops, scallions, parsley, and lemon zest, and season with salt and pepper. Cover and simmer until the fish is cooked through, 2 to 4 minutes. Stir in Tabasco to taste. Remove the pan from the heat and keep warm, partially covered.

step 2

assemble the **tossed salad with cherry tomatoes**

- 5 ounces prewashed salad greens of choice
- 1 cup cherry tomatoes
- Vinaigrette dressing

1. Put the salad greens in a large salad bowl.

2. Rinse the cherry tomatoes and pat dry. Scatter the tomatoes over the greens, drizzle with vinaigrette, and toss. Place on the table, with 4 salad plates for serving.

step 3

prepare the **strawberries with balsamic vinegar**

- 1 pint strawberries
- Balsamic vinegar to taste
- Dark brown sugar, for serving

1. Rinse the strawberries and hull them. Slice in half if large. Place the strawberries in a serving bowl or individual wine glasses and drizzle with balsamic vinegar to taste.

2. Place the brown sugar in a bowl.

step 4

serve

1. Ladle the hot chowder into large soup bowls. Serve the oyster crackers separately, for sprinkling over the chowder.

2. When ready for dessert, place the berries and brown sugar on the table, with 4 small bowls for serving.

New England Seafood Chowder
Single serving is 1/5 of the total recipe
CALORIES 273; PROTEIN 24g; CARBS 21g;
TOTAL FAT 10g; SAT FAT 2g; CHOLESTEROL 46mg;
SODIUM 204mg; FIBER 2g

corn and seafood chowder

garlic bread

cucumber and boston lettuce salad

pears with vanilla ice cream and hot fudge sauce

menu gameplan

shopping list

Canned no-salt-added stewed tomatoes

Low-sodium tomato juice

Fresh cod, scrod, or halibut fillets

Medium shrimp, peeled and deveined

Frozen corn

Fresh parsley (optional)

Ready-to-heat garlic bread

Canned pear halves

Vanilla ice cream

Hot fudge sauce

from the salad bar

Carrot slices

Celery slices

Chopped scallions

Boston lettuce leaves

Cucumber slices

from your pantry

Olive oil

Dried thyme

Salt and pepper

Salad dressing of choice, store-bought or homemade

serves 4 to 6

beforeyoustart

Chill the pears. Place the jar of fudge sauce in a bowl of hot water to soften.

step 1 make the **corn and seafood chowder**

step 2 heat the **garlic bread**

step 3 assemble the **cucumber and boston lettuce salad**

step 4 **serve**

headsup

Both low-sodium tomato juice and no-salt-added stewed tomatoes are called for in the chowder recipe. They keep a lid on the sodium count per serving.

"I think this menu would be terrific for an intimate dinner for 6 or 8. All you'd have to do is double each recipe."

—minutemeals' Chef Joanne

make the **corn and seafood chowder**

1 tablespoon olive oil

1/2 cup carrot slices

1/2 cup celery slices

1/2 cup chopped scallions

2 cans (14 1/2 ounces each) no-salt-added stewed tomatoes

2 cups low-sodium tomato juice

1/4 teaspoon dried thyme or 3/4 teaspoon fresh thyme leaves

Salt and pepper to taste

1 pound cod, scrod, or halibut fillets

1/2 pound peeled and deveined medium shrimp

1 package (10 ounces) frozen corn

2 tablespoons minced parsley (optional)

1. In a large saucepan or Dutch oven, heat the olive oil over medium-high heat until hot. Add the carrots, celery, and scallions and cook, stirring, for 2 minutes.

2. Add the stewed tomatoes, tomato juice, thyme, and salt and pepper. Bring the mixture to a boil.

3. While the chowder is heating, rinse the fish, pat it dry, and cut into 1 1/2-inch chunks. Add the fish, shrimp, and corn to the soup, return the mixture just to the boil, and simmer for 2 minutes, or until the seafood is cooked through. Take care not to overcook the seafood. Remove the pan from the heat.

4. Stir the parsley, if using, into the soup and adjust the seasonings.

step 2

heat the **garlic bread**

1 ready-to-heat garlic bread

Heat the garlic bread according to the directions on the bread wrapper.

step 3

assemble the **cucumber and boston lettuce salad**

3 cups Boston lettuce leaves

1 cup cucumber slices

Salad dressing of choice

Place the lettuce in a salad bowl, add the cucumbers and dressing, and toss. Place the bowl on the table, with 4 salad plates for serving.

step 4

serve

1. Ladle the chowder into deep bowls and serve at once.

2. Place the hot garlic bread on a bread board and place on the table.

3. When ready for dessert, place a drained pear half in each dessert bowl, and top with a small scoop of vanilla ice cream and some hot fudge sauce. Serve at once.

Corn and Seafood Chowder
Single serving is 1/5 of the total recipe
CALORIES 296; PROTEIN 29g; CARBS 26g;
TOTAL FAT 8g; SAT FAT 1g; CHOLESTEROL 108mg;
SODIUM 190mg; FIBER 6g

greek salad

stuffed vine leaves

pita triangles with hummus

chilled plums and bananas
with vanilla yogurt

shopping list

Romaine lettuce hearts

Feta cheese, plain or
tomato-basil, flavored

Pitted kalamata olives

Low-fat Greek-style
vinaigrette dressing

Tomatoes

Pita pockets

Hummus

Prepared stuffed vine leaves

Plums in heavy syrup

Ripe bananas

Vanilla yogurt or
light sour cream

from the salad bar

Red onion slices

Green pepper rings

from your pantry

Salt and pepper

luckyforyou Even the shopping for this
menu is easy. Stuffed vine
leaves, also called stuffed grape leaves, can be found
in cans or jars in the specialty foods section, hummus in
the refrigerated case. Make a quick stop in the produce
department and at the salad bar, and you're done.

serves 4

beforeyoustart

Preheat the oven to 400°F to heat the
pita. Chill the canned plums.

step **1** make the **greek salad**

step **2** heat the **pita triangles**

step **3** plate the **hummus** and
stuffed vine leaves

step **4** assemble the **dessert**

step **5** **serve**

"Though easy to make from scratch, hummus comes in many flavors at the supermarket. I say, when it's hot, take it easy and shop."

—minutemeals' Chef Hillary

step 1
make the **greek salad**

1 bag (12 ounces) hearts of romaine lettuce

4 ounces crumbled plain or tomato-basil-flavored feta cheese

1/2 cup pitted kalamata olives

1/2 cup thin red onion slices

2 cups green pepper rings

1/4 cup low-fat Greek-style store-bought vinaigrette dressing

2 ripe tomatoes

Salt and pepper to taste, for serving

1. Cut the hearts of romaine lettuce into 1-inch pieces. Put the lettuce in a salad spinner, rinse under cold running water, and spin dry.

2. In a large salad bowl, place the crumbled feta, olives, onion, pepper rings, and vinaigrette. Toss gently to coat. Top with the romaine and cover with plastic wrap.

step 2
heat the **pita triangles**

4 to 6 pita pockets

Preheat the oven to 400°F. Cut each pita into 6 triangles. Wrap the triangles in foil and seal well. Place the packet in the oven and heat until just warm, about 3 minutes.

step 3
plate the **hummus** and **stuffed vine leaves**

1 container (8 ounces) prepared hummus

1 can (16 ounces) stuffed vine leaves

1. Put the hummus in a serving dish and place the dish on a serving platter.

2. Arrange the stuffed vine leaves on a plate and place on the table.

step 4
assemble the **dessert**

1 can (16 ounces) plums packed in heavy syrup

2 large ripe bananas

Vanilla yogurt or light sour cream, for serving

Drain the plums, reserving a little of the syrup, and place in a bowl. Slice the bananas into the bowl, add some of the reserved syrup, if desired, and toss gently to coat. Place the yogurt in a small serving bowl. Chill until serving time.

step 5
serve

1. At serving time, season the salad with salt and pepper and toss until well coated. Divide the salad among 4 dinner plates. Cut the tomatoes into wedges and place 2 on each plate.

2. Place the warm pita triangles around the edge of the platter with the hummus and place on the table.

3. When ready for dessert, serve the fruit in small bowls. Pass the yogurt or sour cream as a topping.

Greek Salad
Single serving is 1/4 of the total recipe
CALORIES 178; PROTEIN 6g; CARBS 15g; TOTAL FAT 11g; SAT FAT 0g; CHOLESTEROL 25mg; SODIUM 685mg; FIBER 3g

panzanella with gorgonzola
(italian bread salad with tomatoes and cheese)
mixed olives
fresh figs with port wine

serves 6

shopping list

Fresh figs

Orange (for zest)

Port wine

Tuscan-style bread

Tomatoes

Celery

Red onion

Jarred roasted red peppers

Anchovy fillets

Capers

Basil leaves

Gorgonzola cheese, crumbled

Mixed olives

from your pantry

Sugar

Garlic

Extra virgin olive oil

Salt and pepper

menu gameplan

step **1** prepare the **fresh figs with port wine**

step **2** assemble the **panzanella with gorgonzola**

step **3** plate the **mixed olives**

step **4** **serve**

headsup

Some people see the words "grated zest" and wince. They resent the time it takes and the mess it creates. If you feel that way, try this: Place a piece of plastic wrap directly on the surface of the hand-held box grater, pressing it on so that the surface of the grater comes through. Grate the fruit with the plastic wrap in place. When you're done, lift the plastic wrap off and scrape the zest off the wrap. Not only does it make grating faster, it makes clean-up a lot quicker, too.

"When the summer heat's on, make this menu—there's no cooking at all. Plus, Italian bread salad is absolutely delicious."

—minutemeals' Chef Hillary

step 1

prepare the **fresh figs with port wine**

12 fresh figs

1 orange

1/4 cup port wine

2 tablespoons sugar

1. Rinse the figs and remove the stem on each. Cut the figs in half through the stem ends. Place in a medium bowl.

2. Grate enough of the orange zest to measure 1 teaspoon. Add the zest to the figs with the port and sugar and toss gently to combine. Let stand at room temperature while you make the salad.

step 2

assemble the *panzanella with gorgonzola*

8 ounces crusty Tuscan-style bread

6 large tomatoes

2 large garlic cloves, or more to taste

4 stalks celery from the heart

1 medium red onion

1 jar (12 ounces) roasted red peppers

1 can (4 ounces) anchovy fillets packed in oil

2 tablespoons drained capers

1/2 cup chopped fresh basil leaves

1/2 cup extra virgin olive oil

4 to 6 ounces crumbled Gorgonzola cheese

Salt and pepper to taste

1. Tear the bread into bite-sized pieces and place in a large salad bowl. Core the tomatoes and cut them into large chunks. Add them to the bowl and toss with the bread. Set the bowl aside.

2. Mince the garlic. Chop the celery and red onion. Drain and chop the roasted peppers and anchovies. Add all to the salad bowl along with the capers.

3. Chop enough basil leaves to measure 1/2 cup. Add the basil to the bowl with the olive oil and Gorgonzola. Toss gently to combine, season with salt and pepper, and toss again.

step 3

plate the **mixed olives**

8 ounces mixed olives, such as niçoise, kalamata, or Gaeta

Put the olives in a shallow serving bowl.

step 4

serve

1. At serving time, place the bread salad and bowl of olives on the table, with 4 dinner plates for serving.

2. When ready to serve dessert, place 4 fig halves in each of 4 small bowls. Spoon some of the juices over each portion.

Panzanella with Gorgonzola
Single serving is 1/6 of the total recipe
CALORIES 346; PROTEIN 8g; CARBS 31g;
TOTAL FAT 23g; SAT FAT 4g; CHOLESTEROL 9mg;
SODIUM 568mg; FIBER 7g

pizza pasta salad
pound cake with fresh strawberries

shopping list

Pasta, such as shells or penne

Fresh basil

Presliced mushrooms (from the produce department)

Pre-shredded part-skim mozzarella

Strawberries

Grand Marnier or orange juice

Pound cake

Whipped cream or topping (optional)

from the salad bar

Cherry tomatoes

Green pepper strips

from your pantry

Garlic

Olive oil

Cider vinegar

Dried oregano

Salt and pepper

Grated Parmesan cheese

Confectioners' sugar

serves 4

beforeyoustart

Bring the water to a boil in a large pot, covered, over high heat to cook the pasta.

| step | 1 | make the **pizza pasta salad** |

| step | 2 | prepare the **pound cake with fresh strawberries** |

| step | 3 | **serve** |

 Shredding mozzarella by hand is no longer necessary. By keeping pre-shredded mozzarella in the resealable bag on hand in the cheese drawer of your refrigerator, you save yourself considerable prep time (and mess) in a recipe like this.

"This menu is kid-friendly food at its finest—not surprisingly, the grown-ups love it, too. The ingredients are familiar, their preparation sound."

—minutemeals' Chef Hillary

make the **pizza pasta salad**

4 quarts water

12 ounces shaped pasta, such as shells or penne

1 pint cherry tomatoes

1 cup green pepper strips

1/2 cup chopped fresh basil

2 or 3 garlic cloves

1/3 cup olive oil

1/4 cup cider vinegar

1 teaspoon dried oregano

1 box (8 ounces) presliced mushrooms

1 cup pre-shredded part-skim mozzarella

Salt and pepper to taste

Grated Parmesan cheese, for serving (optional)

1. Cook the pasta: Pour the water into a large pot, salt the water lightly, and cover the pot. Bring the water to a boil over high heat. Add the pasta and cook according to the directions on the package. Drain. Rinse under cold water and drain well again.

2. While the pasta is cooking, rinse the tomatoes, pat dry, and halve. Chop the pepper and enough fresh basil to measure 1/2 cup. Finely chop the garlic. Place all in a large bowl.

3. Add the olive oil, vinegar, oregano, mushrooms, and mozzarella and toss to combine. Season with salt and pepper.

4. Add the cooked pasta and toss well. Taste and correct the seasonings.

step 2

prepare the **pound cake with fresh strawberries**

2 pints strawberries

3 tablespoons confectioners' sugar

1 tablespoon Grand Marnier or orange juice

Store-bought pound cake

Whipped cream or topping (optional)

Rinse, hull, and quarter the strawberries. In a bowl, combine the strawberries with the confectioners' sugar and Grand Marnier or orange juice. Toss gently. Let stand for 5 minutes.

step 3

serve

1. Divide the pasta salad evenly among 4 pasta bowls and serve, with a bowl of Parmesan for sprinkling on top, if desired.

2. When ready for dessert, cut the pound cake into four 1/2-inch-thick slices. Place 1 slice on each of 4 dessert plates. Spoon strawberries with their juices over the top of each slice and garnish with whipped cream, if desired.

Pizza Pasta Salad
Single serving is 1/4 of the total recipe

CALORIES 445; PROTEIN 19g; CARBS 32g; TOTAL FAT 27g; SAT FAT 7g; CHOLESTEROL 23mg; SODIUM 236mg; FIBER 3g

Nutrition Analysis does not include optional Parmesan cheese.

beef and brown rice salad
with roasted vegetables
dried figs, almonds, and dried apricots

shopping list

Quick-cooking brown rice

Balsamic vinaigrette dressing

Roast beef, sliced
(from the deli counter)

Roasted vegetables
(from the deli counter)

Dried figs

Almonds

Dried apricots

from the salad bar

Chopped scallions

Shredded carrots
(or from the produce
department)

Chopped red or green
peppers

from your pantry

Ground cumin

Salt

Cracked black pepper

serves 4

beforeyoustart

Bring the water to a boil in a medium saucepan, covered, over high heat to cook the brown rice.

step	1	make the **beef and brown rice salad with roasted vegetables**
step	2	prepare the **dried figs, almonds, and dried apricots**
step	3	**serve**

 Quick-cooking brown rice makes this minutemeal doable. Don't even entertain using regular brown rice. It takes almost 3 times as long to cook.

"I wanted to create a Mediterranean feel to this menu. The roasted vegetables do that, so does the cumin in the salad."

—minutemeals' Chef Joanne

make the **beef and brown rice salad with roasted vegetables**

1 3/4 cups water

1 1/2 cups quick-cooking brown rice

1/4 cup plus 2 tablespoons store-bought balsamic vinaigrette dressing

1/2 teaspoon ground cumin

1/2 teaspoon salt

1/8 teaspoon cracked black pepper

3/4 pound roast beef, sliced 1/4 inch thick

1/4 cup chopped scallions

1/2 cup shredded carrots

1/2 cup chopped red or green peppers

1/2 to 3/4 pound roasted vegetables

1. Pour the water into a medium saucepan, cover, and bring to a boil over high heat. Stir in the brown rice, bring back to a boil, cover, and reduce the heat to low. Simmer for 10 minutes, or until the water is absorbed and the rice is tender.

2. Stir 1/4 cup of the vinaigrette, the cumin, salt, and pepper into the rice. Spread the rice evenly in a 13- × 9-inch baking pan and place the pan in the freezer to cool down quickly, about 8 minutes.

3. Meanwhile, cut the roast beef into thin strips. In a bowl, combine the roast beef and scallions, add the remaining 2 tablespoons balsamic vinaigrette, and toss gently to coat.

4. To serve, stir the shredded carrots and peppers into the rice salad and mound it in the center of a large chilled platter. Top with the roast beef salad, then arrange the roasted vegetables around the edge.

step 2

prepare the **dried figs, almonds, and dried apricots**

Dried figs

Almonds

Dried apricots

On a platter, a Mediterranean-style one if you have it, place mounds of dried figs, almonds, and dried apricots.

step 3

serve

1. Place the beef and rice salad on the table, with 4 dinner plates for serving.

2. When ready for dessert, place the platter of fruits and almonds in the middle of the table. No plates are needed.

Beef and Brown Rice Salad with Roasted Vegetables
Single serving is 1/4 of the total recipe
CALORIES 416; PROTEIN 30g; CARBS 34g; TOTAL FAT 19g; SAT FAT 3g; CHOLESTEROL 66mg; SODIUM 621mg; FIBER 2g

southeast asian beef salad

grilled pineapple slices
french baguette
coconut ice cream

shopping list

Scallions

Large bunch cilantro

Bunch fresh mint (optional)

Prewashed salad greens
or leaf lettuce

Cucumber

Cherry or grape tomatoes

Rare roast beef, sliced
(from the deli counter)

Limes

Fish sauce (in Asian food
section of supermarket) or
lite soy sauce

Chile paste, with or without
garlic (in Asian food section
of supermarket)

Pineapple slices
(from the produce department)

French baguette

Coconut ice cream

from your pantry

Maple syrup

Unsalted butter

serves 4

step **1** make the **southeast asian beef salad**

step **2** prepare the **grilled pineapple slices**

step **3** **serve**

headsup

Fish sauce is a key Thai ingredient and we call for it in the dressing for the salad. Made from anchovies, salt, and water, it is extremely salty. If you are concerned that you will not be able to use it often enough to justify buying it, use lite soy sauce as a substitute.

"Ethnic cooking really excites me. I like going out to eat, then re-creating the dishes at home. That's what inspired this salad."

—minutemeals' Chef Nancy

step 1

make the **southeast asian beef salad**

For the salad

2 scallions

1 cup chopped cilantro

1/2 cup mint leaves (optional)

8 ounces prewashed salad greens or leaf lettuce

2 small or 1 medium cucumber

2 cups cherry or grape tomatoes

1 pound thinly sliced rare roast beef

For the dressing

1/4 cup fresh lime juice (about 3 large limes)

1/4 cup fish sauce or lite soy sauce

1 to 2 teaspoons maple syrup, or to taste

1/2 teaspoon chile paste, with or without garlic

1. Finely chop the scallions, including most of the green. Trim off the larger stems of the cilantro, then coarsely chop enough of the cilantro sprigs to measure 1 cup. If desired, remove enough mint leaves from the sprigs to measure 1/2 cup, loosely packed.

2. In a medium bowl, toss together the scallions, half the cilantro, the mint leaves, if using, and the salad greens. Mound 1/4 of the salad onto each of 4 dinner plates.

3. Peel the cucumber and cut it in half lengthwise. Lay the cucumber half cut side down and cut thin slices on the diagonal to make half moons. Slice the remaining cucumber half in the same manner. Slice the tomatoes in half. Divide the cucumber pieces and tomatoes among the 4 plates and arrange them decoratively on the edges of the greens.

4. Make the dressing: Squeeze enough fresh limes to measure 1/4 cup juice. In a small bowl, combine the lime juice, fish sauce, 1 to 2 teaspoons maple syrup, and the chile paste until well blended.

step 2

prepare the **grilled pineapple slices**

1 lime

2 tablespoons unsalted butter

1 peeled and cored fresh pineapple, cut into slices

1. Heat a grill pan or heavy skillet over high heat until very hot. Slice the lime into 4 wedges.

2. In a microwave-safe cup, microwave the butter on High about 20 to 30 seconds.

3. Brush the pineapple slices with butter and arrange in a single layer on the hot grill pan. Grill until marks appear, about 1 to 2 minutes. Turn and grill the second side. Transfer the pineapple slices to a serving platter and add the wedges of lime. Place the platter on the table.

step 3

serve

1. Spoon some of the salad dressing over the greens on each plate. Divide the roast beef evenly among the salads, arranging it on the greens. Garnish with the remaining chopped cilantro.

2. Slice the French baguette into pieces and place it in a bread basket. Serve the salads with the bread.

3. When ready for dessert, scoop the coconut ice cream into small bowls and serve.

Southeast Asian Beef Salad
Single serving is 1/4 of the total recipe
CALORIES 296; PROTEIN 36g; CARBS 12g; TOTAL FAT 11g; SAT FAT 4g; CHOLESTEROL 88mg; SODIUM 667mg; FIBER 3g

grilled chicken caesar salad
french bread
iced watermelon

serves 4

shopping list

French bread

Skinless boneless chicken breast halves

Anchovy fillets (optional)

Lemon (for juice)

Prewashed romaine lettuce

Caesar dressing, such as Newman's Own or Ken's Steakhouse

Packaged garlic croutons

from the salad bar

Watermelon chunks (or from the produce department)

Peeled hard-cooked eggs

Red onion slices

from your pantry

Olive oil

Salt and pepper

Grated Parmesan cheese

beforeyoustart

Preheat the oven to 400°F to heat the bread.

step 1 freeze the **watermelon**

step 2 heat the **french bread**

step 3 make the **grilled chicken caesar salad**

step 4 **serve**

luckyforyou We have your interests at heart. We called for store-bought Caesar dressing and prewashed romaine, both of which save a lot of time on the "minute" clock.

"I love Caesar salad. It can be plain, with chicken, or with grilled shrimp—and it's so easy when you use bottled dressing."

—minutemeals' Chef Hillary

step 1

freeze the **watermelon**

Watermelon chunks for 4

Place the watermelon in a shallow bowl and put in the freezer until icy cold, almost semi-frozen.

step 2

heat the **french bread**

1 loaf French bread

Preheat the oven to 400°F. Place the bread in the oven to heat while you make the salad.

step 3

make the **grilled chicken caesar salad**

1 pound skinless boneless chicken breast halves

1 tablespoon olive oil

Salt and pepper to taste

6 anchovy fillets, minced (optional)

4 peeled hard-cooked eggs

1 tablespoon fresh lemon juice (about 1/2 small lemon)

1 bag (10 ounces) prewashed romaine lettuce

1/2 cup red onion slices

1/3 cup store-bought Caesar dressing, such as Newman's Own or Ken's Steakhouse

3 tablespoons grated Parmesan cheese

1/2 cup packaged garlic croutons

1. Preheat the grill pan or grill.

2. Brush the chicken breasts on both sides with the olive oil and season with salt and pepper. Grill the chicken 4 to 5 minutes on each side, or until just cooked through and no pink remains. Transfer to a plate, cover, and keep warm.

3. Mince the anchovies, if using. Thinly slice the hard-cooked eggs. Squeeze enough lemon to measure 1 tablespoon.

4. Combine the lettuce, onion slices, and optional anchovies in a large shallow salad bowl. Cut the chicken into 1/2-inch strips and add them to the salad.

5. Add the salad dressing, grated Parmesan, lemon juice, and salt and pepper and toss to coat evenly. Place slices of egg around the edge.

step 4

serve

1. Divide the Caesar salad evenly among 4 dinner plates. Top each serving with some of the croutons and serve.

2. Slice the French bread into thick slices, arrange in a napkin-lined bread basket, and place on the table.

3. Remove the watermelon from the freezer only when ready to serve. Divide among dessert bowls, and serve at once.

Grilled Chicken Caesar Salad
Single serving is 1/4 of the total recipe
CALORIES 394; PROTEIN 36g; CARBS 9g;
TOTAL FAT 22g; SAT FAT 5g; CHOLESTEROL 282mg;
SODIUM 512mg; FIBER 2g

turkey and walnut salad

tomato and basil focaccia
rice pudding

serves 4 to 6

shopping list

Ripe tomatoes

Focaccia

Fresh basil or prepared pesto

Diced red skin potatoes
(available in airtight bags
in the produce department)

Shelled walnuts

Roasted turkey breast,
in 1 piece
(from the deli counter)

Italian salad dressing, such
as Newman's Own

Prewashed mixed spring or
baby greens, washed
spinach, or other ready-to-
eat salad greens

Rice pudding, with or without
raisins

from your pantry

Salt and pepper

Extra virgin olive oil

Grated nutmeg (optional)

beforeyoustart

Preheat the oven to 400°F to heat the
focaccia.

| step | 1 | prepare the **topping for the tomato and basil focaccia** |

| step | 2 | while the focaccia is heating, make the **turkey and walnut salad** |

| step | 3 | **serve** |

headsup

If you like to use fresh basil
leaves in your cooking, but
don't always use up the whole bunch, look for small bags
of just the leaves that are sold in some supermarkets and
produce stores. The bagged leaves are a terrific convenience item but require a good rinsing before using.

"This salad is really a variation on potato salad, and also lends itself to variation. Try adding in a little crumbled blue cheese."

—minutemeals' Chef Anne

step 1

prepare the **topping for the tomato and basil focaccia**

2 ripe medium tomatoes

1 store-bought plain focaccia

8 leaves fresh basil or
2 to 3 tablespoons prepared pesto

Salt and pepper to taste

Extra virgin olive oil,
for drizzling

1. Preheat the oven to 400°F.

2. Core and slice the tomatoes into rounds.

3. Place the focaccia on a baking sheet. Scatter the basil leaves over the focaccia or spread the pesto over the top. Add the tomato slices to cover the surface and season with salt and pepper. Drizzle olive oil over the top. Bake until the tomatoes soften and the bread is warmed through, about 10 minutes.

step 2

while the focaccia is heating, make the **turkey and walnut salad**

1 to 1½ cups diced red skin potatoes

1 teaspoon water

½ cup shelled walnuts

1 pound roasted turkey breast, in 1 piece

¼ cup store-bought Italian salad dressing, such as Newman's Own, or more to taste

Salt and pepper to taste

8 ounces prewashed mixed spring or baby greens

1. Place the potatoes in a microwave-safe bowl. Add the water. Cover and microwave on High until tender, about 3 minutes. Let stand in the microwave an additional 3 minutes.

2. Spread the walnuts on a small baking sheet. Toast for 6 to 8 minutes, until golden and fragrant. Remove and let cool.

3. While the walnuts toast, remove the skin from the turkey breast and shred the meat.

4. In a medium bowl, combine the potatoes and dressing, and toss. Add the turkey, and toss. Season with salt and pepper and more dressing to taste, if desired.

5. Line a platter with the greens, then mound the salad on top.

step 3

serve

1. Place the salad on the table, with 4 dinner plates for serving.

2. Slide the heated focaccia onto a bread board and serve at once, with a serrated knife for cutting it into squares.

3. When ready for dessert, serve the rice pudding in individual bowls, sprinkled with grated nutmeg, if desired.

Turkey and Walnut Salad
Single serving is ⅕ of the total recipe
CALORIES 325; PROTEIN 30g; CARBS 12g;
TOTAL FAT 18g; SAT FAT 3g; CHOLESTEROL 58mg;
SODIUM 92mg; FIBER 2g

Nutrition Analysis does not include salad dressing,

smoked turkey
with couscous salad on arugula

semolina rolls

nectarines and almond macaroons

serves 4

shopping list

Fresh dill

Plain couscous

White wine vinaigrette dressing

Smoked turkey in 1 piece (from the deli counter)

Grape tomatoes

Prewashed arugula or another peppery green

Nectarines

Almond macaroons

Semolina rolls

from the salad bar

Cucumber slices

Chopped scallions

from your pantry

Fat-free low-sodium chicken broth or vegetable broth (optional)

Salt

Olive oil

step 1 make the **smoked turkey with couscous salad on arugula**

step 2 prepare the **nectarines and almond macaroons**

step 3 serve

 Make the couscous as directed below. (Yes, you do add the vinaigrette to the couscous before it "cooks.") And resist the temptation to add more vinaigrette before you serve the salad. Less dressing is more in this case: The couscous is at its best when it is fluffy, not wet. You can pass additional vinaigrette at the table for those diners who would like more.

"This is my idea of the ideal main-course summer salad. It's easy to make, lightly dressed, pretty, and flavorful—you can even vary it."

—minutemeals' Chef Joanne

step 1

make the **smoked turkey with couscous salad on arugula**

3/4 teaspoon snipped fresh dill or 1/4 teaspoon dried

1 cup water, fat-free low-sodium chicken broth, or vegetable broth

1 cup plain couscous

1/3 cup white wine vinaigrette dressing, plus additional at the table, if desired

1/4 teaspoon salt

3/4 pound smoked turkey in 1 piece

1 cup cucumber slices

2 tablespoons chopped scallions

1 cup grape tomatoes

4 ounces prewashed arugula or another peppery green

Olive oil for dressing the arugula

1. With scissors, snip enough fresh dill to measure 3/4 teaspoon.

2. Pour the broth or water into a medium saucepan, cover, and bring to a boil over high heat. Stir in the couscous, 1/3 cup of the vinaigrette, the dill, and salt. Cover and let stand for 5 minutes, until the liquid is absorbed. Fluff the couscous with a fork, then spread it evenly in a 13- × 9-inch baking pan. Place the pan in the freezer or refrigerator to chill.

3. While the couscous chills, remove the skin from the smoked turkey and cut it into 1/2-inch cubes. Chop the cucumber slices. Finely chop the sliced scallions. Rinse the grape tomatoes and pat dry.

4. Add the turkey, cucumber, and scallions to the chilled couscous and toss to combine.

5. Line a serving platter with the arugula, drizzle with olive oil to taste, and toss to coat. Mound the couscous salad on the arugula. Scatter the grape tomatoes around the edge.

step 2

prepare the **nectarines and almond macaroons**

4 ripe nectarines

Almond macaroons

1. Rinse the nectarines and pat them dry. Place in a pretty bowl.

2. Arrange the macaroons on a serving plate.

step 3

serve

1. Place the salad on the table, with 4 dinner plates for serving. Serve the semolina rolls.

2. When ready for dessert, serve the nectarines with the macaroons. Or crumble the macaroons over the nectarines as a topping.

Smoked Turkey with Couscous Salad on Arugula
Single serving is 1/4 of the total recipe
CALORIES 375; PROTEIN 24g; CARBS 38g; TOTAL FAT 14g; SAT FAT 3g; CHOLESTEROL 35mg; SODIUM 1154mg; FIBER 3g

Nutrition Analysis includes 1/3 cup vinaigrette and water for cooking couscous.

insalata di frutti di mare
(seafood salad italian style)

garlic crostini

lemon sorbet with butter cookies

menu
gameplan

serves 4

beforeyoustart

Preheat the oven to 400°F to heat the crostini.

step	1	make the *insalata di frutti di mare*
step	2	make and bake the **garlic crostini**
step	3	**serve**

shopping list

Bottled clam juice

Bay scallops

Medium shrimp, cooked, peeled, and deveined

Celery stalks

Lemons

Fresh parsley

Prewashed Italian greens

Italian bread

Lemon sorbet

Butter cookies

from the salad bar

Red onion slices

Red pepper strips

from your pantry

Dijon mustard

Garlic

Extra virgin olive oil

Salt and pepper

headsup
Poaching is a very successful way to cook seafood. Being cooked in liquid keeps the shellfish or fish moist. Be alert, though: The liquid should simmer gently, not boil, and it's important that the ingredients not overcook. They toughen if they do.

"This Italian seafood salad is one of the most elegant salads I know. Serve it for dinner parties and celebrations—that's how special it is."

—minutemeals' Chef Hillary

step 1

make the *insalata di frutti di mare*

- 1 bottle (8 ounces) clam juice
- 2 cups water
- 1 pound bay scallops
- 1 pound cooked, peeled, and deveined medium shrimp
- 4 small celery stalks
- 1/2 cup red onion slices
- 1/2 to 3/4 cup thin red pepper strips
- 2 large lemons
- 5 or 6 fresh parsley sprigs
- 1 tablespoon Dijon mustard
- 1 large garlic clove
- 3/4 cup extra virgin olive oil
- Salt and pepper to taste
- 4 cups prewashed Italian greens

1. In a medium skillet, bring the clam juice and water to a boil over high heat. Reduce the heat so that the liquid just simmers and add the bay scallops. Poach for 3 minutes, or until opaque throughout. Do not overcook. Drain immediately in a colander and run under cold water to cool. Transfer the scallops to a large bowl, add the cooked shrimp, and place in the refrigerator to chill.

2. Finely chop the celery, onion slices, and pepper strips. Add to the seafood and place the bowl back in the refrigerator to chill.

3. Juice 1 lemon; cut the remaining lemon into wedges. Stem, then coarsely chop the parsley.

4. In a blender or food processor, combine the lemon juice, mustard, and garlic clove. Add 3/4 cup of the olive oil in a thin stream and process until well blended. Add the parsley and season with salt and pepper. Pour the dressing over the seafood mixture, toss gently, and chill until serving time.

step 2

make and bake the garlic crostini

- 1 loaf Italian bread
- 2 garlic cloves
- 2 tablespoons extra virgin olive oil

1. Preheat the oven to 400°F. Cut the bread into 1/2-inch slices. Peel the garlic cloves and slice them in half.

2. Brush one side of the bread slices with olive oil, put the slices on a baking sheet, and toast about 5 minutes, or until golden. When golden, rub the surface of each slice with the cut side of the garlic cloves. Place the crostini in a napkin-lined basket.

step 3

serve

1. At serving time, line 4 large dinner plates with lettuce leaves. Divide the seafood salad among the plates and garnish each serving with a lemon wedge. Serve.

2. When ready for dessert, scoop the sorbet into small bowls and serve with the butter cookies.

Insalata di Frutti di Mare
Single serving is 1/4 of the total recipe
CALORIES 646; PROTEIN 48g; CARBS 12g;
TOTAL FAT 46g; SAT FAT 7g; CHOLESTEROL 210mg;
SODIUM 785mg; FIBER 3g

shrimp and bread salad

sliced tomatoes and red onion with basil

melon slices with honey and lemon

menu gameplan

serves 4

shopping list

Large tomatoes (beefsteak or vine-ripened)

Red onion

Fresh basil leaves

French or Italian bread

Arugula or red leaf lettuce

Lemon (for juice)

Large shrimp, cooked, peeled, and deveined

Melon slices (from the produce department)

from your pantry

Extra virgin olive oil

Salt and pepper

Mayonnaise

Dijon mustard

Honey

step 1 make the **sliced tomatoes and red onion with basil**

step 2 make the **shrimp and bread salad**

step 3 **serve**

 Vine-ripened tomatoes are readily available at the supermarket at a reasonable price. If you can't find ripe tomatoes for the salad, stay in the no-cook mode and serve cucumber slices with a dusting of fresh dill and scallion greens.

"I had a good time with this menu. Summertime food is fun to me, and the colors alone in this menu make me feel carefree."

—minutemeals' Chef Nancy

make the **sliced tomatoes and red onion with basil**

4 beefsteak tomatoes or
6 large vine-ripened tomatoes

1 medium red onion

Extra virgin olive oil,
for drizzling

Salt and pepper to taste

4 fresh basil leaves

1. With a serrated knife, cut the tomatoes into medium-thin slices. Slice the onion similarly thick. Arrange the tomato and onion slices, alternating them, on a platter.

2. Drizzle olive oil over the salad and season with salt and pepper. Tear the basil leaves into pieces and sprinkle them over the top. Place the salad on the table.

step 2

make the **shrimp and bread salad**

1/4 to 1/2 loaf of French or Italian bread

6 to 8 ounces arugula or
red leaf lettuce

1/2 cup mayonnaise, reduced-fat variety, if desired

1 tablespoon Dijon mustard

2 tablespoons fresh lemon juice
(1 large lemon)

1 tablespoon water

1 pound cooked, peeled,
and deveined large shrimp

Salt and pepper to taste

1. Cut enough of the bread into 1/2-inch cubes to measure 2 generous cups loosely packed. Place in a large bowl. Wash and salad-spin the lettuce dry. Tear the greens into bite-sized pieces.

2. In a small bowl, mix together the mayonnaise, mustard, and lemon juice to taste, adding as much as 2 full tablespoons. Thin the dressing with water to a pourable consistency.

3. Add the shrimp to the bread and lettuce. While tossing the salad, slowly pour in the mayonnaise dressing, adding just enough to cover the ingredients. There should not be so much dressing that it collects in the bottom of the bowl. Season with salt and pepper.

step 3

serve

1. Place the shrimp salad on the table, with 4 dinner plates for serving.

2. Keep the melon slices for dessert in the refrigerator until serving time. When ready for dessert, arrange them on a serving platter and drizzle them with honey, then squeeze fresh lemon juice over the top. Serve.

Shrimp and Bread Salad
Single serving is 1/4 of the total recipe
CALORIES 431; PROTEIN 31g; CARBS 40g;
TOTAL FAT 15g; SAT FAT 3g; CHOLESTEROL 172mg;
SODIUM 792mg; FIBER 3g

shrimp and
white bean salad
warm french bread
strawberries with red wine and pepper

menu
gameplan

shopping list

Medium shrimp, cooked,
peeled, and deveined

White beans

Italian salad dressing

Radicchio

Crusty French bread

Strawberries

Dry red wine

from the salad bar

Red onion slices

Celery slices

Watercress sprigs

from your pantry

Garlic (or preminced jarred
garlic)

Olive oil

Red pepper flakes

Salt and pepper

Freshly ground black pepper

serves 4

beforeyoustart
Preheat the broiler.

| step | 1 | make the **shrimp and white bean salad** |

| step | 2 | heat the **french bread** |

| step | 3 | prepare the **strawberries with red wine and pepper** |

| step | 4 | **serve** |

luckyforyou Washed, stemmed, and
trimmed watercress is avail-
able at salad bars. If it's not, use another slightly tangy
green. You could also opt for a packaged mix and toss
some sliced endive in for crunch.

"While Italy's tuna and white bean salad is renowned, this variation with shrimp is equally enticing—and easy."

—minutemeals' Chef Amanda

step 1

make the **shrimp and white bean salad**

2 garlic cloves

1 pound cooked, peeled, and deveined medium shrimp

1 tablespoon olive oil

1/4 teaspoon red pepper flakes, or to taste

Salt and pepper to taste

1/2 cup red onion slices

1/2 cup celery slices

2 cans (15 ounces each) white beans

1/4 cup store-bought Italian salad dressing

1 small head radicchio, outer leaves removed

1 bunch watercress sprigs, tough stems removed

1. Preheat the broiler. Mince the garlic cloves, if using whole.

2. If necessary, pat dry the shrimp. Place in a single layer in a shallow 13- × 9-inch baking pan.

3. In a small bowl, combine the garlic, olive oil, pepper flakes, and salt and pepper. Pour the mixture over the shrimp and toss to coat evenly. Broil the shrimp, 4 inches from the heat, turning them after 2 minutes, just until heated through. Remove the shrimp from the broiler to a plate to prevent overcooking. Turn the oven to 375°F.

4. Finely chop the onion slices and celery slices and place in a large bowl. Rinse and drain the white beans and add with the salad dressing to the bowl. Toss to coat.

step 2

heat the **french bread**

1 loaf crusty French bread

After the oven has preheated to 375°F for 5 minutes, put the bread in to warm.

step 3

prepare the **strawberries with red wine and pepper**

2 pints strawberries

3 tablespoons dry red wine

Freshly ground black pepper to taste

1. Rinse the strawberries. Hull and cut them in half. Place in a medium bowl.

2. Sprinkle the berries with the red wine and grind fresh pepper over all. Toss gently. Refrigerate until ready to serve.

step 4

serve

1. Finish the salad: Coarsely shred the radicchio. Divide the watercress and radicchio among 4 dinner plates. Spoon some of the bean salad over the greens in the center of the plate and place some of the shrimp, dividing them equally, around the edge. Place the plates on the table.

2. Slice the French bread, place it in a bread basket, and serve.

3. When ready for dessert, spoon the berries and their juices into stemmed glasses or bowls and serve.

Shrimp and White Bean Salad
Single serving is 1/4 of the total recipe
CALORIES 521; PROTEIN 43g; CARBS 60g;
TOTAL FAT 12g; SAT FAT 2g; CHOLESTEROL 172mg;
SODIUM 953mg; FIBER 23g

cucumber, corn, and smoked salmon salad

toasty olive bread

melon and blueberries with honey and lemon

serves 4

shopping list

Red or thin-skinned white potatoes

English cucumber

Sliced smoked salmon

Fresh dill

Prewashed salad greens of choice

Frozen corn

Lemons (for juice)

French baguette

Black or green olive paste

Blueberries

from the salad bar

Cherry tomatoes

Honeydew melon and cantaloupe chunks (or from the produce department)

from your pantry

Dijon mustard

Maple syrup

Extra virgin olive oil

Salt and pepper

Honey

beforeyoustart

Preheat the broiler. Rinse the blueberries in a colander.

| step | 1 | make the **cucumber, corn, and smoked salmon salad** |

| step | 2 | make the **mustard maple vinaigrette** |

| step | 3 | grill the **toasty olive bread** |

| step | 4 | **serve** |

headsup

Smoked salmon is a luxury item so buy it packaged by the half pound in airtight Cryovac—just right for this recipe. Lox is not a substitute.

"Make this salad in celebration of something—a birthday, an anniversary, a homecoming, even a small wedding luncheon."

—minutemeals' Chef Nancy

step 1

make the **cucumber, corn, and smoked salmon salad**

- 4 medium red or white thin-skinned potatoes
- 1 medium English (seedless) cucumber
- 2 teaspoons water
- 1/2 pound sliced smoked salmon
- 1 cup cherry tomatoes
- 2 to 3 tablespoons coarsely chopped fresh dill
- 4 cups prewashed salad greens of choice
- 1 1/2 cups frozen corn, thawed

1. Cut the 4 potatoes and cucumber into 1/2-inch cubes. Place the cucumber cubes in a bowl.

2. Place the potatoes in a microwave-safe bowl with the water. Cover and microwave on High for 4 minutes; let stand, covered, in the microwave for 3 minutes. Stir the potatoes, cover again, and cook another 3 minutes; let stand for 2 to 3 minutes. Remove from the microwave.

3. Cut the smoked salmon into 1/2-inch pieces and add to the bowl with the cucumbers. Rinse the tomatoes, pat dry, slice in half, and place in a small bowl.

4. Discard any thick stems on the dill sprigs. Coarsely chop enough of the dill to measure up to 3 tablespoons. Add the dill to the cooked potatoes and toss gently.

step 2

make the **mustard maple vinaigrette**

- 3 tablespoons fresh lemon juice (about 1 or 2 large lemons)
- 1 tablespoon Dijon mustard
- 2 teaspoons pure maple syrup
- 1/3 cup extra virgin olive oil
- Salt and pepper to taste

1. Squeeze 3 tablespoons fresh lemon juice. Pour 2 tablespoons of the lemon juice into a small bowl or blender.

2. Add the mustard and maple syrup and whisk or blend to combine. Whisking constantly or with the machine running, slowly, in a thin stream, pour in the olive oil. Season with salt and pepper and the remaining 1 tablespoon lemon juice, if needed. (If the dressing is very thick, thin it with a few drops of water.)

3. Toss the dilled potatoes with 2 tablespoons of the dressing.

step 3

grill the **toasty olive bread**

- 4 to 6 slices French baguette (each 1/2 inch thick)
- 1 1/2 tablespoons extra virgin olive oil
- 1/4 cup prepared black or green olive paste

1. Preheat the broiler.

2. Lightly brush one side of each bread slice with olive oil. Place the bread on broiler rack and broil about 2 minutes, until just golden.

3. Spread a thin coating of the olive paste on the toasts. Broil 1 to 2 minutes. Arrange the toasts in a serving basket and place the basket on the table.

step 4

serve

1. Divide the salad greens among 4 dinner plates, mounding them high. Arrange the dilled potatoes, cucumber and smoked salmon, corn, and tomatoes on top. Drizzle the vinaigrette over the salads. Serve any remaining vinaigrette separately.

2. Place the salads on the table and serve with the olive toasts.

3. When ready for dessert, combine the melon chunks and blueberries in a serving bowl. Spoon honey and a squeeze of fresh lemon juice over the top. Toss gently before serving in small bowls.

Cucumber, Corn, and Smoked Salmon Salad
Single serving is 1/4 of the total recipe
CALORIES 497; PROTEIN 24g; CARBS 80g;
TOTAL FAT 14g; SAT FAT 1g; CHOLESTEROL 20mg;
SODIUM 809mg; FIBER 14g

fresh tuna salad niçoise

crusty french bread
french cheeses and fruit

serves 4

shopping list

Assorted French cheeses

Seedless red and green grapes

Fresh figs

Ripe pears

Crusty French bread

Diced, ready-to-cook par-cooked potatoes (in the produce department)

Jarred marinated artichokes

Niçoise or kalamata olives

Ripe tomatoes

Capers

Fresh tuna steam

Anchovy fillets

from the salad bar

Red pepper strips

Cooked green beans

Red onion slices

Prewashed romaine leaves

Peeled hard-cooked eggs

from your pantry

Mustard vinaigrette (store-bought) or oil, vinegar, and Dijon mustard (for home-made dressing)

Olive oil

Salt and pepper

Dried herbes de Provence

step 1 plate the **french cheeses and fruit**

step 2 make the **fresh tuna salad niçoise**

step 3 serve

If you can't find par-cooked potatoes, buy 12 ounces prepared potato salad in vinaigrette from the deli counter. Adjust the seasonings in the salad as needed.

"Precooked and prepped ingredients from the salad bar makes this salade niçoise *possible—otherwise this tasty salad can take forever to make."*

—minutemeals' Chef Katell

step 1

plate the **french cheeses and fruit**

A selection of French cheeses, 1/4 pound each, of: ripe Camembert, chèvre (goat cheese), and Morbier

A selection of seasonal fruits, such as: seedless red and green grapes in bunches, fresh figs, and ripe pears

French bread or crackers or toasts, for serving

1. Remove the wrappers from the cheeses, place the cheeses on a platter, and let stand at room temperature until serving time.

2. Arrange the fruit on another platter. Place the platter in the refrigerator until serving time.

step 2

make the **fresh tuna salad niçoise**

1 bag (1 pound 6 ounces) diced ready-to-cook par-cooked potatoes, such as Naturally Yours (bagged in the produce department)

1 jar (4 ounces) marinated artichoke hearts

1 generous cup red pepper strips

1 cup cooked green beans

1/2 cup red onion slices

1 cup niçoise or kalamata olives

3 ripe tomatoes, cut into wedges

2 tablespoons drained capers

1/4 cup mustard vinaigrette, or more to taste

Olive oil for cooking

1 pound fresh tuna steak, about 1 inch thick

Salt and pepper to taste

Dried herbes de Provence

3 to 4 cups prewashed romaine leaves

4 peeled hard-cooked eggs

6 anchovy fillets, rinsed and patted dry

1. Place the potatoes in a large bowl.

2. Drain the artichoke hearts, reserving some of the marinating oil, if desired, for sprinkling on the salad. Place the artichokes in the bowl.

3. Add the pepper strips, green beans, onion slices, olives, tomatoes, and capers. Drizzle with mustard vinaigrette to taste and toss gently, being careful not to break up the potatoes.

4. In a large nonstick skillet, heat 2 tablespoons olive oil over moderately high heat until hot. Season the tuna with salt and pepper and herbes de Provence. Add the tuna to the skillet and cook for 4 minutes. Turn, season the second side with salt, pepper, and herbes de Provence, and cook 4 minutes, or until just cooked through. Transfer the tuna to a plate and cut it into 4 pieces.

5. Line a wide, shallow salad bowl or a platter with high sides with the lettuce leaves. Slice the hard-cooked eggs into quarters.

6. Arrange the potato salad mixture on the lettuce leaves. Place the tuna pieces on top. Arrange the eggs around the rim and garnish with the anchovy fillets.

step 3

serve

1. Place the salad on the table, with 4 dinner plates for serving and additional salad dressing, on the side, if desired. Serve with the French bread.

2. Before serving dessert, quarter the figs and pears. Place the fruit and cheese platters on the table. Serve the cheese with more French bread.

Fresh Tuna Salad Niçoise
Single serving is 1/4 of the total recipe
CALORIES 507; PROTEIN 39g; CARBS 33g;
TOTAL FAT 25g; SAT FAT 4g; CHOLESTEROL 272mg;
SODIUM 2027mg; FIBER 7g

Nutrition Analysis includes 1/4 cup vinaigrette.

minute
20-minute gourmet

poultry menus

meals

menus

chicken à la king

microwave white rice
mixed lettuces and spinach salad
boston cream pie

shopping list

Minute rice

Skinless boneless
chicken breasts

Fresh parsley

Frozen peas

Jarred diced pimientos

Tomato

Prewashed mixed spring or
baby greens

Dijon vinaigrette dressing,
store-bought or homemade

Boston cream pie

from the salad bar

Mushroom slices (or from the
produce department)

Prewashed baby spinach
leaves (or from the produce
department)

from your pantry

Cucumber slices

Onion

Olive oil

All-purpose flour

Low-fat (2%) milk

Paprika

Salt and pepper

serves 4

step **1** cook the **white rice**

step **2** cook the **chicken à la king**

step **3** assemble the **mixed lettuces and spinach salad**

step **4** **serve**

luckyforyou

If you've run out of time but still want to make this popular main dish, here's how: Don't cook the chicken. Buy roasted turkey breast or smoked turkey breast and simply cube it when you get home. It's already cooked, so all you have to do is stir it in at the end of Step 2.

"This is great comfort food. Sometimes I make this menu even easier, and serve the chicken over warm halved croissants or slices of challah."

—minutemeals' Chef Hillary

step 1

cook the **white rice**

2 cups water

2 cups Minute rice

In a 2-quart microwave-safe bowl, combine the water and rice. Cover and microwave on High for 8 minutes. Let stand, covered, for 5 minutes.

step 2

cook the **chicken à la king**

1 1/2 pounds skinless boneless chicken breasts

1 small onion

4 teaspoons olive oil

1 cup mushroom slices

1/3 cup all-purpose flour

2 cups low-fat (2%) milk

1/4 cup chopped fresh parsley

1/2 cup frozen peas, thawed

1 jar (2 ounces) diced pimiento, drained

1/2 teaspoon paprika

Salt and pepper to taste

1. Cut the chicken into 1/2-inch cubes. Coarsely chop the onion.

2. In a 12-inch nonstick skillet, heat the olive oil over medium-high heat until hot. Add the chicken and chopped onion and cook, stirring, until the chicken pieces are golden brown, about 4 minutes.

3. Add the sliced mushrooms and cook, stirring, for 1 minute. Stir in the flour and cook, stirring constantly, for 1 minute. Gradually pour in the milk and stir to blend. Bring the mixture to a boil and cook, stirring occasionally, until the sauce is thickened, 7 to 10 minutes.

4. Meanwhile, chop enough parsley to measure 1/4 cup. Remove the chicken mixture from the heat and stir in the parsley, peas, pimiento, paprika, and salt and pepper until well combined.

step 3

assemble the **mixed lettuces and spinach salad**

1 tomato

1 bag (5 ounces) prewashed mixed spring or baby greens

4 ounces prewashed baby spinach leaves

1/2 cup cucumber slices

3 tablespoons Dijon vinaigrette dressing

1. Slice the tomato into 8 wedges.

2. In a large salad bowl, combine the lettuces, spinach, cucumber slices, and tomato wedges. Add the vinaigrette, toss, and place the bowl on the table.

step 4

serve

1. Fluff the rice with a fork. Divide the rice among 4 plates and top with some of the chicken. Serve immediately with the salad.

2. When ready for dessert, cut the Boston cream pie into slices, plate, and serve.

Chicken à la King
Single serving is 1/4 of the total recipe
CALORIES 365; PROTEIN 47g; CARBS 19g;
TOTAL FAT 10g; SAT FAT 3g; CHOLESTEROL 109mg;
SODIUM 390mg; FIBER 3g

polynesian chicken

spinach salad

portuguese sweet bread

vanilla ice cream with sliced bananas and chocolate sauce

shopping list

Roasted or barbecued whole chicken (from the prepared foods section or deli counter)

Canned sweet potatoes

Pineapple slices
(fresh from the produce department, or canned)

Lemons (for juice)

Apricot preserves

Sunflower kernels

Prewashed baby spinach leaves (from the salad bar or the produce department)

Portuguese sweet bread

Vanilla ice cream

Ripe bananas

from your pantry

Nonstick cooking spray

Lite soy sauce

Salad dressing of choice, store-bought or homemade

Chocolate sauce

serves 4

beforeyoustart

Preheat the oven 425°F to heat the chicken.

step	1	prepare the **polynesian chicken**
step	2	while the chicken is heating, assemble the **spinach salad**
step	3	**serve**

 Everything in this menu is readily available in almost any supermarket. If you can't find sweet Portuguese bread, substitute another sweet egg bread, like challah.

"I love this one-dish main course. Fresh pineapple, sweet potatoes, and a sweet apricot-soy sauce make it slightly exotic."

—minutemeals' Chef Joanne

step 1

prepare the **polynesian chicken**

1 (3-pound) roasted or barbecued whole chicken

1 can (15 ounces) sweet potatoes

1 1/2 cups peeled and cored fresh pineapple slices or 1 can (16 ounces) sliced pineapple rings packed in juice

1/4 cup fresh lemon juice (2 lemons)

3/4 cup apricot preserves

2 tablespoons lite soy sauce

1. Preheat the oven to 425°F. Line a large rimmed baking sheet or shallow roasting pan with aluminum foil. Generously coat with nonstick cooking spray.

2. Cut the chicken into pieces and place them on the baking sheet. Drain the sweet potatoes. Arrange them and the fresh pineapple slices in one layer around the chicken on the baking sheet.

3. Squeeze 1/4 cup fresh lemon juice into a small bowl. Add the apricot preserves and soy sauce and stir to combine. Spoon the glaze over the chicken, sweet potatoes, and pineapple. Bake for 10 to 12 minutes, until the chicken is heated through.

step 2

while the chicken is heating, assemble the **spinach salad**

1/4 cup sunflower kernels

1 bag (10 ounces) prewashed baby spinach leaves

Salad dressing of choice

1. Place the sunflower kernels in a small baking pan and toast them in the oven with the chicken about 5 minutes, until fragrant. Remove to a plate and let cool.

2. Meanwhile, place the spinach in a bowl. Add the toasted sunflower kernels and dressing and toss. Place the bowl on the table.

step 3

serve

1. Transfer the chicken, sweet potatoes, and pineapple to a platter and drizzle with the juices in the pan. Place the platter on the table.

2. Place the sweet bread on a cutting board with a serrated knife and place on the table.

3. When ready for dessert, scoop the ice cream into bowls. Slice bananas over the top and pour chocolate sauce over all. Serve.

Polynesian Chicken
Single serving is 1/4 of the total recipe
CALORIES 774; PROTEIN 94g; CARBS 60g; TOTAL FAT 18g; SAT FAT 0g; CHOLESTEROL 304mg; SODIUM 603mg; FIBER 1g

chicken breasts
with scallion-ginger sauce

jasmine rice

steamed green beans

tangerines and
almond cookies

menu gameplan

serves 4

step **1** microwave the **jasmine rice**

step **2** prepare the **steamed green beans**

step **3** cook the **chicken breasts with scallion-ginger sauce**

step **4** **serve**

shopping list

Jasmine rice

Green beans

Skinless boneless chicken breast halves

Sesame seeds (optional)

Scallions

Gingerroot

Tangerines

Almond cookies

from your pantry

Butter

Salt and pepper

Canola oil

Garlic

Fat-free reduced-sodium chicken broth

Lite soy sauce

Cornstarch

luckyforyou If you want to really cut back on the amount of chopping in this menu, use pre-chopped garlic and ginger, available in jars in the produce sections of most supermarkets.

"Here you get the delectable flavors of an Asian stir-fry without all the chopping. How? The chicken breasts are cooked whole."

—minutemeals' Chef Tina

step 1

microwave the **jasmine rice**

- 1 cup jasmine rice
- 1 teaspoon butter

Microwave the jasmine rice in a microwave-safe bowl with the amount of water and for the time given on the package. When done, remove the bowl from the microwave oven and let stand, still covered, for 5 minutes, before fluffing the rice with a fork. Be sure to uncover the casserole carefully, averting your face, so that the steam does not burn. Stir in the butter and keep warm, covered.

step 2

prepare the **steamed green beans**

- 1 pound green beans

1. Trim the green beans and rinse them.

2. Pour water into a 3-quart saucepan to measure 1 inch. Place a steamer basket in the pan, cover, and bring the water to a boil over high heat. Place the beans in the basket, cover the pan, and steam for 8 to 10 minutes, or until crisp-tender.

3. Remove the pan from the heat, transfer the beans to a bowl, and keep warm, covered.

step 3

cook the **chicken breasts with scallion-ginger sauce**

- 4 skinless boneless chicken breast halves (5 ounces each)
- Salt and pepper to taste
- 2 tablespoons sesame seeds, for garnish (optional)
- 1 tablespoon canola oil
- 8 scallions
- 1 tablespoon minced ginger (1 medium knob gingerroot)
- 3 garlic cloves
- 1 cup fat-free reduced-sodium chicken broth
- 1/4 cup lite soy sauce
- 2 tablespoons cornstarch

1. One at a time, place a chicken breast half between 2 pieces of plastic wrap. With a meat mallet or the bottom of a heavy skillet, pound lightly to an even thickness. Remove the paper and season the breasts on both sides with salt and pepper.

2. If desired for garnish, in a small skillet, toast the sesame seeds over medium heat, stirring, until golden. Remove the pan from the heat and tip onto a plate.

3. In a large nonstick skillet, heat the canola oil over medium-high heat until hot. Add the chicken breasts and cook, turning them once, until nicely browned on both sides and cooked through, 8 to 10 minutes. Transfer the chicken to a plate and keep warm.

4. While the chicken is cooking, trim and thinly slice the scallions. Mince enough ginger to measure 1 tablespoon; mince the garlic.

5. In the nonstick skillet, cook the scallions, ginger, and garlic over medium heat, stirring, until softened and fragrant, 1 to 2 minutes, being careful not to let the garlic burn.

6. In a cup, stir together the chicken broth, soy sauce, and cornstarch, until blended. Pour into the skillet, bring to a boil, and cook, stirring constantly, until thickened, about 2 minutes.

step 4

serve

1. Spoon a serving of hot rice onto each of 4 dinner plates. Place 1 chicken breast half on top of the rice, and spoon some of the scallion-ginger sauce over all. Arrange a serving of green beans on the side. If desired, sprinkle each serving with some of the toasted sesame seeds and serve.

2. When ready for dessert, place the tangerines in a bowl and place on the table with small plates for the peels. Serve with the almond cookies.

Chicken Breasts with Scallion-Ginger Sauce
Single serving is 1/4 of the total recipe
CALORIES 226; PROTEIN 32g; CARBS 8g;
TOTAL FAT 7g; SAT FAT 0g; CHOLESTEROL 76mg;
SODIUM 646mg; FIBER 0g

☆ chicken chasseur
(chicken in mushroom sauce)

buttered egg noodles

green salad

french bread

fat-free vanilla fudge ice cream

shopping list

Skinless boneless
chicken breast halves

Crushed tomatoes

Fresh herb, such as basil,
tarragon, chives, or parsley

Lemon (for juice)

Prewashed mixed spring or
baby greens

French bread

Fat-free vanilla fudge
ice cream

from the salad bar

Onion slices

Mushroom slices (or from the
produce department)

from your pantry

Fine egg noodles

Butter

Garlic

Salt and pepper

Olive oil

Dried herbes de Provence

Wine vinegar

serves 4

beforeyoustart

Bring the water to a boil in a large
saucepan, covered, over high heat to
cook the noodles.

step 1 cook the **buttered egg noodles**

step 2 make the **chicken chasseur**

step 3 assemble the **green salad**

step 4 **serve**

headsup
You maximize the effect of a
fresh herb added to any dish if
you chop it just before using and add it just before serving.

"To make this menu as French as possible I used herbes de Provence. If you don't have it, substitute a combination of dried thyme and basil."

—minutemeals' Chef Anne

step 1

cook the **buttered egg noodles**

3 quarts water

Salt to taste

1 package (12 ounces) fine egg noodles

1 to 2 tablespoon butter, softened

Pour the water into a large saucepan, salt lightly, and cover. Bring to a boil over high heat. Add the noodles, stir to separate, and cook according to the directions on the package until tender. Drain, return to the pan, add the butter, and toss to combine. Cover and keep warm.

step 2

make the **chicken chasseur**

2 or 3 garlic cloves

1 1/4 pounds skinless boneless chicken breast halves

Salt and pepper to taste

2 tablespoons olive oil

1 cup onion slices

2 cups mushroom slices

1 teaspoon dried herbes de Provence

1 can (14 1/2 ounces) crushed tomatoes

3 tablespoons minced fresh basil, tarragon, chives, or parsley, or any combination

Juice of 1/2 lemon

1. Smash the garlic cloves with the flat side of a large knife. Rinse the chicken breasts, pat dry, then season with salt and pepper.

2. In a large nonstick skillet, heat 1 tablespoon of the oil over medium-high heat until hot. Add the chicken and cook for 1 minute on each side. Remove to a plate.

3. Add the remaining 1 tablespoon oil to the skillet. Add the onions, mushrooms, smashed garlic cloves, salt and pepper, and herbes de Provence. Cook, stirring occasionally, for 3 minutes, or until the vegetables are softened.

4. Add the tomatoes and stir to combine. Reduce the heat to medium low and return the chicken to the skillet. Bring the sauce to a boil and cover. Reduce the heat and simmer for 10 minutes, or until the chicken is just cooked through. Remove the pan from the heat and keep warm.

step 3

assemble the **green salad**

1 bag (5 ounces) prewashed mixed spring or baby greens

Olive oil to taste

Wine vinegar to taste

Place the greens in a salad bowl. Add olive oil and vinegar and toss. Place the bowl on the table.

step 4

serve

1. Chop enough fresh herb to measure 3 tablespoons. Add to the chicken with lemon juice to taste and stir to combine. Remove the whole garlic cloves, if desired, and correct the seasoning. Transfer the chicken to a serving platter and place on the table.

2. Divide the noodles among 4 dinner plates to serve as a bed for the chicken.

3. Slice the French bread, place it in a bread basket, and serve.

4. When ready for dessert, scoop the ice cream in small bowls and serve.

Chicken Chasseur
Single serving is 1/4 of the total recipe
CALORIES 389; PROTEIN 49g; CARBS 13g;
TOTAL FAT 15g; SAT FAT 3g; CHOLESTEROL 128mg;
SODIUM 407mg; FIBER 3g

chicken breasts en papillote
(chicken and fresh vegetables baked in foil)
curried couscous
honeydew slices with raspberry sauce

menu gameplan

shopping list

Thin-sliced chicken cutlets

Fresh basil leaves

Dry white wine

Couscous

Raspberry sauce or quick-thaw raspberries

from the salad bar

Carrot slices

Red pepper strips

Snow peas, trimmed

Honeydew melon slices (or from the produce department)

from your pantry

Salt and pepper

Olive oil

Fat-free reduced-sodium chicken broth

Curry powder

serves 4

beforeyoustart

Preheat the oven to 400°F to bake the foil packages.

step 1 assemble and bake the **chicken breasts en papillote**

step 2 while the chicken is baking, make the **curried couscous**

step 3 **serve**

luckyforyou

We are not asking you to cut out parchment paper in the shape of a butterfly (*papillote* means butterfly in French) for these packets. We've kept it simple. Make the packages with aluminum foil. If you want to make it *really* simple, buy Reynolds Wrapper Pop-Up sheets, which are already cut. (Use 2 sheets per package.)

"No clean-up is my idea of bliss! Also, 300 calories for a main dish is hard to beat, especially when it's tasty."

—minutemeals' Chef Hillary

step 1

assemble and bake the **chicken breasts en papillote**

4 thin-sliced chicken cutlets (1¼ pounds total weight)

Salt and pepper to taste

¼ cup chopped fresh basil leaves

1 cup carrot slices

1 cup thin red pepper slices

24 small trimmed snow peas

8 teaspoons olive oil

¼ cup dry white wine

1. Preheat the oven to 400°F. Cut out 4 12-inch squares of heavy-duty aluminum foil.

2. Rinse the chicken cutlets and pat dry. Season on both sides with salt and pepper.

3. Chop enough basil leaves to measure ¼ cup. In a medium bowl, combine the basil, carrot, and pepper slices, and snow peas.

4. Drizzle each square of foil with 2 teaspoons olive oil. Place a cutlet on each square, and top with ¼ of the vegetable mixture; sprinkle 1 tablespoon white wine over the top. Crimp the edges of the foil airtight to form 4 well-sealed packages. Place the 4 packets on a baking sheet. Bake 7 minutes.

step 2

while the chicken is baking, make the **curried couscous**

2 cups fat-free reduced-sodium chicken broth or water

2 teaspoons curry powder

1 tablespoon olive oil or butter

Salt and pepper to taste

1½ cups plain couscous

1. In a 1-quart saucepan with a lid, combine the chicken broth or water, curry powder, olive oil or butter, and salt and pepper. Cover and bring to a boil over high heat.

2. Stir in the couscous. Remove the pan from the heat, cover, and let stand for 5 minutes, until all the liquid is absorbed. Fluff the couscous with a fork and keep it warm.

step 3

serve

1. At serving time, place 1 foil package on each of 4 dinner plates. Using scissors and averting your face to avoid the steam that escapes, cut open the foil.

2. Serve the couscous with the chicken, either alongside or on a separate plate.

3. When ready for dessert, divide the melon slices among 4 dessert plates and either top with the raspberry sauce or serve it separately.

Chicken Breasts en Papillote
Single serving is ¼ of the total recipe
CALORIES 297; PROTEIN 34g; CARBS 7g;
TOTAL FAT 12g; SAT FAT 2g; CHOLESTEROL 82mg;
SODIUM 104mg; FIBER 3g

⭐ chicken breasts
with orange sauce

orzo with olive oil
green beans with almonds
apple pie with cinnamon ice cream

menu
gameplan

serves 4

shopping list

Orzo

Green beans

Slivered almonds

Skinless boneless chicken breast halves

Lemons (for juice)

Bitters

Apple pie

Cinnamon ice cream

from your pantry

Olive oil

Butter

All-purpose flour

Orange juice

Salt and pepper

beforeyoustart

Bring the water to a boil in a large saucepan, covered, over high heat to cook the orzo.

step **1** cook the **orzo with olive oil**

step **2** microwave the **green beans;** add the **almonds**

step **3** cook the **chicken breasts with orange sauce**

step **4** **serve**

**headsup** Take care not to overcook the chicken. The white meat of chicken dries out and becomes chewy. Cut into one of the pieces at its thickest point slightly before it is due to be done. (The meat should no longer be pink and the juices should run clear.)

"This menu is versatile, simple enough for a weekday dinner and stylish enough for dinner-party fare."

—minutemeals' Chef Katell

step 1

cook the **orzo with olive oil**

3 quarts water

Salt to taste

Orzo for 4 servings

Olive oil, for drizzling

Pour the water into a large saucepan, salt lightly, and cover. Bring to a boil over high heat. Add the orzo and cook for about 7 minutes, until *al dente*. Drain in a colander, return to the saucepan, and keep warm, covered.

step 2

microwave the **green beans;** add the **almonds**

1 1/2 pounds small green beans

2 tablespoons water

1 tablespoon butter

1/3 cup blanched slivered almonds

1. Trim the green beans and rinse.

2. Place the water in a microwave-safe dish and add the beans. Cover with plastic wrap and microwave on High for 2 minutes.

3. Meanwhile, in a small skillet, melt the butter over medium heat. Add the almonds and cook, stirring occasionally, until lightly toasted and fragrant, about 3 or 4 minutes. (Be careful not to let them over-brown.) Add the almond mixture to the green beans and toss to combine. Keep warm, covered.

step 3

cook the **chicken breasts with orange sauce**

2 tablespoons butter

4 skinless boneless chicken breast halves (5 ounces each)

2 tablespoons all-purpose flour

1 cup orange juice

2 tablespoons fresh lemon juice (1 lemon), or more to taste

1 teaspoon aromatic bitters, or to taste

Salt and pepper to taste

1. In a large heavy skillet, melt 1 tablespoon of the butter over medium-high heat. Add the chicken breasts in a single layer. Cook until golden on one side, 1 to 2 minutes; turn and cook until golden on the other, about 3 minutes total time. Be careful not to overcook.

2. Reduce the heat to low and cook until the chicken is done, 6 to 8 minutes, depending upon how thick the breasts are. Do not overcook.

3. While the chicken is cooking, in a medium saucepan, melt the remaining 1 tablespoon butter over medium heat. Add the flour and cook, stirring constantly, until well blended.

4. Gradually stir in the orange juice and cook, stirring constantly, until thickened, about 2 to 3 minutes. Add the lemon juice and bitters, and stir until combined. Season with salt and pepper.

step 4

serve

1. Transfer the orzo to a serving bowl and drizzle with olive oil to taste. Toss gently and place on the table.

2. Place the green beans on the table. Arrange the chicken breasts on a platter and pour the orange sauce over them. Serve the chicken either on a bed of the orzo or alongside.

3. When ready for dessert, cut the pie into slices, plate, and top with a scoop of the ice cream. Serve.

Chicken Breasts with Orange Sauce
Single serving is 1/4 of the total recipe
CALORIES 237; PROTEIN 30g; CARBS 11g;
TOTAL FAT 8g; SAT FAT 4g; CHOLESTEROL 92mg;
SODIUM 88mg; FIBER 0g

⭐ chicken piccata
sautéed snow peas and cherry tomatoes
crusty rolls
brownies

shopping list
Lemons
Thin-sliced chicken cutlets
Dry sherry
Capers
Crusty rolls
Brownies

from the salad bar
Cherry tomatoes
Snow peas

from your pantry
Garlic
Salt and pepper
All-purpose flour
Olive oil
Butter

menu gameplan

serves 4

step 1 cook the **chicken piccata**

step 2 heat the **crusty rolls**

step 3 sauté the **snow peas and cherry tomatoes**

step 4 **serve**

headsup
Thin-sliced chicken cutlets are key to the success of this variation on the renowned Italian favorite, veal piccata. Not only will the cutlets, as opposed to even small chicken breast halves, cook more quickly, they require little if any trimming.

"Fresh lemon adds more than you can imagine to a dish, and this piccata recipe is a perfect example."

—minutemeals' Chef Hillary

step 1

cook the **chicken piccata**

3 large lemons

2 large garlic cloves

4 thin-sliced chicken cutlets (1¼ pounds total weight)

Salt and pepper to taste

¼ cup all-purpose flour

1½ tablespoons olive oil

½ cup dry sherry

2 tablespoons drained capers

2 tablespoons butter

1. Slice 1 of the lemons into 8 thin slices. From the remaining lemons, squeeze ¼ cup juice. Mince the garlic.

2. Season the chicken on both sides with salt and pepper. Dredge the cutlets, one at a time, in the flour.

3. In a 12-inch nonstick skillet, heat the oil over medium-high heat until hot. Add the chicken and sauté for 4 to 5 minutes per side, or until golden brown. Transfer to a platter, and keep warm, covered.

4. Add the minced garlic to the skillet and cook, stirring, for 30 seconds, being careful not to let it brown. Add the sherry, lemon juice, and capers and combine, stirring and scraping the bottom of the pan with a wooden spoon to release the browned bits. Reduce the sauce over medium-high heat by half, stirring occasionally. Remove the pan from the heat and add the 8 lemon slices. Keep warm, covered.

step 2

heat the **crusty rolls**

4 crusty rolls, such as sourdough or French

Place the rolls in a toaster oven to heat while you sauté the snow peas and tomatoes.

step 3

sauté the **snow peas and cherry tomatoes**

¼ cup cherry tomatoes

2 garlic cloves

1 tablespoon olive oil

12 ounces snow peas, strings removed and trimmed

Salt and pepper to taste

1. Rinse the tomatoes and pat dry. Halve to measure ½ cup. Slice the garlic into slivers.

2. In a 10-inch skillet, heat the olive oil over high heat until hot. Add the slivered garlic and cook, stirring, 30 seconds. Add the snow peas and cook, stirring, for 2 minutes, or until bright green. Turn off the heat and add the tomatoes. Toss until just warmed through. Season with salt and pepper.

step 4

serve

1. Return the chicken to the pan and reheat in the sauce over low heat until just warmed through. Swirl in the butter until melted.

2. At serving time, divide the chicken and sauce among 4 dinner plates.

3. Divide the snow pea and tomato sauté among the plates. Remove the rolls from the oven and serve in a bread basket.

4. When ready for dessert, cut the brownies into squares and serve on a platter.

Chicken Piccata
Single serving is ¼ of the total recipe
CALORIES 305; PROTEIN 30g; CARBS 9g; TOTAL FAT 13g; SAT FAT 1g; CHOLESTEROL 90mg; SODIUM 243mg; FIBER 0g

macadamia nut-crumbed chicken breasts

basmati rice
gingery banana chutney
coconut cream pie

shopping list

Basmati rice

Bananas

Cilantro

Lime (for juice)

Crystallized ginger

Skinless boneless
chicken breast halves

Macadamia nuts

Coconut cream pie

from your pantry

Butter

Ground cinnamon

Ground cardamom (optional)

Maple syrup

Salt and pepper

Fine dry bread crumbs

All-purpose flour

Eggs

Vegetable oil

serves 6

step 1   cook the **basmati rice**

step 2   prepare the **chutney**

step 3   cook the **macadamia nut-crumbed chicken breasts**

step 4   **serve**

headsup

Nuts, whether you are toasting them in the oven or cooking them in a skillet, tend to burn easily due to their high fat content. This includes nuts that are used as coating. Be careful to sauté the macadamia-coated cutlets over medium-low heat and to keep a watch on the side that is cooking.

"This menu is elegant and unusual—a conversation piece all of its own, and perfect for company."

—minutemeals' Chef Nancy

step 1

cook the **basmati rice**

1 cup basmati rice

Cook the rice in a medium saucepan in the amount of water and for the time suggested on the package. Keep warm, covered.

step 2

prepare the **chutney**

4 large firm-ripe bananas

4 tablespoons chopped cilantro

$1/2$ lime

2 to 3 tablespoons chopped crystallized ginger

1 tablespoon butter

$1/4$ teaspoon ground cinnamon

$1/8$ teaspoon ground cardamom (optional)

2 tablespoons maple syrup

3 tablespoons water

Pinch of salt, for serving

1. Peel and dice the bananas into $1/2$-inch pieces. Chop enough cilantro to measure 4 tablespoons. Juice the lime. Chop enough crystallized ginger to measure up to 3 tablespoons.

2. In a small saucepan, melt the butter over medium heat. Add the crystallized ginger, cinnamon, and cardamom, if using, and cook for 30 seconds. Add the bananas, maple syrup, and water, lower the heat, and cover the pan. Cook, stirring frequently, until the bananas are tender, about 3 to 4 minutes. Remove the pan from the heat.

step 3

cook the **macadamia nut-crumbed chicken breasts**

6 skinless boneless chicken breast halves (5 to 6 ounces each)

$3/4$ cup macadamia nuts

$3/4$ cup fine dry bread crumbs

$1/2$ cup all-purpose flour

3 large eggs

Salt and pepper to taste

2 tablespoons vegetable oil

2 tablespoons butter

1. Place the chicken breasts in a single layer between 2 pieces of plastic wrap and pound lightly with a meat mallet or a rolling pin until they are somewhat evened out and flattened.

2. Place the macadamia nuts with $1/2$ cup of the bread crumbs in a food processor or blender and pulse until finely ground. In a shallow bowl, combine the ground crumb/nut mixture with the remaining $1/4$ cup bread crumbs.

3. Place the flour in another shallow bowl. Lightly beat the eggs in a third shallow bowl with salt and pepper.

4. Dip a chicken breast into the flour, then into the eggs, then into the nut-crumb mixture; pat the crumbs on to adhere. Set the breast on a plate and repeat with remaining chicken.

5. Heat the vegetable oil and butter in a large heavy skillet over medium heat until the butter is melted. Reduce the heat to medium-low and add the chicken breasts in a single layer. (If the heat is too high, the coating will burn.) Cook until golden on one side, 3 to 4 minutes. Turn and cook until golden on the other, about 3 minutes. Remove to a serving platter.

step 4

serve

1. Finish the chutney: Add the lime juice, a pinch of salt, and the cilantro and stir to combine. Taste and add more sweetener, if necessary. Transfer to a serving bowl.

2. Transfer the rice to a bowl. Place the platter of chicken on the table. Serve the chicken on or alongside the rice, with the chutney as garnish.

3. When ready for dessert, cut the pie into slices, plate, and serve.

Macadamia Nut-Crumbed Chicken Breasts
Single serving is $1/6$ of the total recipe

CALORIES 529; PROTEIN 36g; CARBS 40g; TOTAL FAT 25g; SAT FAT 4g; CHOLESTEROL 184mg; SODIUM 276mg; FIBER 3g

Nutrient Analysis includes banana chutney.

☆ chicken fajitas
all the fixings
frozfruit bars

menu
gameplan

shopping list

Flour tortillas
(7-inch diameter)

Dried Mexican seasoning
blend (available in jars in
the spice section)

Limes

Thin-sliced chicken cutlets

Ripe avocado

Fresh hot chile peppers

Cilantro

Salsa

Sour cream or
plain nonfat yogurt

Pre-grated Monterey Jack
or Cheddar cheese

Frozfruit bars

from the salad bar

Red or yellow onion slices

Green pepper slices

from your pantry

Garlic

Olive oil

Salt and pepper

Tomato paste

Fat-free reduced-sodium
chicken broth

Olive oil cooking spray

serves 6

beforeyoustart

Preheat the oven to 350°F to heat
the tortillas.

step **1** heat the **tortillas**

step **2** make the **fajita filling**

step **3** prepare the **fixings**

step **4** **serve**

luckyforyou Bell peppers come de-ribbed,
seeded, and sliced at
the salad bar. Buying them ready to cook saves a lot of
time here.

"Fajitas make great party fare. The filling can be doubled or tripled easily. For additional flavor, try grilling the chicken on the barbecue."

—minutemeals' Chef Miriam

step 1

heat the **tortillas**

12 flour tortillas (7-inch diameter)

Preheat the oven to 350°F. Wrap the stack of tortillas in aluminum foil and heat for 10 minutes. (If using a microwave oven instead, place the tortillas between sheets of paper towels and heat according to the instructions for your microwave.)

step 2

make the **fajita filling**

For the vegetables

3 garlic cloves

2 tablespoons olive oil

2 cups red or yellow onion slices

2 cups green pepper slices

2 teaspoons dried Mexican seasoning blend (available in jars in the spice section)

Salt and pepper to taste

2 tablespoons tomato paste

1/2 cup fat-free reduced-sodium chicken broth or water

Juice of 1 lime

For the chicken

6 thin-sliced chicken cutlets (2 pounds total)

Salt and pepper to taste

1 teaspoon Mexican seasoning blend

Olive oil cooking spray

Juice of 1 lime

1. Finely chop the garlic.

2. In a 12-inch nonstick skillet, heat the olive oil over medium-high heat until hot. Add the onions, peppers, Mexican seasoning, and salt and pepper and cook, stirring often, for 5 minutes, until the vegetables start to soften.

3. Add the minced garlic and tomato paste and cook, stirring, for 1 minute. Stir in the broth or water. Cover and cook over medium heat, stirring occasionally, for 5 minutes, or until the vegetables are tender. Add the juice of 1 lime, or to taste, and correct the seasonings. Remove the skillet from the heat.

4. Cook the chicken: Season the cutlets on both sides with salt and pepper and the Mexican seasoning blend.

5. Spray a grill pan or heavy skillet with the olive oil cooking spray and heat over medium-high heat until hot. Add the chicken and cook for 2 to 3 minutes per side, or until cooked through but still moist. Transfer to a cutting board.

step 3

prepare the **fixings**

Ripe avocado, preferably Haas

Fresh hot chile peppers, such as jalapeño or serrano chiles

Cilantro

Limes

Salsa

Sour cream or plain nonfat yogurt

Pre-grated Monterey Jack or Cheddar cheese

Select your favorite fajita accompaniments. Peel and chop the avocado. Seed and chop some fresh chiles, if using. Coarsely chop some cilantro, including the stems. Cut the limes into wedges. Put each accompaniment in a separate bowl and place on the table.

step 4

serve

1. Reheat the vegetables.

2. Meanwhile, slice the chicken cutlets into strips.

3. Put the vegetables on a platter, top with the chicken strips, and sprinkle with fresh lime juice.

4. To serve, place 2 warm tortillas on each of 6 dinner plates; immediately top with some of the chicken and vegetables, and garnish with one or all of the accompaniments. Roll up and serve (with lots of napkins).

5. When ready for dessert, serve the fruit bars directly from the freezer.

Chicken Fajitas
Single serving is 1/6 of the total recipe
(2 fajitas per serving)

CALORIES 241; PROTEIN 6g; CARBS 36g;
TOTAL FAT 9g; SAT FAT 0g; CHOLESTEROL 0mg;
SODIUM 231mg; FIBER 2g

Nutrient Analysis does not include any fixings such as sour cream, avocado, cheese, and so on.

☆ chicken ratatouille

couscous with roasted garlic
romaine vinaigrette
french bread
caramel custard

menu
gameplan

shopping list

Small eggplant

Chicken tenders

Tomatoes

Packaged couscous with roasted garlic and olive oil

Prewashed romaine lettuce

French bread

Caramel custard

from the salad bar

Green pepper slices

Zucchini slices

Mushroom slices (or from the produce department)

from your pantry

Garlic

Olive oil

Salt and pepper

Dried basil

Dried thyme

Fat-free reduced-sodium chicken broth

Vinaigrette dressing, store-bought or homemade

serves 4

step	1	make the **chicken ratatouille**
step	2	prepare the **couscous with roasted garlic**
step	3	assemble the **romaine vinaigrette**
step	4	**serve**

luckyforyou Chicken tenders really save a lot of time here. If you don't see tenders in your market, buy chicken cut for stir-fry instead.

step 1

make the chicken ratatouille

4 garlic cloves

1 small eggplant (about 3/4 pound)

1 pound chicken tenders

2 tablespoons olive oil

Salt and pepper to taste

1 cup green pepper slices

1 cup zucchini slices

1 cup mushroom slices

1/2 teaspoon dried or 1 1/2 teaspoons chopped fresh basil leaves

1/4 teaspoon dried or 3/4 teaspoon fresh thyme leaves

2 medium tomatoes

1. Slice the garlic cloves. Quarter the eggplant lengthwise, then slice the quarters crosswise. Cut the chicken tenders in half crosswise.

2. In a large nonstick skillet, heat 1 tablespoon of the olive oil over medium-high heat until hot. Add the chicken pieces, season with salt and pepper, and cook, tossing, for 2 to 3 minutes, or until cooked through. Remove to a plate.

3. Add the remaining 1 tablespoon olive oil to the skillet. Add the sliced garlic, the eggplant, pepper, zucchini, mushrooms, salt and pepper, and the herbs. Cook, stirring occasionally, for 3 minutes, or until the vegetables are softened.

4. Cut the tomatoes into 8 pieces each. Add to the skillet. Bring the vegetables to a boil and cover. Simmer for 2 minutes, or until the tomatoes have just softened. Return the chicken to the skillet and cook, uncovered, just until the chicken is heated through, about 3 minutes.

step 2

prepare the couscous with roasted garlic

1 1/4 cups water or fat-free reduced-sodium chicken broth

1 tablespoon olive oil

1 box (5.8 ounces) couscous with roasted garlic and olive oil

In a medium saucepan, combine the water or chicken broth and olive oil. Cover and bring to a boil over high heat. Stir in the couscous, cover, and remove the pan from the heat. Let stand for 5 minutes, or until all the liquid has been absorbed.

step 3

assemble the romaine vinaigrette

1/2 bag (5 ounces) prewashed romaine lettuce

1/4 cup vinaigrette dressing

Place the romaine in a salad bowl. Add the dressing and toss. Place the bowl on the table.

step 4

serve

1. Fluff the couscous with a fork, then spread on a large serving platter.

2. Correct the seasonings in the ratatouille, spoon it over the couscous, and serve.

3. Place the bread on a bread board and put on the table.

4. When ready for dessert, unmold the individual custards onto dessert plates, being sure to include the caramel sauce.

Chicken Ratatouille
Single serving is 1/4 of the total recipe
CALORIES 250; PROTEIN 29g; CARBS 15g;
TOTAL FAT 9g; SAT FAT 0g; CHOLESTEROL 66mg;
SODIUM 85mg; FIBER 5g

☆ chicken tetrazzini

tomato and romaine salad
breadsticks
raspberry sorbet and chocolate biscotti

menu
gameplan

shopping list

Dried spaghetti or linguine

Skinless boneless chicken breast halves

Tomatoes

Prewashed romaine lettuce

Italian salad dressing, store-bought or homemade

Breadsticks

Raspberry sorbet

Chocolate biscotti

from the salad bar

Mushroom slices (or from the produce department)

Chopped scallions

from your pantry

Salt

Olive oil

Garlic

Whole milk

All-purpose flour

Grated Parmesan cheese

Dried basil

serves 4

beforeyoustart

Bring the water to a boil in a large pot, covered, over high heat to cook the pasta. Preheat the broiler.

step 1 cook the **pasta;** make the **chicken tetrazzini**

step 2 assemble the **tomato and romaine salad**

step 3 serve

headsup
Not *all* pre-grated Parmesan cheese is equally flavorful, or to be recommended. When we don't have the time to grate the fresh ourselves—always the first option—we like the cheese sold in plastic containers in large supermarkets near the deli counter or produce section, not the kind in cardboard shakers on the shelves. The texture and flavor of the non-shaker variety are much closer to the real McCoy. Be sure to store in the refrigerator to preserve that flavor.

"Think Chicken Tetrazzini whenever you have leftover cooked spaghetti or linguine on hand. You will have a major ingredient already prepped."

—minutemeals' Chef Joanne

step 1

cook the **pasta;** make the **chicken tetrazzini**

For the pasta

4 quarts water

Salt to taste

8 ounces dried spaghetti or linguine

1 tablespoon olive oil

For the chicken

2 garlic cloves

4 skinless boneless chicken breast halves (1¼ pounds total)

2 tablespoons olive oil

1½ cups mushroom slices

½ cup chopped scallions

1½ cups whole milk

2 tablespoons all-purpose flour

¼ cup grated Parmesan cheese

½ teaspoon dried basil or 1½ teaspoons chopped fresh basil

¼ teaspoon salt

1. Cook the pasta: Pour the water into a large pot, salt lightly, and cover. Bring to a boil over high heat. Add the spaghetti, stir to separate the strands, and cook, according to the package directions until *al dente*. Drain well. Return to the pot, toss with the olive oil, and keep warm, covered.

2. Cook the chicken: Slice the garlic cloves. Rinse the chicken breast halves, pat dry, and slice each crosswise into 8 pieces. Preheat the broiler.

3. In a large nonstick skillet, heat 1 tablespoon of the olive oil over medium-high heat until hot. Add the sliced chicken and cook for 5 minutes, turning the pieces often. Add the remaining 1 tablespoon oil, mushrooms, scallions, and garlic. Stir-fry just until the chicken is cooked through and white in color throughout.

4. In a quart jar with lid, combine the milk, flour, 2 tablespoons of the Parmesan, basil, and salt. Seal the jar with the lid and shake until the mixture is smooth. Pour over the chicken in the skillet and cook, stirring constantly, until the sauce has thickened.

5. Transfer the cooked spaghetti to a shallow flameproof 11- or 12-inch baking dish, top with the chicken mixture, and sprinkle with the remaining 2 tablespoons Parmesan. Place the dish under the broiler about 4 inches from the heat and broil until the top is lightly browned, about 1 minute.

step 2

assemble the **tomato and romaine salad**

2 large ripe tomatoes

½ bag (5 ounces) prewashed romaine lettuce

¼ cup Italian salad dressing

1. Rinse the tomatoes and slice thin.

2. Place the romaine in a large shallow salad bowl. Arrange the tomato slices around the edge of the bowl and drizzle with the dressing. Place the bowl on the table.

step 3

serve

1. Take the chicken tetrazzini to the table and serve directly from the baking dish.

2. Toss the salad at the table.

3. Place the breadsticks in a basket and place on the table.

4. When ready for dessert, scoop the raspberry sorbet into bowls and garnish each with a chocolate biscotti or two.

Chicken Tetrazzini
Single serving is ¼ of the total recipe
CALORIES 462; PROTEIN 43g; CARBS 41g;
TOTAL FAT 14g; SAT FAT 3g; CHOLESTEROL 86mg;
SODIUM 461mg; FIBER 1g

chicken fingers
with dipping sauces
apple wedges and orange sections
cherry tomatoes and cucumber spears
ice cream sandwiches

menu gameplan

shopping list

Apples, such as Golden Delicious or Gala

Cucumbers

Blue cheese dressing

Honey barbecue sauce

Skinless boneless chicken breasts

Cap'n Crunch cereal

Cornflakes

Onion powder

Garlic powder

Ice cream sandwiches

from the salad bar

Orange wedges or sections

Cherry tomatoes

from your pantry

Ketchup

Egg

Whole milk

All-purpose flour

Pepper

Canola oil

serves 4 to 6

step **1** plate the **fruit and vegetables**

step **2** plate the **dipping sauces**

step **3** make the **chicken fingers**

step **4** serve

headsup

The chicken fingers become crispy on the outside because they're fried in hot oil. Be very careful when cooking with hot oil, especially when adding anything to it. It can splatter and burn a cook badly.

"Everybody adores these chicken fingers, and asks for the recipe. You feel like the best cook in the world. Picky-eating kids like them, too."

—minutemeals' Chef Carolyn

step 1

plate the **fruit and vegetables**

3 crisp apples, such as Golden Delicious or Gala

Orange wedges or sections

Cherry tomatoes

3 medium cucumbers

1. Cut the apples into wedges and remove the cores. Arrange the wedges on a plate with the orange wedges.

2. Rinse the tomatoes, pat dry, and place in the middle of a deep plate. Trim the ends off the cucumbers and cut the cucumbers lengthwise into spears. Place the spears around the rim of the plate. Place the fruit and the vegetable platters on the table.

step 2

plate the **dipping sauces**

Blue cheese dressing

Honey barbecue sauce

Ketchup

Place each of the dipping sauces in a shallow bowl and place the bowls on the table.

step 3

make the **chicken fingers**

2 pounds skinless boneless chicken breasts

2 cups Cap'n Crunch cereal

1 1/2 cups cornflakes

1 large egg

1 cup whole milk

1 cup all-purpose flour

1 teaspoon onion powder

1 teaspoon garlic powder

1/2 teaspoon pepper

Canola oil, for frying

1. Rinse the chicken and pat dry. Cut into 32 pieces.

2. Coarsely crush both the cereals with a rolling pin; place in a pie plate. In a bowl, beat the egg with the milk until combined. In a plastic food storage bag, combine the flour, onion and garlic powders, and pepper; shake to mix.

3. In a large heavy deep skillet, heat 1 inch canola oil over medium heat until hot but not smoking.

4. As the oil heats, add batches of chicken to the seasoned flour, close the bag, and shake to coat. Remove the pieces to a plate. Dip the floured chicken, 1 piece at a time, into the egg mixture, then into the cereal, coating all sides.

5. Carefully place the chicken, a few pieces at a time, in the hot oil and fry until golden brown and cooked through, about 3 to 5 minutes, depending on the size. As the chicken is done, remove to paper towels to drain. Continue to fry chicken, adding more oil as needed to the skillet, being sure to heat it until hot before adding the next batch of chicken.

step 4

serve

1. Place the chicken fingers on individual plates and eat with the dipping sauce of choice. Use the blue cheese dressing on the vegetables and on the chicken, too.

2. When ready for dessert, serve the ice cream sandwiches (with lots of napkins for the small fry) directly from the freezer.

Chicken Fingers
Single serving is 1/5 of the total recipe

CALORIES 444; PROTEIN 30g; CARBS 37g; TOTAL FAT 19g; SAT FAT 2g; CHOLESTEROL 107mg; SODIUM 253mg; FIBER 3g

Nutrient Analysis does not include dipping sauces.

sesame chicken fingers
on soba noodles
cucumber salad with pickled ginger
green tea ice cream

serves 4

shopping list

Chicken tenders

Sesame seeds

Lemon

Soba noodles
(in the produce department)

Mirin

European "seedless" cucumber

Pickled sushi ginger

Green tea ice cream

from your pantry

Dijon mustard

All-purpose flour

Pepper

Canola oil

Lite soy sauce

Toasted sesame oil

Rice vinegar

beforeyoustart

Bring the water to a boil in a large pot, covered, over high heat to cook the soba noodles.

| step | 1 | cook the **sesame chicken fingers** |

| step | 2 | cook the **soba noodles** |

| step | 3 | prepare the **cucumber salad with pickled ginger** |

| step | 4 | **serve** |

luckyforyou

There is a great way to simplify this menu if you are running short on time. Serve a green salad instead of the soba noodles. Don't even take the time to measure the dressing. Just toss the greens with equal parts soy sauce, toasted sesame oil, and rice vinegar.

"Want Japanese, but don't feel like going out to eat? Try this Japanese-inspired meal, with a lot of the traditional flavors and textures."

—minutemeals' Chef Nancy

step 1

cook the **sesame chicken fingers**

2 tablespoons Dijon mustard

1 1/2 pounds chicken tenders

1/3 cup sesame seeds

3 tablespoons all-purpose flour

Pepper to taste

6 tablespoons canola oil

1 lemon, for serving

1. Place the mustard in a small bowl. Lay the chicken tenders side by side on a cutting board. Brush with mustard on both sides.

2. Heat 2 heavy 10-inch skillets over medium-high heat.

3. On a plate, combine the sesame seeds and flour and season with pepper. When the pans are hot, add about 3 tablespoons canola oil to each. (You are not deep-frying, but you will need a little more oil than if you were sautéing.)

4. Dip the mustard-brushed tenders in the sesame-flour mixture. Shake off excess. When the oil is hot, add some of the tenderloins to each pan in a single layer and cook until golden, about 2 to 3 minutes. Turn and cook the second side in same manner, until cooked through. With a spatula or tongs, remove the pieces to a large plate.

step 2

cook the **soba noodles**

4 quarts water

8 ounces soba noodles or fresh pasta

2 tablespoons lite soy sauce

2 tablespoons mirin

2 teaspoons toasted sesame oil

1. Pour the water into a large pot. Cover and bring to a boil over high heat. Add the noodles and cook according to the package directions until tender, about 7 to 8 minutes. Drain well.

2. Meanwhile, in a medium bowl, combine the soy sauce, mirin, and sesame oil.

3. Add the drained noodles to the bowl and toss.

step 3

prepare the **cucumber salad with pickled ginger**

1 medium English "seedless" cucumber

1 to 2 tablespoons chopped pickled sushi ginger

1 1/2 tablespoons rice vinegar

1 tablespoon lite soy sauce

1. Peel the cucumber and cut it in half lengthwise. Slice the cucumber thinly on the diagonal to make half moons and place in a medium bowl. Chop enough pickled ginger to measure 2 tablespoons, or to taste.

2. Add the pickled ginger, rice vinegar, and soy sauce to the bowl and toss gently to combine. Place the bowl on the table.

step 4

serve

1. Arrange the soba noodles on a platter and top with the chicken fingers.

2. Cut the lemon into 4 wedges and add to the platter for each diner to squeeze onto his or her chicken and soba.

3. When ready for dessert, scoop the green tea ice cream into small bowls and serve.

Sesame Chicken Fingers on Soba Noodles
Single serving is 1/4 of the total recipe
CALORIES 830; PROTEIN 46g; CARBS 48g;
TOTAL FAT 47g; SAT FAT 7g; CHOLESTEROL 109mg;
SODIUM 716mg; FIBER 5g
Nutrient Analysis includes soba noodles.

thai chicken curry
jasmine rice
mango sorbet

menu
gameplan

serves 4

step 1 cook the **jasmine rice**

step 2 make the **thai chicken curry**

step 3 **serve**

shopping list

Jasmine rice

Skinless boneless
chicken breast halves

Gingerroot

Onion slices
(from the salad bar)

Yellow curry paste

Unsweetened coconut milk

Cilantro

Mango chutney

Mango sorbet

from your pantry

Garlic

Butter

Canola oil

Fat-free reduced-sodium
chicken broth

Salt

luckyforyou
If you're short on time and the thought of having to cut chicken into 1-inch pieces is more than you can bear, use chicken cut for stir-fry instead. The strips will probably cook a little faster than the squares, so keep an eye out for doneness and forget about the shape.

"Thai food is fascinating. If you've never tried it, this curry is a great place to start. It's comforting and exotic at the same time."

—minutemeals' Chef Nancy

cook the **jasmine rice**

1 1/2 cups jasmine rice

Cook the jasmine rice in a medium saucepan in the amount of water and for the time suggested on the package. Keep warm, covered.

make the **thai chicken curry**

1 1/4 pounds skinless boneless chicken breasts halves

3/4 teaspoon minced garlic (1 small clove)

3/4 teaspoon chopped ginger (1 small piece of gingerroot)

1 tablespoon butter

1 tablespoon canola oil

1/4 cup onion slices

2 tablespoons yellow curry paste

1 cup fat-free reduced-sodium chicken broth

1/2 cup unsweetened coconut milk

1/4 cup finely chopped cilantro, or to taste

Salt to taste

Mango chutney, for serving

1. Rinse the chicken breasts and pat dry. Cut into 1-inch pieces.

2. Chop the garlic and enough ginger to measure 3/4 teaspoon each.

3. In a large nonstick skillet, melt the butter with the canola oil over medium-high heat. Add the onion, garlic, and ginger. Sauté, stirring, for 2 minutes, until the onion is softened.

4. Add the chicken pieces, and cook, stirring, for 2 minutes. Add the yellow curry paste and cook, stirring, for 1 or 2 minutes, until the chicken pieces are well coated with the paste.

5. Add the chicken broth and coconut milk, bring to a simmer, and cook gently for 8 to 10 minutes, until the chicken is cooked through.

6. While the chicken cooks, finely chop enough cilantro to measure 1/4 cup.

serve

1. Add salt to the curry, if necessary, transfer it to a shallow serving dish, and sprinkle with the chopped cilantro. Serve the chutney in a small bowl to be passed at the table.

2. Fluff the rice with a fork, transfer it to it a serving bowl, and place on the table.

3. When ready for dessert, scoop the mango sorbet into small bowls and serve.

Thai Chicken Curry
Single serving is 1/4 of the total recipe
CALORIES 272; PROTEIN 30g; CARBS 3g;
TOTAL FAT 15g; SAT FAT 7g; CHOLESTEROL 80mg;
SODIUM 199mg; FIBER 0g

flat but flavorful grilled chicken

red and green salad

garlic bread

cheesecake with blueberry topping

menu
gameplan

shopping list

Fresh oregano

Skinless boneless chicken breast halves

French bread

Cherry tomatoes (from the salad bar)

Prewashed mixed spring or baby greens

Italian salad dressing, store-bought or homemade

Cheesecake with blueberry topping

from your pantry

Salt and pepper

Extra virgin olive oil

Garlic-flavored olive oil

serves 4

beforeyoustart

Preheat the oven to 400°F to heat the garlic bread. Preheat the grill, if using.

| step | 1 | marinate and cook the **flat but flavorful grilled chicken** |

| step | 2 | make the **garlic bread** |

| step | 3 | assemble the **red and green salad** |

| step | 4 | **serve** |

luckyforyou Pounding meat evens out its thickness and also tender-izes it. Sometimes, though, it's a step in a recipe that no one wants to undertake. In that case, buy thin-sliced chicken cutlets. Just be careful not to overcook them on the grill. Some cutlets can be paper-thin.

"I love how light this chicken is and how fresh and clean the flavors are. It was inspired by a trip to northern Italy."

—minutemeals' Chef Nancy

step 1

marinate and cook the **flat but flavorful grilled chicken**

2 tablespoons chopped fresh oregano

4 skinless boneless chicken breast halves (about 1¼ pounds total)

Salt and pepper to taste

2 tablespoons extra virgin olive oil

1. Preheat the grill, if using. Chop enough oregano to measure 2 tablespoons.

2. If the butcher cannot flatten the chicken breasts for you, place 1 between 2 large pieces of plastic wrap. With a wooden rolling pin or meat mallet, gently pound the breast to an even ¼-inch thickness. Repeat with the remaining 3 chicken breasts. Season on both sides with salt and pepper.

3. In a pie plate, combine the olive oil and oregano. One at a time, add the pounded chicken breasts and turn to coat with the herbed oil. Stack the chicken in the marinade and let marinate while you move on to making the garlic bread.

4. To grill the chicken: Place the chicken breasts on the heated grill or grill pan and cook the first side until you can see the meat on the sides of the breast begin to turn opaque and the breast has grill marks, about 3 minutes, depending upon how hot the grill is. Turn and grill another 3 to 4 minutes, about 5 to 7 minutes total cooking time. Remove from the heat to prevent overcooking.

step 2

make the **garlic bread**

1 small loaf of French bread

2 tablespoons garlic-flavored olive oil

Salt to taste

1. Preheat the oven to 400°F.

2. Slice the loaf in half horizontally. Brush the cut sides with the flavored olive oil and sprinkle with salt. Place, cut side up, on a cookie sheet and heat until golden brown, about 7 to 10 minutes.

step 3

assemble the **red and green salad**

1 pint ripe cherry tomatoes

1 bag (5 ounces) prewashed mixed spring or baby greens

¼ cup Italian salad dressing

1. Rinse the tomatoes and pat dry. Halve, if desired.

2. Place the greens in a bowl, add the tomatoes and dressing, and toss.

step 4

serve

1. Mound ¼ of the salad on each of 4 dinner plates and lay a grilled chicken breast on top.

2. Slice the garlic bread, place in a bread basket, and place on the table.

3. When ready for dessert, cut the cheesecake into slices, plate, and serve.

Flat but Flavorful Grilled Chicken
Single serving is ¼ of the total recipe
CALORIES 200; PROTEIN 29g; CARBS 0g;
TOTAL FAT 9g; SAT FAT 0g; CHOLESTEROL 75mg;
SODIUM 85mg; FIBER 0g

grilled chicken
with peanut sauce

jasmine rice

avocado, tomato,
and cucumber salad

pineapple ice

menu
gameplan

serves 4 (with great leftovers)

beforeyoustart

If not using a grill pan, preheat the
broiler.

step 1   cook the **jasmine rice**

step 2   make the **avocado, tomato, and cucumber salad**

step 3   make the **grilled chicken with peanut sauce**

step 4   **serve**

shopping list

Jasmine rice

Avocado

Tomato

English cucumber

Cilantro

Mango

Lime (for juice)

Chicken tenders

Prepared Thai peanut sauce
(from Asian specialty foods
section in most supermarkets)

Pineapple ice

from your pantry

Soy sauce or Thai fish sauce

Maple syrup or brown sugar

Canola oil

Salt

headsup   With a bottled ingredient that
you have never tried before,
as in the peanut sauce in this meal, always taste it before
adding it to the dish. This is particularly true with Thai
ingredients. Thai cooking is frequently very spicy.

"The peanut sauce associated with Thai cooking has a marvelous sweet, hot, nutty flavor. Good news—it keeps beautifully in the refrigerator."

—minutemeals' Chef Nancy

step 1

cook the **jasmine rice**

2 cups jasmine rice

Cook the rice in a large saucepan in the amount of water and for the time suggested on the package. Keep warm, covered.

step 2

make the **avocado, tomato, and cucumber salad**

1 ripe avocado

1 large tomato

1 small English cucumber

1/4 cup loosely packed cilantro leaves

1 ripe mango

1 tablespoon soy sauce or Thai fish sauce

1 teaspoon maple syrup or brown sugar

Juice of 1 lime

1. Cut the avocado in half lengthwise. Remove the pit. Place the avocado, skin side down, on the cutting board. Cut the flesh in a crosshatch pattern. With a spoon, scoop the diced avocado into a salad bowl.

2. Cut tomato and cucumber into chunks. Remove enough cilantro leaves from the stems to measure 1/4 cup, loosely packed.

3. With a vegetable peeler, peel the mango. Slice the fruit off the large flat oval pit. Cut the mango into pieces about the size of the cut-up avocado.

4. Add the mango, tomato, cucumber, soy sauce, maple syrup, cilantro leaves, and juice of 1 lime to the salad bowl. Toss gently to combine. Taste and adjust the seasonings. Place the bowl on the table.

step 3

make the **grilled chicken with peanut sauce**

About 1 pound chicken tenders

1 tablespoon plus 1 cup prepared Thai peanut sauce

1 tablespoon canola oil

Salt to taste

1. Heat a grill pan over low heat until hot. Or, preheat the broiler.

2. Meanwhile, place the chicken tenders in a bowl and add the 1 tablespoon peanut sauce, canola oil, and salt. Toss to coat.

3. Lightly oil the heated grill pan or broiler-pan rack.

4. If using grill pan: Lay the chicken tenders in one layer on the hot grill pan. Without moving them, grill until sear marks appear and the tenders release from the grill, about 2 minutes. Turn and continue grilling until opaque in the thickest part.

5. If using broiler: Place the tenders on a broiler-pan rack. Broil 3 to 4 inches from the heat until slightly golden. Turn and broil until the tenders test done as described above. Transfer to a serving platter.

6. Meanwhile, in a small saucepan, bring the remaining 1 cup peanut sauce to a simmer over low heat, stirring frequently.

step 4

serve

1. Pour the heated peanut sauce over the chicken and place the platter on the table.

2. Fluff the rice and place in a serving bowl. Serve as a bed for the grilled chicken or alongside.

3. When ready for dessert, scoop the pineapple ice into small bowls and serve.

Grilled Chicken with Peanut Sauce
Single serving is 1/4 of the total recipe
CALORIES 215; PROTEIN 31g; CARBS 10g;
TOTAL FAT 5g; SAT FAT 1g; CHOLESTEROL 66mg;
SODIUM 1007mg; FIBER 2g

☆ tarragon chicken
with mushrooms and onions

basmati rice

broccoli and red pepper salad

pecan pie à la mode

menu **gameplan**

serves 6

shopping list

Basmati rice

Skinless boneless chicken breast halves

Fresh tarragon

Large mushroom caps

Frozen or canned boiled onions

Dry white wine

Prewashed mixed spring or baby greens

Pecan pie

Butter pecan ice cream

from the salad bar

Broccoli florets (or from the produce department)

from your pantry

Red pepper slices

Garlic

Olive oil

Salt and pepper

Fat-free reduced-sodium chicken broth

All-purpose flour

Vinaigrette dressing, store-bought or homemade

step **1** cook the **basmati rice**

step **2** cook the **tarragon chicken with mushrooms and onions**

step **3** prepare the **broccoli and red pepper salad**

step **4** **serve**

luckyforyou The onions in the tarragon chicken are essential to the dish. You have two options for buying them: frozen or canned. Don't even entertain the notion of peeling individual fresh ones from scratch. There isn't the time.

"This menu is elegant—chicken and tarragon is a classic combination. And unlike a lot of French-inspired recipes, there's no complicated cooking here.

—minutemeals' Chef Joanne

step 1
cook the **basmati rice**

1½ cups basmati rice

Cook the rice in a medium saucepan in the amount of water and for the time suggested on the package. Keep warm, covered.

step 2
cook the **tarragon chicken with mushrooms and onions**

6 skinless boneless chicken breast halves (5 ounces each)

4 garlic cloves

1½ teaspoons chopped fresh tarragon leaves or ½ teaspoon dried

2 tablespoons olive oil

Salt and pepper to taste

6 large mushrooms caps

6 thawed frozen or canned boiled onions

1 can (14½ ounces) fat-free reduced-sodium chicken broth

½ cup dry white wine

3 tablespoons all-purpose flour

Fresh tarragon sprigs, for garnish (optional)

1. Rinse the chicken and pat dry. Slice the garlic. Chop enough fresh tarragon leaves, if using, to measure 1½ teaspoons.

2. In a large nonstick skillet, heat the olive oil over medium-high heat until hot. Add the chicken breasts and sprinkle with ½ the fresh or dried tarragon. Sauté for 5 minutes.

Turn, season with salt and pepper and the remaining tarragon, and sauté 5 minutes, or until the chicken is cooked through. Remove to a plate and keep warm, loosely covered.

3. Add the mushrooms, onions, and garlic to the skillet. Cook, turning occasionally, for 3 minutes, or until the mushrooms have browned and the onions are hot throughout. Place the mushrooms and onions on a serving platter.

4. Add the chicken broth to the skillet, stirring to loosen the garlic and browned-on bits. Bring to a boil.

5. Meanwhile, in a small bowl, stir the white wine into the flour until smooth. Whisk into the boiling broth in the skillet and cook, stirring, until the sauce is thickened. Return the chicken to the skillet and cook just until heated through, 1 to 2 minutes. Remove the pan from the heat, and keep warm.

step 3
prepare the **broccoli and red pepper salad**

3 cups water

Salt to taste

3 cups broccoli florets

1 cup red pepper slices

¼ cup vinaigrette dressing, plus more to taste

1 bag (5 ounces) prewashed mixed spring or baby greens

1. Pour the water into a 2-quart saucepan, salt lightly, and cover. Bring to a boil over high heat. Add the broccoli, return the water to a boil, and cover; cook 1 minute. Drain well, transfer to a medium bowl, and add the pepper strips and dressing. Toss to combine.

2. Divide the salad greens among 6 salad plates and top with broccoli salad. Place the plates on the table.

step 4
serve

1. Place the chicken breasts on the serving platter with the mushrooms and onions. Drizzle with a little of the sauce from the pan. Garnish with tarragon sprigs, if desired.

2. Spoon the remaining sauce into a serving bowl. Place the chicken and sauce on the table.

3. Fluff the rice, transfer it to a serving bowl, and place on the table.

4. When ready for dessert, cut the pie into slices, plate, place on dessert plates, and top with a small scoop of the butter pecan ice cream. Serve.

Tarragon Chicken with Mushrooms and Onions
Single serving is ⅙ of the total recipe
CALORIES 249; PROTEIN 31g; CARBS 12g; TOTAL FAT 6g; SAT FAT 1g; CHOLESTEROL 75mg; SODIUM 89mg; FIBER 1g

tortilla casserole

refried beans

yellow tomato and avocado salad

pineapple and honeydew chunks with cinnamon thins

menu gameplan

shopping list

Cooked chicken

Corn tortillas (6-inch diameter)

Frozen Southwestern-style corn and roasted red peppers

Salsa

Shredded Mexican cheese mixture

Black or pinto beans

Cilantro (optional)

Yellow tomatoes

Ripe avocado

American-style salad greens

Cinnamon thins

from the salad bar

Chopped scallions

Pineapple chunks
(or from the produce department)

Honeydew melon chunks
(or from the produce department)

from your pantry

Fat-free reduced-sodium chicken broth

All-purpose flour

Ground cumin

Olive oil

Chili powder

Salad dressing of choice, store-bought or homemade

beforeyoustart

Combine the precut fruits for dessert in a bowl and place in the freezer.

step 1 make the **tortilla casserole**

step 2 make the **refried beans**

step 3 assemble the **yellow tomato and avocado salad**

step 4 **serve**

headsup

The Mexican cheese blend called for in the casserole is sometimes called Nacho and Taco mix and is usually stocked with the other pre-shredded cheeses in the dairy section of the supermarket. The blend combines Colby and Monterey Jack.

"I love food like this. It's Southwestern comfort food. Sometimes I spice it up a bit by adding hot salsa."

—minutemeals' Chef Joanne

step 1

make the **tortilla casserole**

2 cups shredded cooked chicken (use leftover chicken or two 5-ounce packages refrigerated plain carved chicken breast from the supermarket)

10 corn tortillas (6-inch diameter)

1 cup fat-free reduced-sodium chicken broth

2 tablespoons all-purpose flour

1/2 teaspoon ground cumin

1 package (10 ounces) frozen Southwestern-style corn and roasted red peppers, thawed

1 jar (11 1/2 to 12 ounces) salsa

1 cup shredded Mexican cheese mixture

1. Preheat the broiler if you are going to brown the top of the casserole. Grease a shallow 2-quart microwave-safe baking dish.

2. Shred the chicken, if necessary. Cut the stack of tortillas into quarters.

3. In a 1-quart saucepan, whisk together the broth, flour, and cumin. Cover and bring to a boil over medium-high heat. Cook, stirring, until the sauce has thickened. Stir in the chicken.

4. Assemble the casserole: In the prepared baking dish, layer 1/3 of the tortilla pieces. Top with the corn and peppers with any sauce,

1/2 of the remaining tortilla pieces, the chicken mixture, the remaining tortilla pieces, salsa, and, finally, the cheese. Cover loosely with a piece of waxed paper, making sure that it does not touch the cheese. Microwave on High 8 to 10 minutes, or until the center of the casserole is hot.

5. If you want to brown the cheese on top, remove the piece of waxed paper and run the dish under the broiler for 1 to 2 minutes, until the cheese is lightly browned.

step 2

meanwhile, make the **refried beans**

2 cans (15 to 16 ounces each) black or pinto beans

1 tablespoon olive oil

1/3 cup chopped scallions

1 teaspoon chili powder

2 tablespoons chopped fresh cilantro (optional)

1. Drain and rinse the beans.

2. In a large nonstick skillet, heat the olive oil over medium-high heat until hot. Add the scallions and cook, stirring, for 2 minutes. Add the beans and chili powder and cover. Cook, covered, stirring occasionally, until very hot throughout.

step 3

assemble the **yellow tomato and avocado salad**

2 small yellow tomatoes

1 large ripe avocado

1/2 bag (12-ounce size) prewashed American-style salad greens

Salad dressing of choice

1. Cut the tomatoes into thin slices. Peel, pit, and slice the avocado.

2. Divide the greens among 4 salad plates. Top each with 1/4 of the tomato and avocado slices. Place the salads and the dressing on the table.

step 4

serve

1. Place the casserole on the table.

2. Spoon the refried beans into a serving dish. Chop 2 tablespoons cilantro, if desired, and sprinkle on the beans.

3. When ready for dessert, divide the iced fruits among dessert bowls and serve with the cinnamon thins as an accompaniment.

Tortilla Casserole
Single serving is 1/4 of the total recipe
CALORIES 767; PROTEIN 41g; CARBS 84g;
TOTAL FAT 32g; SAT FAT 11g; CHOLESTEROL 84mg;
SODIUM 2069mg; FIBER 4g
Nutrient Analysis includes refried beans.

☆ asian turkey pot stickers

sesame dipping sauce

grated carrot salad

chilled apricots with crumbled macaroons

menu
gameplan

serves 4

shopping list

Pickled ginger or fresh gingerroot

Lean ground turkey

Square wonton wrappers (in refrigerated Asian foods section of supermarket)

Golden or dark raisins

Apricot halves packed in syrup (one 16-ounce jar)

Almond macaroons

from the salad bar

Grated or shredded carrots (or from the produce department)

Chopped scallions

from your pantry

Worcestershire sauce

Toasted sesame oil

Canola oil

Fat-free reduced-sodium chicken broth

Lite soy sauce

Rice vinegar or lemon juice

Maple syrup or brown sugar

Vinaigrette dressing, store-bought or homemade

beforeyoustart

Place the jar or apricots in the refrigerator until serving time.

step 1 make the **asian turkey pot stickers**

step 2 combine the **sesame dipping sauce**

step 3 make the **grated carrot salad**

step 4 serve

headsup

Pot stickers are usually served with their browned bottoms up. Before turning them out on a platter make sure you've cooked the pot stickers all the way through. And if you've plated them and think they still need a few more minutes of cooking, there is a simple solution. Just microwave them.

"Pot stickers are pan-fried dumplings, and people love them. I was delighted when I found a way to make them in only 20 minutes!"

—minutemeals' Chef Nancy

step 1

make the **asian turkey pot stickers**

2 tablespoons chopped pickled ginger or grated fresh gingerroot

1¼ pounds lean ground turkey

½ cup chopped scallions

2 tablespoons Worcestershire sauce

2 teaspoons toasted sesame oil

24 square wonton wrappers, each 3 inches (in refrigerated Asian foods section of supermarket)

3 tablespoons canola oil

¾ cup fat-free reduced-sodium chicken broth

1. Chop enough pickled or fresh ginger to measure 2 or 3 tablespoons.

2. In a large bowl, combine the turkey, scallions, 2 tablespoons of the ginger, Worcestershire sauce, and sesame oil, tossing to mix.

3. Lay 12 of the wonton wrappers on the counter. Place a heaping tablespoon of the turkey filling in the middle of each skin. Bring the sides of the skins up and press to make them hold on the sides, then slightly down, forming a flat bottom. (Filling will show at the top.) Repeat with the remaining 11 wrappers.

4. Heat a heavy 12-inch skillet over medium-high heat. As it heats, finish making dumplings with the remaining 12 wonton wrappers and filling.

5. Add the canola oil to the hot skillet and heat until hot. Add the dumplings (crowding them in is fine) and sauté until the bottoms brown, about 1 minute. Add the chicken broth and cover the pan. Lower the heat and steam the dumplings until the liquid is absorbed, about 5 minutes.

step 2

while the dumplings cook, combine the **sesame dipping sauce**

¼ cup lite soy sauce

3 tablespoons rice vinegar or lemon juice

1 tablespoon maple syrup or brown sugar

1 teaspoon toasted sesame oil

Stir all the ingredients together in a small serving bowl. Place the bowl, with a small ladle or serving spoon, on the table.

step 3

make the **grated carrot salad**

2 cups (16 ounces) grated or shredded carrots

4 to 6 tablespoons golden or dark raisins

Vinaigrette dressing

Place the carrots, raisins, and dressing in a salad bowl and toss to coat. Place the bowl on the table.

step 4

serve

1. Turn the dumplings out onto a platter and serve at once, with the sesame dipping sauce as an accompaniment.

2. When ready for dessert, divide the chilled apricot halves among dessert bowls and crumble macaroons over each serving. Serve with additional macaroons, if desired.

Asian Turkey Pot Stickers
Single serving is ¼ of the total recipe
CALORIES 404; PROTEIN 43g; CARBS 52g; TOTAL FAT 2g; SAT FAT 1g; CHOLESTEROL 69mg; SODIUM 527mg; FIBER 3g

turkey and fettuccine
with mushroom garlic cream sauce

broccoli with smoked almonds

dutch apple pie

menu
gameplan

shopping list

Cooked turkey meat

Fresh parsley

Button mushroom slices
(from the produce department)

Oyster mushrooms

Dry sherry

Fat-free half-and-half

Broccoli florets
(from the salad bar or the
produce department)

Smoked almonds

Fresh fettuccine or
other fresh strand pasta

Dutch apple pie

from your pantry

Garlic

Butter

Fat-free reduced-sodium
chicken broth

Salt and pepper

serves 4

beforeyoustart

Bring the water to a boil in a large pot,
covered, over high heat to cook the
fettuccine.

step	1	cook the **turkey** in **mushroom garlic cream sauce**
step	2	make the **broccoli with smoked almonds**
step	3	cook the **fettuccine**
step	4	**serve**

lucky**foryou** Fresh pasta cooks quickly,
in about ½ the time you
would allow for the dried. It is an ideal quick-cooking
minutemeal ingredient. Even if it's frozen, you can add it
frozen to the boiling water in the pasta pot, and it will
still take less time to cook than the dried.

"Who doesn't need a new way to use the leftover holiday turkey? I did, which is why I created this menu."

—minutemeals' Chef Nancy

step 1

cook the **turkey** in **mushroom garlic cream sauce**

4 cups diced roasted turkey breast or skinless leftover cooked turkey

2 tablespoons chopped fresh parsley

8 ounces button mushroom slices

8 ounces oyster mushrooms

4 garlic cloves

2 tablespoons butter

1/4 cup dry sherry

1 cup fat-free reduced-sodium chicken broth

1 cup fat-free half-and-half

Salt and pepper to taste

1. Dice enough leftover cooked turkey to measure 4 cups. Finely chop enough parsley to measure 2 tablespoons.

2. Place the button and oyster mushrooms and garlic cloves in a food processor and pulse until very finely chopped.

3. Heat a deep 10-inch skillet over medium heat. Cut up the butter and add it to the hot skillet. When melted, scrape the mushroom-garlic mixture into the skillet. Cook, stirring frequently, until the mushrooms release their moisture and then begin to dry, about 3 minutes.

4. Add the sherry, increase the heat to high, and boil until reduced by half, about 4 minutes. Add the chicken broth and boil about 4 minutes, or until slightly thickened.

5. Add the half-and-half and boil, stirring occasionally, for 4 to 5 minutes, until slightly thickened. Season with salt and pepper. Stir in the diced turkey. Cook until heated through, stirring occasionally. Remove from the heat and keep warm, covered.

step 2

make the **broccoli with smoked almonds**

4 cups broccoli florets

1 teaspoon water

4 to 6 tablespoons chopped smoked almonds

1. Place the broccoli florets in a large microwave-safe serving bowl and add the water. Cover and microwave on High until the florets are crisp-tender, 3 to 4 minutes. Let the broccoli stand in the oven for 2 to 3 minutes before removing.

2. Meanwhile, coarsely chop the almonds. Add to the broccoli and toss to combine.

step 3

cook the **fettuccine**

3 quarts water

Salt to taste

1 pound fresh fettuccine or other fresh strand pasta

Pour the water into a large pot, salt lightly, and cover the pot. Bring to a boil over high heat. Add the fettuccine, stir to separate the strands, and cook according to the directions on the package, until *al dente*, 3 to 4 minutes. Drain well. Transfer to a large shallow serving dish.

step 4

serve

1. Pour the turkey and mushroom mixture over the fettuccine and toss to combine. Sprinkle the parsley over the top. Place on the table.

2. Serve the broccoli.

3. When ready for dessert, cut the pie into slices, plate, and serve.

Turkey and Fettuccine with Mushroom Garlic Cream Sauce
Single serving is 1/4 of the total recipe

CALORIES 821; PROTEIN 87g; CARBS 84g; TOTAL FAT 17g; SAT FAT 4g; CHOLESTEROL 178mg; SODIUM 433g; FIBER 13g

Nutrient Analysis includes fettuccine.

spicy turkey burgers
on whole-grain buns
ginger carrot soup with yogurt
orange wedges

menu
gameplan

serves 4

step	1	make the **ginger carrot soup with yogurt**
step	2	make the **spicy turkey burgers on whole-grain buns**
step	3	**serve**

shopping list

Carrots

Gingerroot

Plain yogurt

Lean ground turkey

Chinese chile paste with garlic (available in Asian foods section of many supermarkets)

Whole-grain burger buns

Oranges

from the salad bar

Lettuce leaves

Tomato slices

from your pantry

Onion

Olive oil

Salt and pepper

Lite soy sauce

Toasted sesame oil

Canola oil

Spicy mustard

Ketchup

headsup

Chinese chile paste with garlic accounts for the spiciness in the burgers. A word of warning: It is *very* hot. If you are serving these burgers to small folk or to anyone who prefers mildly seasoned food, substitute Worcestershire sauce, A-1, or steak sauce to taste. Avoid the chile paste entirely.

"Pressed for time? Just make the burgers and serve them with a big salad. It's still a great dinner."

—minutemeals' Chef Nancy

step 1

make the **ginger carrot soup with yogurt**

6 cups water

1 pound sweet carrots

2 to 2 1/2 cups diced onion
(1 medium-large onion)

1 tablespoon grated ginger
(1 small knob gingerroot)

2 tablespoons olive oil

Salt and pepper to taste

1/2 cup plain yogurt, for serving

1. Pour the water into a large saucepan, cover, and bring to a boil over high heat.

2. Scrub the carrots. In a food processor fitted with the grating blade, grate them.

3. Dice the onion to measure 2 to 2 1/2 cups. Peel the ginger, then grate enough to measure 1 tablespoon.

4. In a medium soup pot, heat the olive oil over medium-high heat until hot. Add the onion and ginger and lower the heat to medium. Cook, stirring, until the onion is tender, about 5 minutes. Add the carrots and cook 1 minute.

5. Add 5 cups of boiling water and increase the heat to high. When the soup boils, reduce the heat to a simmer, and cook until the carrots are tender, about 5 minutes.

6. Pour the carrot mixture carefully into the food processor or a blender and puree until smooth, about 1 minute, adding some of the additional remaining cup of water, if desired, to thin it. Return the soup to the pot and season with salt and pepper.

step 2

make the **spicy turkey burgers on whole-grain buns**

1 1/2 pounds lean ground turkey

2 tablespoons lite soy sauce

2 teaspoons toasted sesame oil

2 teaspoons Chinese chile paste
with garlic, or less to taste

4 teaspoons canola oil

4 whole-grain burger buns

4 lettuce leaves

4 tomato slices

Spicy mustard and ketchup
as condiments

1. In a medium bowl, blend together the turkey, shoyu or soy sauce, sesame oil, and chile paste. Form the meat into 4 patties.

2. In a 10-inch nonstick skillet heat the canola oil over medium heat until hot. Add the patties and cook about 5 minutes per side, or until cooked through.

step 3

serve

1. Place a bun on each serving plate. Top one half of each with a lettuce leaf and tomato. Place a burger on each of the remaining sides. Serve with mustard and ketchup or other favorite condiments.

2. Ladle the soup into bowls and top each serving with 2 tablespoons yogurt.

3. Serve the soup and the burgers at the same time.

4. When ready for dessert, cut the oranges into wedges, place on a platter, and serve with napkins.

Spicy Turkey Burgers on Whole-Grain Buns
Single serving is 1/4 of the total recipe

CALORIES 479; PROTEIN 35g; CARBS 24g;
TOTAL FAT 27g; SAT FAT 6g; CHOLESTEROL 137mg;
SODIUM 708mg; FIBER 2g

Nutrient Analysis includes buns.

turkey cutlets
in mustard cream sauce
glazed baby carrots
warm croissants
orange sorbet with chocolate shavings

serves 4

shopping list

Thin-sliced turkey cutlets

Frozen succotash or corn

Light sour cream

Moutarde de Maille mustard, or Dijon mustard

Dry sherry or Madeira (optional)

Partially blanched baby carrots (from the produce department)

Croissants

Orange sorbet

from the salad bar

Onion slices

Celery sticks (or from the produce department)

from your pantry

Salt and pepper

Butter

Fat-free reduced-sodium chicken broth

Dried thyme

Dried rosemary

Cornstarch

Sugar

Semisweet chocolate bar or squares

step 1 cook the **turkey cutlets in mustard cream sauce**

step 2 cook the **glazed baby carrots**

step 3 heat the **croissants**

step 4 serve

headsup There are a lot of mustards on the market. For the cream sauce, we recommend moutarde de Maille, which is full-bodied in flavor, without being overly sharp. If you don't have it, use Dijon. Don't even consider the ballpark variety!

"I know that some cooks are leery of making cream sauce. This one is different, though, and a snap to make."

—minutemeals' Chef Nancy

cook the **turkey cutlets in mustard cream sauce**

4 thin-sliced turkey cutlets (1 1/4 pounds)

Salt and pepper to taste

1 cup onion slices

1/2 cup celery sticks

2 tablespoons butter

1 1/2 cups fat-free reduced-sodium chicken broth

1 package (10 ounces) frozen succotash or corn

1/2 teaspoon dried thyme

1/2 teaspoon dried rosemary, crumbled

1/2 cup light sour cream

1 tablespoon cornstarch

2 teaspoons moutarde de Maille or Dijon mustard, or more to taste

1 to 2 tablespoons dry sherry or Madeira (optional)

1. Pat the turkey cutlets dry with paper towels and season with salt and pepper. Roughly chop the onion slices and celery.

2. In a nonstick 12-inch skillet, melt 1 tablespoon of the butter over medium-high heat, add the turkey cutlets in one layer, and cook for 30 seconds on each side. Transfer the cutlets to a plate and cover loosely to keep warm.

3. Melt the remaining tablespoon of butter in the skillet. Add the chopped onions and celery and cook, stirring occasionally, for 2 minutes. Add the chicken broth, frozen vegetables, and herbs, season with salt and pepper, and cover. Bring to a boil, lower the heat, and simmer, covered, for 5 minutes.

4. In small bowl, whisk together the sour cream, cornstarch, and mustard. Add the sour cream mixture to the skillet and cook, stirring, until the sauce is lightly thickened. (Do not let the mixture boil or the sour cream will curdle.) Remove the pan from the heat.

5. Add the cooked cutlets to the sauce with the sherry, if using. Stir to combine and keep warm, covered.

step 2

cook the **glazed baby carrots**

1 package (12 ounces) partially blanched baby carrots

1 tablespoon butter

1 teaspoon sugar, or to taste

Salt and pepper to taste

In a skillet large enough to hold them in one layer, arrange the carrots. Add just enough water to cover, and add the butter, sugar, and salt and pepper. Bring to a boil, and simmer, stirring occasionally, until almost all the water is evaporated and the carrots are glazed and just tender. Transfer to a serving bowl and place on the table.

step 3

heat the **croissants**

4 to 6 croissants

Heat the croissants in a toaster oven until hot.

step 4

serve

1. Serve the turkey cutlets and sauce with the warm croissants. Or, halve the croissants horizontally and serve the turkey cutlets and sauce over them.

2. When ready for dessert, scoop the sorbet into bowls. With a cheese slicer or sharp knife, shave curls of chocolate over the top. Serve.

Turkey Cutlets in Mustard Cream Sauce
Single serving is 1/4 of the total recipe
CALORIES 277; PROTEIN 23g; CARBS 27g; TOTAL FAT 10g; SAT FAT 1g; CHOLESTEROL 46mg; SODIUM 362mg; FIBER 2g

turkey cutlets tonnato

green bean salad
parmesan toasts
lemon sorbet with frozen raspberries

shopping list

Frenched frozen green beans

Cornichons

Fresh parsley

Tuna packed in olive oil

Anchovy fillets

Dry white wine

Capers

Lemon (for juice)

Thin-sliced turkey cutlets

Italian bread

Lemon sorbet

Frozen raspberries

from your pantry

Vinaigrette dressing, store-bought or homemade

Garlic

Mayonnaise

Salt and pepper

Olive oil

Butter

Grated Parmesan cheese

serves 4

beforeyoustart

Preheat the oven to 400°F to heat the bread. Remove the raspberries from the freezer to thaw.

step	1	prepare the **green bean salad**
step	2	make the **tuna sauce;** cook the **turkey cutlets**
step	3	make the **parmesan toasts**
step	4	**serve**

 *Vitello Tonnato* is the classic Italian dish that has made *tonnato* sauce famous. *Vitello* in Italian means veal, and, as anyone who buys veal knows, it is very expensive, even on sale. Turkey cutlets are affordable and make a fine substitute.

"This is a dinner-party menu if there ever was one. If you want to stretch it a bit, serve sliced tomatoes garnished with basil."

—minutemeals' Chef Hillary

step 1

prepare the **green bean salad**

1 box (10 ounces) Frenched frozen green beans

1/4 cup vinaigrette dressing

Cook the beans according to the directions on the package just until crisp-tender. Drain well and shake dry. In a bowl, toss them with the dressing; set aside.

step 2

make the **tuna sauce;** cook the **turkey cutlets**

For the tuna sauce

2 large garlic cloves

1/4 cup cornichons

2 tablespoons finely chopped fresh parsley

1 can (6 ounces) tuna packed in olive oil

4 anchovy fillets

1 cup dry white wine

1/2 cup mayonnaise

1 tablespoon drained capers

2 tablespoons lemon juice (1 large lemon)

For the turkey

4 thin-sliced turkey cutlets (about 1 1/4 pounds total), each 1/4 inch thick

Salt and pepper to taste

1 1/2 tablespoons olive oil

1. Make the tuna sauce: Smash the garlic cloves with the flat side of a large knife. Drain and slice the cornichons. Finely chop enough parsley to measure 2 tablespoons; reserve all.

2. Drain the oil from the tuna into a 12-inch nonstick skillet and heat over medium-high heat until hot. Add the garlic and cook, stirring, for 30 seconds.

3. Add the tuna, anchovies, cornichons, and wine. Bring to a boil and simmer over high heat for 5 minutes until slightly reduced. Scrape the mixture into a food processor or blender and blend until smooth. Transfer to a small metal bowl and set over a larger bowl filled with ice. Stir occasionally until chilled.

4. While the sauce chills, cook the turkey: Pat the cutlets dry with paper towels. Season with salt and pepper.

5. Wipe out the skillet, add the olive oil, and heat over high heat until hot. Add the turkey cutlets and cook for 3 minutes per each side, or until cooked through. Arrange the cutlets in the center of a serving platter, overlapping them slightly.

step 3

make the **parmesan toasts**

1/2 loaf Italian bread

3 tablespoons butter, softened

2 tablespoons grated Parmesan cheese

1. Preheat the oven to 400°F.

2. Cut the bread into 8 slices, each 1/2 inch thick.

3. In a small bowl, cream the butter and Parmesan until blended. Butter the bread and place the slices on a cookie sheet. Heat for 5 minutes. Put the toasts in a napkin-lined basket, and put on the table.

step 4

serve

1. Finish the tuna sauce: Stir in the mayonnaise, capers, lemon juice, and parsley, along with any juices that have collected on the turkey platter. Blend well. Season with salt and pepper. Spoon the sauce down the center of the cutlets.

2. Spoon the green bean salad around the turkey cutlets. Place the platter on the table.

3. When ready for dessert, scoop the sorbet into small bowls, garnish each with raspberries, and serve.

Turkey Cutlets Tonnato
Single serving is 1/4 of the total recipe
CALORIES 342; PROTEIN 29g; CARBS 2g;
TOTAL FAT 27g; SAT FAT 22g; CHOLESTEROL 28mg;
SODIUM 584mg; FIBER 0g

italian turkey meatballs
with sautéed cherry tomatoes
fresh spinach pasta
ripe pears and walnuts

shopping list

Fresh spinach linguine or other fresh strand pasta

Pine nuts (*pignoli*)

Extra-lean ground turkey

Fresh basil

Fresh oregano

Red cherry or grape tomatoes

Yellow cherry or grape tomatoes

Ripe pears

Walnut halves

from your pantry

Salt

Olive oil

Fine dry bread crumbs

Egg

Freshly ground black pepper

serves 4

beforeyoustart

Bring the water to a boil in a large pot, covered, over high heat to cook the pasta.

step	1	cook the **fresh spinach pasta**
step	2	make the **italian turkey meatballs**
step	3	make the **sautéed cherry tomatoes**
step	4	**serve**

 luckyforyou There's an easy solution if you find yourself out of bread crumbs just as you are about to start the meatballs. (And who hasn't had that happen?) Grind Saltines or unsweetened shredded wheat to a powder in a blender or food processor and use those crumbs instead. Remember to add less salt to the turkey mixture if you've added Saltine crumbs.

"Everyone loves meatballs and these ones are light and delicious because they're made with lean ground turkey and flavored with basil and pine nuts."

—minutemeals' Chef Nancy

step 1

cook the **fresh spinach pasta**

4 quarts water

Salt to taste

1 pound fresh spinach linguine or other fresh strand pasta

1 tablespoon olive oil

Pour the water into a large pot, salt lightly, and cover. Bring to a boil over high heat. Add the pasta and stir to separate the strands. Cook according to the directions on the package, until *al dente*, 3 to 5 minutes. Drain. Return to the pan, add the olive oil, and toss. Keep warm, covered.

step 2

make the **italian turkey meatballs**

6 tablespoons pine nuts

3/4 to 1 cup fine dry bread crumbs

1 1/4 pounds extra-lean ground turkey

1/2 teaspoon salt

1 large egg

2 tablespoons fresh basil leaves, or more to taste

Freshly ground black pepper to taste

2 tablespoons olive oil

1. In a food processor or blender, process the pine nuts and 1/2 cup of the bread crumbs until very finely ground.

2. In a large bowl, combine the ground turkey, ground crumb mixture, salt, and egg. Slice the 2 tablespoons (or more) fresh basil into fine shreds and add to the meat with a few grinds of pepper. Mix thoroughly with your hands, adding more of the remaining bread crumbs, if necessary, so that the mixture holds together.

3. With oiled hands, form the mixture into 30 or so (depending upon the amount of meat and crumbs you have used) 1-inch meatballs. When you are almost finished forming the meatballs, heat a 12-inch heavy skillet over medium-high heat.

4. Add the olive oil to the skillet and when it is hot, add the meatballs in a single layer. Brown, turning them gently with a spatula, on all sides, until cooked through, about 10 to 12 minutes.

step 3

while the meatballs cook, make the **sautéed cherry tomatoes**

2 tablespoons coarsely chopped fresh oregano

1 1/2 tablespoons olive oil

1 pint red cherry or grape tomatoes

1 pint yellow cherry or grape tomatoes (If you can only find red tomatoes, use 2 pints of the reds.)

Salt and pepper to taste

1. Chop enough of the fresh oregano to measure 2 tablespoons.

2. Heat the olive oil in a 12-inch skillet over high heat until hot. Add the tomatoes. Cover and cook, shaking the pan occasionally, until the tomatoes collapse, about 7 to 10 minutes. (If most of the tomatoes are cooked but a few of them have not collapsed, simply pierce those ones with a knife tip.) Season with salt and pepper, add the oregano, and remove the pan from the heat. Pour the sautéed tomatoes over the meatballs, stir gently to combine, and cook, stirring, until heated through.

step 4

serve

1. Divide the pasta among 4 dinner plates and top with a generous serving of the meatballs and their sauce. Serve.

2. When ready for dessert, place a whole pear on each dessert plate. Serve with forks and knives. Place the walnut pieces in a small bowl and pass at the table.

Italian Turkey Meatballs
Single serving is 1/4 of the total recipe
CALORIES 304; PROTEIN 32g; CARBS 8g;
TOTAL FAT 17g; SAT FAT 2g; CHOLESTEROL 102mg;
SODIUM 447mg; FIBER 1g

☆ microwave turkey pot pie
with biscuit topping
mixed green salad
clementines and almond biscotti

menu
gameplan

shopping list

Buttermilk biscuits

Prewashed salad greens of choice

Roasted turkey breast, in 1 piece

Frozen mixed corn, carrots, and peas

Fresh parsley

Lemon juice

Clementines

Almond biscotti

from your pantry

Vinaigrette dressing, store-bought or homemade

Fat-free reduced-sodium chicken broth

Dried herbes de Provence

Salt and pepper

Milk

Cornstarch

serves 4

beforeyoustart

Preheat the oven to 350°F to heat the biscuits.

| step | 1 | heat the **biscuit topping** |

| step | 2 | assemble the **mixed green salad** |

| step | 3 | make the **turkey pot pie** |

| step | 4 | **serve** |

luckyforyou

At one time, and it wasn't that long ago, roasted turkey breast was only available at delicatessens, which meant that it was not very easy to get. Now it's sold freshly cooked in supermarkets as a matter of course. It's even available with different seasonings. It's a terrific convenience item when you consider how long it takes to roast even a small turkey breast.

"A topping of biscuits means this pot pie is simple to make. This is pure comfort food—just what you want when you're 'holidayed-ed out...'"

—minutemeals' Chef Miriam

step 1

heat the **biscuit topping**

4 to 6 packaged buttermilk biscuits

Preheat the oven to 350°F. Heat the biscuits according to the directions on the package. Keep warm while you make the filling for the pot pie.

step 2

assemble the **mixed green salad**

1 bag (5 ounces) prewashed salad greens of choice

1/4 cup vinaigrette dressing

Place the greens in a salad bowl, add dressing, and toss to coat. Place the bowl on the table.

step 3

make the **turkey pot pie**

4 cups leftover turkey or chicken pieces, skin removed, or 1 pound roasted turkey breast, in 1 piece

1 can (14 1/2 ounces) fat-free reduced-sodium chicken broth

1 package (16 ounces) frozen mixed corn, carrots, and peas

1 teaspoon dried herbes de Provence

Salt and pepper to taste

1/2 cup milk

3 tablespoons cornstarch

Fresh parsley, for serving

Fresh lemon juice to taste, for serving

1. Cut the leftover turkey or chicken into bite-sized pieces. Remove the skin, if any, from the turkey and cut the meat into small chunks.

2. In a 2 1/2-quart microwave-safe casserole, combine the chicken broth, frozen vegetables, herbes de Provence, and salt and pepper. Cover and microwave on High, stirring once, for 10 minutes.

3. Meanwhile, in a small bowl, stir together the milk and cornstarch until blended.

4. Stir the cornstarch mixture into the casserole. Cover and microwave on High for 2 minutes. Stir, cover again, and microwave on High for 2 minutes more.

5. Add the diced turkey to the casserole, stir to combine, and add salt and pepper. Cover and microwave on High for 2 or 3 minutes, or until heated through.

step 4

serve

1. Chop enough parsley to measure 3 tablespoons. Remove the pot pie from the microwave and stir in the parsley and lemon juice.

2. Put the warm biscuits on top of the pot pie and serve. If you have heated additional biscuits, serve them as bread. Serve at once.

3. When ready for dessert, serve the clementines in a bowl and the biscotti on a plate.

Microwave Turkey Pot Pie with Biscuit Topping
Single serving is 1/4 of the total recipe
CALORIES 469; PROTEIN 42g; CARBS 40g; TOTAL FAT 16g; SAT FAT 4g; CHOLESTEROL 85mg; SODIUM 546mg; FIBER 3g

Nutrient Analysis includes biscuits.

white turkey chili
vegetable tostadas
chocolate chunks, almonds, and raisins

menu gameplan

shopping list

Cooked turkey breast

Chopped green chiles

White beans

Frozen stir-fry vegetables

Corn or flour tortillas
(6- or 7-inch diameter)

Salsa

Pre-shredded cheese,
such as Monterey Jack
 or Colby

Almonds

Raisins

Onion

from your pantry

Garlic

Olive oil

Ground cumin

Fat-free reduced-sodium
chicken broth

Salt

Tabasco sauce

Chocolate chunks

serves 4

beforeyoustart
Preheat the broiler.

step	1	make the **white turkey chili**
step	2	prepare the **vegetable tostadas**
step	3	**serve**

luckyforyou There's yet another possible
variation on this chili theme:
Try cooked pork loin, available in the prepared foods
sections of many supermarkets, for the turkey. You'll have
to dice it first.

"If the vegetable tostadas don't fit into your schedule, simply serve warm flour tortillas and a big green salad."

—minutemeals' Chef Nancy

make the **white turkey chili**

- 1¹/2 pounds roasted turkey breast or leftover turkey
- 1 medium-to-large onion
- 3 or 4 garlic cloves
- 1 can (4 ounces) chopped green chiles
- 1 tablespoon olive oil
- 1 tablespoon ground cumin
- 2 cans (16 ounces each) white beans
- 2 cans (14¹/2 ounces each) fat-free reduced-sodium chicken broth
- Salt to taste, for serving
- Tabasco sauce to taste, for serving

1. Remove the skin on the roasted turkey breast and chop the meat to measure 4 cups. Finely chop the onion. Crush the garlic in a garlic press. Drain the chiles.

2. In a soup pot, heat the olive oil until hot. Add the onion and cook over medium-high heat, stirring, for 3 minutes, or until soft. Stir in the crushed garlic, cumin, and chiles and cook for 1 minute.

3. Drain and rinse the white beans. Add the beans, chicken broth, and turkey to the pot, cover, and bring the mixture to a boil. Lower the heat, remove cover, and simmer the chili, stirring occasionally, for 10 minutes, until the flavors have blended.

prepare the **vegetable tostadas**

- 2 cups packaged frozen stir-fry vegetables
- 4 corn or flour tortillas (6- or 7-inch diameter)
- ³/4 cup salsa
- 4 ounces (1 cup) pre-shredded cheese, such as Monterey Jack or Colby

1. Preheat the broiler.

2. Place the vegetables in a colander and run under hot water until thawed. Place the tortillas on a large baking sheet.

3. Spread 3 tablespoons of the salsa on each tortilla all the way to the edges. Spread ¹/2 cup of the vegetables on top of each. Sprinkle ¹/4 cup of the cheese over each. Broil 4 inches from the heat for about 1 to 2 minutes, until the cheese is melted. Transfer to a large platter and place on the table.

serve

1. Season the chili with salt and Tabasco sauce. Ladle into wide shallow bowls and serve at once with the tostadas.

2. When ready for dessert, place mounds of the chocolate, almonds, and raisins on a round platter and serve as is.

White Turkey Chili and Vegetable Tostadas
Single serving is part of ¹/4 total recipe
CALORIES 637; PROTEIN 66g; CARBS 57g;
TOTAL FAT 17g; SAT FAT 1g; CHOLESTEROL 30g;
SODIUM 656mg; FIBER 8g

minute

20-minute gourmet

meat menus

meals

menus

☆ beef and asparagus stir-fry

chinese-style rice
vanilla ice cream with candied ginger

menu
gameplan

serves 4

step	1	cook the **chinese-style rice**
step	2	prepare the **vanilla ice cream with candied ginger**
step	3	make the **beef and asparagus stir-fry**
step	4	**serve**

shopping list

Short-grain rice
Vanilla ice cream
Candied ginger
Gingerroot
Beef strips cut for stir-fry
Asparagus
Black bean sauce

from your pantry

Garlic
Lite soy sauce
Cornstarch
Fat-free reduced-sodium beef or chicken broth
Dry sherry
Sugar
Canola oil

heads up

Ideally, when trimming asparagus, you want to bend the end of each stalk until it naturally snaps off. That means you trim the bunch one stalk at a time. In a minutemeal, there isn't time for that. So try this: Do not remove the rubber bands that hold the bunch together at the bottom and the top. Rinse the bunch, then with a large sharp knife and the rubber bands still in place, cut firmly down through the stalks about 1 inch up from the ends. One step, and it's done.

"If 'ordering out' no longer works for you, try cooking Chinese in! This stir-fry is a great place to start—it's so easy."

—minutemeals' Chef Connie

step 1

cook the **chinese-style rice**

- 1 cup short-grain rice
- 1 3/4 cups water for cooking

Rinse the rice in a strainer under cold water. Tip it into a 2 1/2-quart saucepan and add the water. Cover the pan and bring to a boil over high heat. Reduce the heat to low and simmer for 15 minutes, or until all the water is absorbed. Keep warm, covered.

step 2

prepare the **vanilla ice cream with candied ginger**

- 1 pint vanilla ice cream
- 1/4 cup candied ginger, or to taste

1. Spoon the ice cream into a serving bowl and let stand at room temperature to soften slightly.

2. With a sharp knife or scissors, cut the candied ginger into small pieces. Scatter the pieces over the ice cream and with a spoon swirl it in. Place the bowl in the freezer until serving time.

step 3

make the **beef and asparagus stir-fry**

- 1 piece gingerroot, 1 inch long
- 4 garlic cloves (purchase already peeled, if possible)
- 3 tablespoons lite soy sauce
- 3 tablespoons plus 2 teaspoons cornstarch
- 1 1/4 to 1 1/2 pounds beef strips cut for stir-fry
- 1 pound asparagus, pencil-thin stalks if possible
- 1/2 cup fat-free reduced-sodium beef or chicken broth
- 2 tablespoons dry sherry
- 1 tablespoon black bean sauce
- 1 teaspoon sugar
- 2 tablespoons canola oil

1. Peel the ginger. Finely chop the ginger and garlic.

2. In a medium bowl, stir the soy sauce into 3 tablespoons of the cornstarch until blended. Add the ginger and garlic. Add the beef and rub the seasonings into the strips, coating them completely.

3. Rinse the asparagus. Trim the ends of the stalks with a sharp knife. Cut the stalks into 1 1/2-inch pieces.

4. Prepare the sauce: In a measuring cup, stir together the broth, sherry, black bean sauce, remaining 2 teaspoons cornstarch, and sugar until blended.

5. Heat a wok or large heavy skillet over high heat until hot. Add 1 tablespoon of the canola oil and swirl to coat the pan. Add the asparagus and toss to coat. Stir-fry over high heat, tossing, about 3 minutes, until crunchy but cooked. Remove to a large serving bowl.

6. Add the remaining 1 tablespoon oil to the pan and heat until hot. Add the beef, toss to separate the strips, and stir-fry until cooked medium-rare, about 3 to 5 minutes. Taste for doneness; the meat should be tender and cooked. Return the asparagus to the pan. Stir the sauce combination, add it to the pan, and bring to a boil, tossing. Cook, tossing, until heated through and the sauce is slightly thickened. Transfer to a serving bowl.

step 4

serve

1. Remove the ice cream from the freezer to stand at room temperature until serving time.

2. Spoon the hot rice into 4 large bowls and place on the table. Top with some of the asparagus beef stir-fry. Serve with chopsticks, if desired.

3. When ready for dessert, serve the ice cream in small bowls, with additional candied ginger, if desired.

Beef and Asparagus Stir-Fry
Single serving is 1/4 of the total recipe
CALORIES 472; PROTEIN 56g; CARBS 26g; TOTAL FAT 15g; SAT FAT 4g; CHOLESTEROL 128mg; SODIUM 473mg; FIBER 3g
Nutrient Analysis includes rice.

steak au poivre
(steak with crushed peppercorns)

pan-fried potatoes
with onions

steamed spinach

fresh fruit tart

shopping list

Diced potatoes with onions
(available bagged in
refrigerated section of
produce department)

Bagged baby spinach

Shallots

Shell steaks

Dry red wine

Fresh fruit tart

from your pantry

Vegetable oil

Salt and pepper

Whole black peppercorns

Butter

Reduced-sodium beef broth

serves 4

step 1 make the **pan-fried potatoes with onions**

step 2 prepare the **steamed spinach**

step 3 cook the **steak au poivre**

step 4 **serve**

headsup

Dry red wine is used in the sauce for the *steak au poivre*. When it comes to selecting a wine to cook with, this rule applies: It should be a wine you would like to drink. In this case, you have a whole bottle (less 1/2 cup) to enjoy with the meal.

"Steak au poivre is a classic French preparation that's perfect for a special-occasion dinner. It's fancy without being complicated."

—minutemeals' Chef Anne

step 1

make the **pan-fried potatoes with onions**

3 tablespoons vegetable oil

1 bag (20 ounces) diced potatoes with onions

Salt and pepper to taste

In a large nonstick skillet, heat the vegetable oil over medium heat until hot. Add the potatoes with onions and cook, tossing occasionally, for 10 to 12 minutes, or until evenly browned. (If you like them crispy, cook them for a minute or two longer.) Season with salt and pepper. Keep warm, partially covered.

step 2

prepare the **steamed spinach**

1 bag (20 ounces) baby spinach

Salt and pepper to taste

1. Put the spinach in a large colander and run under cold water. Do not shake the water off the leaves.

2. Transfer the spinach to a large saucepan. Cover and put the pan over high heat. Steam the spinach for 2 minutes, or until wilted. Remove the pan from the heat, season with salt and pepper, and reserve, covered.

step 3

cook the **steak au poivre**

2 tablespoons crushed black peppercorns, or more to taste

2 shallots

4 shell steaks (about 8 ounces each)

Salt to taste

2 tablespoons vegetable oil

2 tablespoons butter

1/2 cup dry red wine

1/2 cup reduced-sodium beef broth

1. Coarsely crush enough peppercorns to measure 2 tablespoons. Peel and thinly slice the shallots.

2. Salt the steaks lightly. Sprinkle the steaks equally on both sides with the crushed peppercorns, then with the palm of your hand press them into the meat.

3. In a large heavy skillet, heat the vegetable oil over high heat until very hot, almost smoking. Carefully add the steaks and cook for 3 minutes. Turn and cook for 2 minutes for medium-rare, or longer, if desired. Remove the steaks to a platter and keep warm. Discard any fat in the pan.

4. Add 1 tablespoon of butter to the pan and heat over medium heat until melted. Add the shallots and cook, stirring, until softened. Pour in the wine and cook over medium-high heat until reduced by three quarters. Stir in the beef broth and cook for 1 minute. Swirl the remaining 1 tablespoon butter into the sauce, stirring until melted and well combined.

step 4

serve

1. Pour the sauce over the steaks and place the platter on the table.

2. Put the spinach in one serving bowl and the pan-fried potatoes in another and serve.

3. When ready for dessert, cut the tart into slices, plate, and serve.

Steak au Poivre
Single serving is 1/4 of the total recipe
CALORIES 662; PROTEIN 67g; CARBS 2g;
TOTAL FAT 39g; SAT FAT 15g; CHOLESTEROL 218mg;
SODIUM 151mg; FIBER 0g

barbecued flank steak

corn on the cob with garlic butter

coleslaw

crusty french rolls

fresh cherries and chocolate

shopping list

Fresh corn on the cob

Flank steak

Barbecue sauce

Prepared coleslaw
(from the deli counter)

Crusty rolls

Cherries

from your pantry

Salt and pepper

Garlic

Butter

Olive oil

Paprika

Semisweet chocolate bars or squares

serves 4

beforeyoustart

Bring the water to a boil in a large pot, covered, over high heat to cook the corn. Preheat the grill or broiler. Rinse the cherries and let them drain during dinner.

step **1** cook the **corn on the cob with garlic butter**

step **2** grill the **barbecued flank steak**

step **3** plate the **coleslaw**

step **4** **serve**

heads**up**

Flank steak is a thin lean cut of beef. Two important points when cooking it: Don't overcook it, and cut it paper thin across the grain. If cut into chunks, like boneless sirloin, flank steak is chewy.

"Summertime cooking doesn't get any easier than this. Ask the kids to shuck the corn, then light up the grill, and enjoy."

—minutemeals' Chef Joanne

step 1

cook the **corn on the cob with garlic butter**

3 quarts water

Salt to taste

8 ears husked fresh corn on the cob

8 garlic cloves

1 stick (8 tablespoons) butter

1. Pour the water into a large pot, salt lightly, and cover. Bring to a rolling boil over high heat. Add the corn, cover, and boil for 5 minutes.

2. Meanwhile, crush the garlic cloves in a garlic press. In a small microwave-safe bowl, combine the butter and pressed garlic. Cover and microwave on High for 25 seconds.

3. Drain the corn well, arrange it on a napkin-lined large platter, and cover to keep warm. Place the platter and garlic butter on the table.

step 2

grill the **barbecued flank steak**

1 flank steak (1$1/2$ pounds)

2 tablespoons olive oil

$1/4$ teaspoon salt

$1/8$ teaspoon pepper

1 cup barbecue sauce, or more to taste

1. Preheat the barbecue grill or place the broiler rack 4 inches from the heat and preheat the broiler.

2. Trim the flank steak and remove the white membrane directly on the surface of the meat, if necessary. Brush the steak on both sides with the olive oil, and sprinkle with the salt and pepper. Place on the grill or under the broiler and cook for 3 minutes. Remove, brush $1/2$ cup of the barbecue sauce over the steak, and grill sauce side down or broil sauce side up for 2 minutes.

3. Turn the steak and grill for 3 minutes. Spread with the remaining barbecue sauce and grill or broil as directed above to desired doneness, about 2 minutes longer. Transfer to a rimmed cutting board or a platter and let stand for a minute or two before slicing.

step 3

plate the **coleslaw**

1 pound coleslaw

Ground paprika to taste

Put the coleslaw in a serving bowl and sprinkle the top with paprika. Place the bowl on the table.

step 4

serve

1. Cut the steak across the grain into very thin slices. Transfer the slices to a platter, then pour any juices that have accumulated over the meat. Place the platter on the table.

2. Place the rolls in a basket and place on the table.

3. Serve the corn drizzled with or rolled in the garlic butter with plenty of salt and freshly ground black pepper.

4. When ready for dessert, place the cherries in a bowl and serve with chunks of semisweet chocolate.

Barbecued Flank Steak
Single serving is $1/4$ of the total recipe
CALORIES 458; PROTEIN 27g; CARBS 32g;
TOTAL FAT 23g; SAT FAT 8g; CHOLESTEROL 71mg;
SODIUM 1734mg; FIBER 0g

☆ chicken fried steak

cream gravy

succotash

buttermilk biscuits

sliced pineapple with
coconut macaroons

menu gameplan

shopping list

Round steaks

Buttermilk biscuits

Frozen succotash

Chopped scallions
(from the salad bar)

Half-and-half

Pineapple slices
(from the produce department)

Coconut macaroons

from your pantry

Eggs

Milk

All-purpose flour

Salt and pepper

Canola oil

Butter

Fat-free reduced-sodium
chicken broth

Cayenne pepper

Worcestershire sauce

serves 4

step 1 cook the **chicken fried steaks**

step 2 heat the **buttermilk biscuits**

step 3 cook the **succotash**

step 4 make the **cream gravy**

step 5 **serve**

headsup
Some supermarkets sell packages of thinly sliced beef "for braciole." If yours does not, buy thin-cut round steak.

"Don't be confused: It's not chicken, it's beef, and it's fried and served with delicious gravy—comfort food of the best kind."
—minutemeals' Chef Miriam

step 1
cook the **chicken fried steaks**

4 round steaks (1 1/4 to 1 1/2 pounds), cut as for bracciole, about 1/4 inch thick

2 large eggs

1/4 cup milk

1 1/2 cups all-purpose flour for dredging

Salt and pepper to taste

Canola oil for frying

1. Pat the steaks dry with paper towels.

2. In a shallow bowl, beat the eggs together with the milk until combined.

3. Spread the flour out on a large plate. Dip 1 steak at a time into the egg mixture, letting the excess drip off, then into the flour, shaking off any excess. Place on a baking sheet and season on both sides with salt and pepper. Prepare the remaining 3 steaks in the same manner.

4. Heat a large heavy skillet, preferably cast iron, over medium-high heat until hot. Add 1/4 inch canola oil and heat until hot, almost smoking. Carefully add 2 steaks and fry for 2 minutes. Turn and fry for 2 minutes, or until golden brown and crisp. Transfer the steaks to a large platter and keep warm. Add more oil to the skillet, if necessary, and cook the remaining 2 steaks in the same manner.

5. Carefully pour the hot oil out of the skillet and discard it; wipe the skillet clean with paper towels.

step 2
heat the **buttermilk biscuits**

1 package buttermilk biscuits

In a toaster oven, warm the biscuits according to the directions on the package.

step 3
cook the **succotash**

1 package (10 ounces) frozen succotash

In a medium saucepan, cook the succotash according to the directions on the package. Drain, place in a serving bowl, and keep warm, covered.

step 4
make the **cream gravy**

1 tablespoon butter

1/2 cup chopped scallions

1 cup fat-free reduced-sodium chicken broth

1/2 cup half-and-half

2 tablespoons all-purpose flour

Salt to taste

Cayenne pepper to taste

Worcestershire sauce to taste

1. In the skillet in which you cooked the steaks, melt the butter over medium heat. Add the scallions and cook, stirring, for 2 minutes.

2. In a bowl, stir together the broth, half-and-half, and flour until blended. Add to the skillet, and bring to a boil, stirring. Simmer, stirring occasionally, until thickened, about 2 minutes. Add salt, cayenne, and Worcestershire sauce to taste.

step 5
serve

1. Put 1 steak on each dinner plate, spoon cream gravy over it, and serve with the succotash and the warm biscuits. Serve the remaining cream gravy separately.

2. When ready for dessert, divide the pineapple among 4 dessert plates. Serve with the macaroons.

Chicken Fried Steak
Single serving is 1/4 of the total recipe
CALORIES 649; PROTEIN 36g; CARBS 20g; TOTAL FAT 46g; SAT FAT 10g; CHOLESTEROL 189mg; SODIUM 133mg; FIBER 0g

Nutrient Analysis does not include gravy.

sliced steak
with asian vegetables

sesame rice

watercress and bean sprout salad

vanilla frozen yogurt with gingersnap crumble

menu
gameplan

serves 4

step 1	cook the **sesame rice**
step 2	cook the **sliced steak with asian vegetables**
step 3	assemble the **watercress and bean sprout salad**
step 4	**serve**

shopping list

Jasmine rice

Sesame seeds

Boneless sirloin steak

Frozen mixed broccoli, carrots, and water chestnuts

Prewashed stemmed watercress

Asian-style salad dressing

Vanilla frozen yogurt

Gingersnaps

from the salad bar

Mushroom slices
(or from the produce department)

Chopped scallions

Bean sprouts

from your pantry

Peanut oil

Toasted sesame oil

Salt and pepper

Lite soy sauce

Cornstarch

Ground ginger

Sugar

luckyfor**you** We've relied on presliced mushrooms and scallions and frozen mixed vegetables for quick preparation. These are handy shortcuts no matter what you might be preparing.

step 1

cook the **sesame rice**

3/4 cup jasmine rice

2 teaspoons peanut oil

1 tablespoon sesame seeds

1/2 teaspoon toasted sesame oil

1. In a medium saucepan, cook the jasmine rice in the amount of water and for the time suggested on the package.

2. While the rice cooks, heat the peanut oil in a small skillet over medium heat until hot. Add the sesame seeds and cook, stirring, until golden. Do not let them burn. Stir in the sesame oil. Stir the mixture into the hot rice and toss to combine. Keep warm, covered.

step 2

cook the **sliced steak with asian vegetables**

1 1/2 pounds boneless sirloin steak, at least 1 inch thick

Salt and pepper to taste

1 1/2 tablespoons peanut oil

3 tablespoons lite soy sauce

1 cup mushroom slices

1/2 cup chopped scallions

1 bag (16 ounces) frozen mixed broccoli, carrots, and water chestnuts, thawed

3/4 cup water

2 teaspoons cornstarch

1/2 teaspoon ground ginger

1/2 teaspoon sugar

1. Pat the steak dry with paper towels and season on both sides with salt and pepper.

2. In a large heavy skillet, heat 1 tablespoon of the peanut oil over medium-high heat until hot. Add the steak and cook for 3 minutes. Drizzle 1 tablespoon of the soy sauce over the meat and turn. Sauté for 3 to 5 minutes, or until cooked to desired doneness. Remove to a rimmed cutting board and keep warm, covered.

3. Add the remaining 1/2 tablespoon peanut oil to the skillet with the mushrooms and scallions. Stir-fry over medium-high heat for 2 to 3 minutes. Add the thawed mixed vegetables and 1/4 cup of the water, cover, and cook for 5 minutes, or until the vegetables are just tender, stirring occasionally.

4. Meanwhile, thinly slice the steak.

5. In a small bowl, stir together the remaining 1/2 cup water, the remaining 2 tablespoons soy sauce, the cornstarch, ground ginger, and sugar until blended. Add to the skillet and cook, stirring occasionally, until the sauce comes to a boil, thickens, and becomes shiny.

step 3

assemble the **watercress and bean sprout salad**

1 bag (4 ounces) prewashed stemmed watercress

1/2 cup bean sprouts

1/4 cup Asian-style salad dressing

Combine the watercress and bean sprouts in a salad bowl. Add the dressing and toss. Place the bowl on the table.

step 4

serve

1. Transfer the vegetables to a large serving platter. Arrange the steak slices in the center. Drizzle with any drippings from the cutting board and the sauce from the skillet.

2. Spoon the rice into a bowl and serve.

3. When ready for dessert, scoop the yogurt into small bowls and crush gingersnaps over the top of each serving. Serve with additional gingersnaps, if desired.

Sliced Steak with Asian Vegetables
Single serving is 1/4 of the total recipe

CALORIES 433; PROTEIN 39g; CARBS 17g; TOTAL FAT 24g; SAT FAT 8g; CHOLESTEROL 103mg; SODIUM 486mg; FIBER 1g

beef stroganoff
egg noodles
cucumber salad
black forest cake

---

shopping list

Beef tenderloin

Fresh parsley (optional)

Sour cream

Medium-width yolk-free egg noodles

Kosher salt

Black Forest cake

from the salad bar

Onion slices

Mushroom slices (or from the produce department)

Cucumber slices

from your pantry

Canola oil

Butter

Salt and pepper

All-purpose flour

Fat-free reduced-sodium chicken or beef broth

Dijon mustard

Rice vinegar or white wine vinegar

serves 6

beforeyoustart

Bring the water to a boil in a large pot, covered, over high heat to cook the egg noodles.

| step | 1 | make the **beef stroganoff** |

| step | 2 | cook the **egg noodles** |

| step | 3 | plate the **cucumber salad** |

| step | 4 | **serve** |

headsup Sour cream curdles if it boils and that will ruin this famous dish. Be sure to remove the pan from the heat before adding the sour cream, and in the event that the mixture needs reheating, do so over low heat only.

"Beef Stroganoff is creamy and comforting, with an old-fashioned feel about it—just what you want for dinner in winter."

—minutemeals' Chef Nancy

step 1

make the **beef stroganoff**

1 1/2 pounds beef tenderloin

2 tablespoons chopped fresh parsley, for garnish (optional)

1 tablespoon canola oil

1 1/2 tablespoons butter

1 1/2 cups thin onion slices

8 ounces mushroom slices

Salt and pepper to taste

1 tablespoon all-purpose flour

1 cup fat-free reduced-sodium chicken or beef broth

2 teaspoons Dijon mustard

1 cup sour cream (light, if desired)

1. Pat the beef tenderloin dry with paper towels, then slice into 1- × 1/4-inch strips. Chop 2 tablespoons parsley for garnish, if desired.

2. In a large nonstick skillet, heat the canola oil over medium-high heat until hot. Add the beef strips and cook, tossing, until no longer pink. Transfer with a slotted spoon to a plate.

3. In the skillet, melt the butter over medium-high heat. When the mixture begins to sizzle, add the onion slices and cook, stirring, for 4 to 5 minutes, until softened. Add the mushrooms and cook, stirring, for 4 to 5 minutes, until soft. Season with salt and pepper.

4. Stir in the flour and cook, stirring, for 30 seconds. Add the broth slowly, whisking well to combine. Bring the mixture to a boil, lower the heat, and cook 1 minute.

5. Stir in the mustard until blended. Add the tenderloin strips, and simmer until just heated through, about 2 minutes.

step 2

cook the **egg noodles**

4 quarts water

Salt to taste

3/4 pound medium-width yolk-free egg noodles

1 tablespoon butter, or more to taste

Pour the water into a large pot, salt lightly, and cover. Bring to a boil over high heat. Add the noodles and 1 teaspoon salt. Cook according to the directions on the package, until soft but not mushy. Drain. Transfer the noodles to a serving bowl and add the butter. Toss to coat. Keep warm, covered.

step 3

plate the **cucumber salad**

Cucumber slices for 6

Rice vinegar or white wine vinegar to taste

Kosher salt to taste

Arrange the cucumber slices on a plate, overlapping them slightly, and drizzle with vinegar. Season with kosher salt. Place the plate on the table.

step 4

serve

1. Remove the skillet with the tenderloin from the heat and stir in the sour cream. If necessary, add more broth (or water) to thin the sauce to the desired consistency. Season with salt and pepper. (If you need to reheat the stroganoff, heat it gently—do not let it boil.)

2. Spoon the noodles onto a platter, top with the stroganoff, and garnish with the chopped parsley, if using.

3. When ready to serve dessert, slice the cake into generous pieces, plate, and serve.

Beef Stroganoff with Egg Noodles
Single serving is 1/6 of the total recipe

CALORIES 682; PROTEIN 30g; CARBS 48g;
TOTAL FAT 41g; SAT FAT 18g; CHOLESTEROL 121mg;
SODIUM 121mg; FIBER 1g

roquefort burgers
tomato and pepper toss
lemon meringue pie

serves 4

shopping list

Large burger buns

Ground sirloin

Roquefort or blue cheese

Tomatoes

Green pepper strips
(from the salad bar)

Lemon meringue pie

from your pantry

Salt

Freshly ground black pepper

Your favorite burger
condiments

Extra virgin olive oil

Balsamic vinegar

step 1 make the **roquefort burgers**

step 2 make the **tomato and pepper toss**

step 3 **serve**

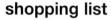 **headsup** If you don't have a grill pan for cooking the burgers, use a large nonstick skillet. You'll have to spray it with cooking spray to prevent burgers made with sirloin from sticking. A word about heat and nonstick cookware: Because of the specialized surface, cooking over high heat is not recommended.

"I love these burgers. The first bite, when you taste the melted cheese inside, it's just heavenly."

—minutemeals' Chef Nancy

step 1

make the **roquefort burgers**

4 large burger buns

1¹/₂ pounds ground sirloin

About 1 teaspoon each of salt and freshly ground black pepper

4 to 6 ounces crumbled Roquefort or blue cheese

Your favorite condiments, for serving

1. In a large toaster oven, toast the buns lightly. Place one bun on each dinner plate.

2. Break up the sirloin and season with the salt and fresh pepper. Divide the meat equally into 4 mounds. Form the Roquefort, 2 tablespoons at a time, into nuggets, then flatten each into a disk about the size of a 50-cent piece.

3. Halve the mounds. Flatten the halves into patties about ¹/₄ inch thick. Place 1 disk of the cheese on each of the 4 patties, being sure to leave a ¹/₄-inch edge all the way around. Top with one of the remaining patties. Flatten each burger gently between the palms of your hands, then pinch the edge of the two patties together firmly to seal. (This prevents the cheese from melting out the sides.)

4. Heat a grill pan over high heat until hot. Place the burgers in the pan, without crowding them, and reduce the heat to medium. Cook about 4 to 5 minutes per side, to the desired doneness. Place 1 burger on the bottom half of each bun. Top with the remaining half or serve open face.

step 2

while the burgers cook, make the **tomato and pepper toss**

2 large (or 3 medium) ripe tomatoes

1 cup thinly sliced green pepper strips

1¹/₂ to 2 tablespoons extra virgin olive oil

2 to 3 teaspoons balsamic vinegar

Salt and pepper to taste

Rinse and core the tomatoes and dice into ¹/₂-inch cubes. Place in a salad bowl. Add the pepper strips, olive oil, vinegar, and salt and pepper to taste and toss to combine. Place the bowl on the table.

step 3

serve

1. Serve the burgers with your favorite condiments and the vegetable toss.

2. When ready for dessert, cut the pie into slices, plate, and serve.

Roquefort Burgers
Single serving is ¹/₄ of the total recipe
CALORIES 485; PROTEIN 45g; CARBS 22g; TOTAL FAT 24g; SAT FAT 7g; CHOLESTEROL 132mg; SODIUM 869mg; FIBER 2g

Nutrient Analysis includes bun.

saucy mini meat cakes

parsleyed new potatoes

mixed greens vinaigrette

rice pudding with whipped cream

shopping list

Lean ground beef

Fresh parsley

Pre-scrubbed small new potatoes (in bags in the produce department)

Cherry tomatoes (from the salad bar)

Prewashed mixed salad greens

Rice pudding

Instant whipped cream

from your pantry

Steak sauce or barbecue sauce

Italian-style seasoned dry bread crumbs

Milk

Egg

Dijon mustard

Dried thyme

Salt and pepper

Olive or vegetable oil

Butter

Vinaigrette dressing, store-bought or homemade

serves 4

step **1** make the **saucy mini meat cakes**

step **2** boil the **parsleyed new potatoes**

step **3** assemble the **mixed greens vinaigrette**

step **4** **serve**

luckyforyou If mashed potatoes are the family favorite, simply smash the potatoes you've cooked for parsleyed potatoes. Add milk or chicken broth and mash to the desired consistency.

"I love meatloaf. Pan-frying individual 'cakes' means you can have it in only 20 minutes."

—minutemeals' Chef Paul

step 1

make the **saucy mini meat cakes**

- 1½ pounds lean ground beef
- 6 tablespoons steak sauce or barbecue sauce
- ⅓ cup Italian-style seasoned dry bread crumbs
- ⅓ cup milk
- 1 large egg
- 1 tablespoon grainy Dijon mustard
- ¼ teaspoon dried thyme
- ¼ teaspoon salt
- ⅛ teaspoon pepper
- 1 tablespoon olive or vegetable oil

1. In a large bowl, place the ground beef, 3 tablespoons of the steak sauce, the bread crumbs, milk, egg, mustard, thyme, salt, and pepper. Work with your hands until combined. Form the mixture into 4 rough 4-inch patties, each about 1 inch high.

2. In a large nonstick skillet, heat the oil over high heat. Add the patties, cook 1 minute, and then reduce the heat to medium. Cook for 5 minutes, or until browned on the underside.

3. Turn the patties and cover the skillet. Cook for 6 minutes longer, or until no longer pink in the center.

4. Transfer each loaf to a dinner plate and spoon some of the remaining 3 tablespoons steak sauce over each.

step 2

boil the **parsleyed new potatoes**

- 3 tablespoons chopped fresh parsley
- 1½ pounds pre-scrubbed small new potatoes
- 2 tablespoons butter
- ½ teaspoon salt

1. Chop enough parsley to measure 3 tablespoons.

2. In a 1½-quart shallow saucepan or 10-inch skillet, arrange the potatoes; add water just to cover. Cover the pan and bring to a boil over medium-high heat. Cook, covered, for 13 minutes, or until fork-tender.

step 3

assemble the **mixed greens vinaigrette**

- 1 cup cherry tomatoes
- 1 bag (5 ounces) prewashed mixed salad greens of choice
- ¼ cup vinaigrette dressing

1. Rinse the cherry tomatoes and pat dry.

2. Place the greens in a bowl, add the vinaigrette, and toss. Divide the salad among 4 salad plates, divide the cherry tomatoes among the salads, and place the plates on the table.

step 4

serve

1. Drain the potatoes well and return them to the pan. Add the butter, chopped parsley, and salt; toss gently to coat.

2. Place 1 meat cake on each of 4 dinner plates and spoon some of the parsleyed potatoes alongside.

3. When ready for dessert, spoon the rice pudding into bowls, garnish each serving with whipped cream, and serve.

Saucy Mini Meat Cakes
Single serving is ¼ of the total recipe
CALORIES 308; PROTEIN 35g; CARBS 9g;
TOTAL FAT 13g; SAT FAT 1g; CHOLESTEROL 156mg;
SODIUM 434mg; FIBER 0g

hamburger stroganoff

buttered noodles
green peas with mint
apple crumb cake

menu
gameplan

shopping list

Wide egg noodles

Onion slices
(from the salad bar)

Lean ground beef,
such as ground round

Sour cream

Frozen green peas

Fresh mint

Apple crumb cake

from your pantry

Salt and pepper

Butter

Canola oil

Garlic

Tomato paste

Dried thyme

All-purpose flour

Fat-free reduced-sodium
beef broth

serves 4

beforeyoustart

Bring the water to a boil in a large pot, covered, over high heat to cook the noodles.

step **1** cook the **buttered noodles**

step **2** make the **hamburger stroganoff**

step **3** cook the **green peas with mint**

step **4** **serve**

luckyforyou Tomato paste is available in tubes. Squeeze out what you need, reseal the tube, and store. No more throwing out nearly whole cans anymore.

"This menu is too good to be true. It's across the board kid- and adult-friendly, and it's easy to make."

—minutemeals' Chef Sharon

step 1

cook the buttered noodles

3 quarts water

Salt to taste

12 ounces wide egg noodles

1 tablespoon butter

1. Pour the water into a large pot, salt lightly, and cover. Bring to a boil over high heat. Add the noodles and cook, stirring occasionally, 8 to 10 minutes, until tender. Drain in a colander.

2. Return the noodles to the pot, add the butter, and toss until melted. Keep warm, covered.

step 2

make the hamburger stroganoff

1 tablespoon canola oil

1/2 cup onion slices

1 pound lean ground beef, such as ground round

1 garlic clove

1 tablespoon tomato paste

1/2 teaspoon dried thyme

1 tablespoon all-purpose flour

1 cup fat-free reduced-sodium beef broth

Salt and pepper to taste

1/2 cup sour cream

1. In a large nonstick skillet, heat the canola oil over medium-high heat until hot. Add the onion and cook, stirring, for 3 minutes, until softened. Add the ground beef and sauté, tossing, until lightly browned.

2. Meanwhile, mince the garlic clove. Add to the meat and cook, stirring, for 1 minute.

3. Stir in the tomato paste and thyme, then sprinkle in the flour and stir to combine. Stir in the broth until fully incorporated. Cook for 3 to 4 minutes, until the mixture thickens slightly. Season with salt and pepper.

4. Remove the pan from the heat and stir in the sour cream. Place the pan over low heat and warm the stroganoff just until heated through. Do not let it boil.

step 3

cook the green peas with mint

1 package (10 ounces) frozen green peas

1 tablespoon chopped fresh mint

1 tablespoon butter

1. In a medium saucepan, cook the peas on the stovetop or in the microwave oven according to the directions on the package.

2. Meanwhile, chop enough mint to measure 1 tablespoon.

3. Drain the peas, add the butter and chopped mint, stirring to combine, and keep warm, covered.

step 4

serve

1. Divide the noodles among 4 dinner plates and spoon the stroganoff over them.

2. Spoon a serving of minted peas onto each plate.

3. If desired, warm the apple crumb cake in a low oven while you have dinner. Serve in squares.

Hamburger Stroganoff
Single serving is 1/4 of the total recipe
CALORIES 672; PROTEIN 47g; CARBS 68g;
TOTAL FAT 25g; SAT FAT 4g; CHOLESTEROL 118mg;
SODIUM 634mg; FIBER 1g

Nutrient Analysis includes egg noodles.

hamburger pie

mixed green salad

garlic bread

butter crunch ice cream
and shortbread cookies

shopping list

Ground chuck (85% lean)

Chopped tomatoes with basil

Pre-shredded mozzarella
with grated Parmesan and
Romano cheeses

Ready-to-heat garlic bread

Prewashed mixed spring or
baby greens

Italian salad dressing,
store-bought or homemade

Butter crunch ice cream

Shortbread cookies

from your pantry

Onion

Canola oil

Salt and pepper

Mustard

Worcestershire sauce

Dried oregano

serves 4

beforeyoustart

Place the broiler rack 4 inches from the
heat and preheat the broiler.

step **1** make the **hamburger pie**

step **2** heat the **garlic bread**

step **3** assemble the **mixed green salad**

step **4** **serve**

headsup

Ground chuck is an inexpensive
and flavorful cut of beef. It is
also higher in fat than ground round, which would also be
suitable for the pie. Avoid meat labeled simply "all beef,"
which has the highest fat content of all the ground beef
varieties.

"I've worked in some very sophisticated restaurants, and I still look forward to hamburger pie for dinner."

—minutemeals' Chef Katell

step 1

make the **hamburger pie**

½ cup chopped onion
(1 small onion)

1 tablespoon canola oil

1 pound ground chuck
(85% lean)

Salt and pepper to taste

1 teaspoon mustard

1 teaspoon Worcestershire
sauce, or more to taste

1 cup canned chopped
tomatoes with basil, drained

½ teaspoon dried oregano

1 cup combined pre-shredded
mozzarella with grated Parmesan
and Romano cheeses

1. Chop the onion to measure
½ cup.

2. In a large ovenproof skillet, with a heatproof handle, heat the canola oil over medium-high heat until hot. Add the onion and cook, stirring, just until softened. Add the meat and salt and pepper, and cook, breaking up the pieces with the side of the spoon, until no longer pink. If necessary, pour off any excess liquid from the skillet. Stir in the mustard and Worcestershire sauce.

3. Drain the tomatoes. Spread the tomatoes over the meat mixture in the skillet and sprinkle with the oregano. Scatter the cheese evenly over the top. Run the skillet under the broiler and broil for 3 to 4 minutes, until the cheese is melted.

step 2

heat the **garlic bread**

1 ready-to-heat garlic bread

In a toaster oven, heat the bread according to the directions on the package.

step 3

assemble the **mixed green salad**

1 bag (5 ounces) prewashed
mixed spring or baby greens

¼ cup Italian salad dressing

Place the greens in a salad bowl. Add the dressing and toss. Place the bowl on the table.

step 4

serve

1. Serve the hamburger pie directly from the skillet.

2. Place the garlic bread in a bread basket and place on the table.

3. When ready for dessert, scoop the ice cream into bowls and serve with the cookies.

Hamburger Pie
Single serving is ¼ of the total recipe
CALORIES 446; PROTEIN 30g; CARBS 6g;
TOTAL FAT 33g; SAT FAT 13g; CHOLESTEROL 103mg;
SODIUM 423mg; FIBER 0g

meatball and pepper subs
greens and beans salad
brownies

menu gameplan

serves 4

beforeyoustart
Place the jar of bean salad in the refrigerator to chill.

step **1** make the **meatball and pepper subs**

step **2** assemble the **greens and beans salad**

step **3** **serve**

shopping list
Ground round
Whole-wheat bread
Italian bread
Jarred three bean salad
Brownies

from the salad bar
Onion slices
Green pepper slices
Red pepper slices
Boston lettuce leaves

from your pantry
Pasta sauce
Salt
Olive oil
Dried basil

luckyforyou
This meatball recipe becomes totally doable when you use already sliced onions and peppers from the salad bar. And, if you can enlist a meatball shaper as a kitchen assistant, the recipe goes even faster.

"These sandwiches make a fun simple supper or a great lunch when you know you're going to have a late dinner."

—minutemeals' Chef Joanne

make the **meatball and pepper subs**

3/4 pound ground round

1 jar (14 ounces) prepared pasta sauce

1 slice whole-wheat bread

1/2 teaspoon salt, or to taste

2 tablespoons olive oil

1 cup onion slices

1 cup green pepper slices

1 cup red pepper slices

Dried basil leaves

1 loaf (20 inches) Italian bread

1. In a large bowl, combine the ground round and 1/4 cup of the pasta sauce. Crumble the bread into the bowl and add the salt. Stir until combined. On a sheet of waxed paper, shape the mixture into a 4-inch square and cut into 16 chunks. With your hands, shape each chunk into a meatball.

2. In a very large nonstick skillet (or 2 nonstick skillets), heat the olive oil over medium heat. Add the meatballs and cook them, turning frequently, until browned well on all sides.

3. Add the onion and pepper slices and cook, stirring frequently, for 3 minutes. Add the remaining pasta sauce and a pinch of dried basil and bring the mixture to a boil. Cook until the meatballs are no longer pink inside, about 3 minutes longer.

4. Cut one side of the Italian bread horizontally, leaving the other side attached. Open up the loaf and spoon the meatballs, peppers, and as much of the sauce as possible over the bread. Cut the loaf crosswise into 4 equal pieces. Serve with the remaining sauce passed separately.

step 2

meanwhile, assemble the **greens and beans salad**

8 large Boston lettuce leaves, rinsed

1 jar (16 ounces) three bean salad

1. Rinse the lettuce leaves and pat dry. Drain the bean salad.

2. Place 2 lettuce leaves on each of 4 salad plates to form lettuce cups. With a slotted spoon, divide the chilled bean salad among the lettuce cups. Place the salads on the table.

step 3

serve

1. Serve the subs with lots of napkins and/or forks and knives.

2. When ready for dessert, serve the brownies.

Meatball and Pepper Subs
Single serving is 1/4 of the total recipe
CALORIES 543; PROTEIN 29g; CARBS 68g;
TOTAL FAT 20g; SAT FAT 1g; CHOLESTEROL 50mg;
SODIUM 1324mg; FIBER 7g

monte cristo sandwiches

coleslaw

cantaloupe with honeyed blueberries

menu
gameplan

shopping list

Sliced smoked ham, such as Black Forest or Westphalian (from the deli counter)

Sliced Swiss cheese (from the deli counter)

Sliced roasted turkey breast (from the deli counter)

Gherkins

Prepared coleslaw (from the deli counter)

Blueberries

Cantaloupe

Lime

from your pantry

Butter

Sliced firm-textured white or whole-wheat bread

Dijon mustard

Eggs

Milk

Salt

Cayenne pepper

Honey

serves 4

step **1** make the **monte cristo sandwiches**

step **2** plate the **coleslaw**

step **3** prepare the **cantaloupe with honeyed blueberries**

step **4** **serve**

luckyforyou

There isn't cause for even one concern in a menu like this. The ingredients are straightforward, the shopping for them will be easy, and, better still, nearly everything can be done well in advance. All that's left is to assemble the sandwiches and grill them.

"Anything that's grilled in butter is my idea of bliss. How could anyone resist a sandwich that's this rich and tasty?"

—minutemeals' Chef Miriam

step 1

make the **monte cristo sandwiches**

4 tablespoons butter, softened

8 slices firm-textured white or whole-wheat bread

Dijon mustard

6 ounces sliced smoked ham, such as Black Forest or Westphalian

6 ounces sliced Swiss cheese

6 ounces sliced roasted turkey breast

4 large eggs

1/2 cup milk

Salt to taste

Cayenne pepper to taste

Gherkins for serving

1. Place a griddle or 2 medium skillets over medium heat. Melt the butter on the griddle or divide it between the skillets until it is no longer foamy.

2. Meanwhile, spread one side of each slice of bread with some of the mustard. Top 4 of the slices with some of the ham, cheese, and turkey. Top each with 1 slice of the remaining bread, pressing down to form 4 compact sandwiches.

3. To make the batter, in a shallow bowl, whisk the eggs together with the milk and salt and cayenne to taste.

4. Dip each sandwich on both sides into the batter, coating it well.

5. When the foam from the butter subsides, add the sandwiches to each hot surface. Cook for 4 minutes, turn with a metal spatula, and cook for 4 minutes more, or until golden brown. (Use the back of the spatula to press each sandwich down as a way of melting the cheese.)

step 2

plate the **coleslaw**

1 pound prepared coleslaw

Spoon the coleslaw into a serving bowl and place on the table.

step 3

prepare the **cantaloupe with honeyed blueberries**

1/2 pint blueberries

2 tablespoons honey

1 ripe cantaloupe

1 lime

1. Rinse the blueberries and remove any stems. Blot dry with paper towels and place in a bowl. Add the honey and toss gently to combine.

2. Cut the cantaloupe into quarters and remove the seeds and strings. Place a piece on each of 4 dessert plates and top with blueberries. Cut the lime into 4 wedges and add 1 wedge to each plate. Refrigerate until serving time.

step 4

serve

1. Transfer the sandwiches to a cutting board and cut each in half on the diagonal. Divide the triangles among 4 plates, garnish with gherkins, and serve while still warm.

2. Serve the dessert well chilled.

Monte Cristo Sandwiches
Single serving is 1/4 of the total recipe
CALORIES 670; PROTEIN 40g; CARBS 54g;
TOTAL FAT 33g; SAT FAT 14g; CHOLESTEROL 300mg;
SODIUM 1379mg; FIBER 6g

veal marsala
(veal in wine sauce)
risotto milanese
sliced tomatoes with basil
crusty italian bread
tiramisù

menu
gameplan

shopping list

Boxed risotto Milanese style

Frozen peas

Vine-ripened tomatoes

Fresh basil

Shallot

Veal scaloppine

Dry Marsala wine

Italian bread

Tiramisù

from your pantry

Butter

Fat-free reduced-sodium chicken broth

Grated Parmesan cheese

Salt and pepper

Extra virgin olive oil

Canola oil

serves 4

step **1** make the **risotto milanese**

step **2** prepare the **sliced tomatoes with basil**

step **3** cook the **veal marsala**

step **4** **serve**

headsup
Marsala is a dessert wine from Sicily that is often used in cooking. You can purchase it dry or sweet. You need only a small amount of the dry to make the sauce for the veal. Chill the bottle and serve it in small glasses as an aperitif.

"From the way this menu tastes you'd think it was far more complicated. The veal and risotto complement each other beautifully."

—minutemeals' Chef Anne

step 1

make the **risotto milanese**

1 tablespoon butter

1 box risotto Milanese style

3 cups fat-free reduced-sodium chicken broth or water

1/2 cup frozen peas

1/4 cup grated Parmesan cheese

Salt and pepper to taste

1. In a medium saucepan, melt the butter over medium heat. Add the rice and cook for 1 to 2 minutes, stirring, to coat.

2. Add the broth or water with the risotto seasoning packet. Stir well, reduce the heat to a simmer, and cook, stirring occasionally, for 10 minutes.

3. Stir in the frozen peas and cook, stirring once, for 5 to 6 minutes. When done, the rice should be cooked through but firm and the mixture should be creamy.

step 2

prepare the **sliced tomatoes with basil**

4 medium vine-ripened tomatoes

Fresh basil leaves

Extra virgin olive oil for drizzling

1. Rinse the tomatoes and basil leaves and pat dry.

2. With a serrated knife, cut the tomatoes into thin slices. Arrange the slices on a platter and scatter the basil, torn into pieces, if desired, over the top. Drizzle with olive oil. Place the platter on the table.

step 3

cook the **veal marsala**

1 shallot

4 veal scaloppine (about 1 pound)

Salt and pepper to taste

1 tablespoon butter

1 tablespoon canola oil

1/2 cup dry Marsala wine

3/4 cup fat-free reduced-sodium chicken broth

1. Finely chop the shallot.

2. Lightly season the veal on both sides with salt and pepper.

3. In a large nonstick skillet, melt the butter with the canola oil over medium-high heat. Add the veal and cook for about 1 minute. Turn and cook for 1 minute. Remove the veal to a plate and keep warm.

4. Add the chopped shallot to the skillet and sauté, stirring, for 1 minute. Add the Marsala and reduce over high heat by one half.

5. Add the chicken broth and reduce by one quarter. Lower the heat to a simmer, return the veal to the pan, and cook for 1 minute or so, just to heat through. Do not overcook. Transfer the veal to a platter and pour the sauce over it.

step 4

serve

1. Place the platter with the veal on the table.

2. Place the bread on a bread board and place on the table.

3. Stir the Parmesan and salt and pepper into the risotto, transfer to a serving bowl, and serve at once.

4. When ready for dessert, spoon portions of the tiramisù on dessert plates and serve.

Veal Marsala
Single serving is 1/4 of the total recipe
CALORIES 318; PROTEIN 21g; CARBS 1g;
TOTAL FAT 24g; SAT FAT 7g; CHOLESTEROL 88mg;
SODIUM 82mg; FIBER 0g

microwave southwestern chili
with all the fixin's
warm flour tortillas
flan

menu
gameplan

shopping list

Flour tortillas (7-inch diameter)

Lean ground beef

Black beans

Crushed tomatoes in puree

Cilantro

Ripe avocado

Sour cream or plain yogurt

Pre-grated Cheddar or
Monterey Jack cheese

Flan or caramel custards

from the salad bar

Onion slices

Green pepper slices

from your pantry

Garlic

Olive oil

Chili powder or Cajun
seasoning

Dried oregano

Salt and pepper

Onion

Hot sauce

serves 6

beforeyoustart

Preheat the oven to 350°F to heat
the tortillas.

step **1**   warm the **flour tortillas**

step **2**   make the **microwave southwestern chili**

step **3**   prepare the **accompaniments**

step **4**   **serve**

headsup
Chili doesn't have to be served only as a main course. Use it as a topping for burgers or hot dogs or as the filling for Southwestern Sloppy Joes or for omelets.

"I was determined to see if a microwave chili was possible in 20 minutes. It is, and it's delicious."

—minutemeals' Chef Miriam

step 1

warm the **flour tortillas**

6 to 12 flour tortillas
(7-inch diameter)

Preheat the oven to 350°F. Wrap the stack of tortillas in aluminum foil and place in the oven to heat while you make the chili.

step 2

make the **microwave southwestern chili**

1 cup onion slices

1 cup green pepper slices

2 garlic cloves

1 tablespoon olive oil

1 tablespoon chili powder or Cajun seasoning

$1/2$ teaspoon dried oregano, crumbled

Salt and pepper to taste

1 pound lean ground beef

1 can (16 ounces) black beans, drained

1 can (28 ounces) crushed tomatoes in puree

3 tablespoons minced cilantro

1. In a food processor, coarsely chop the onion and pepper slices and garlic. Scrape into a $2^1/2$-quart microwave-safe casserole.

2. Add the olive oil, chili powder, and oregano, season with salt and pepper, and stir to combine. Cover and microwave on High, stirring once, for 3 minutes.

3. Add the beef and stir to break up the pieces. Season with salt and pepper. Cover and microwave on High, stirring once, for 5 minutes.

4. Rinse and drain the black beans. Add the tomatoes and beans to the casserole. Cover and microwave on High, stirring twice, 8 to 10 minutes, or until flavorful.

5. Mince enough cilantro to measure 3 tablespoons.

step 3

while the chili is cooking, prepare the **accompaniments**

Ripe avocado

Onion

Sour cream or plain yogurt

Pre-grated Cheddar or Monterey Jack cheese

Hot sauce

1. Peel and chop the avocado (or buy it already chopped from the salad bar). Chop the onion.

2. Place each accompaniment in a separate bowl and arrange on the table.

step 4

serve

1. Remove the tortillas from the foil, wrap in a large cloth napkin, and place on a plate on the table.

2. Stir the cilantro into the chili. Ladle into large bowls and serve.

3. When ready for dessert, serve the flan in dessert bowls.

Microwave Southwestern Chili with All the Fixin's
Single serving is $1/6$ of the total recipe
CALORIES 233; PROTEIN 19g; CARBS 23g; TOTAL FAT 9g; SAT FAT 0g; CHOLESTEROL 45mg; SODIUM 652mg; FIBER 6g
Nutrient Analysis includes the fixin's.

herbed rib lamb chops

orzo

tomato, olive, and feta salsa

baklava

menu
gameplan

shopping list

Fresh rosemary

Lemon juice

Rib lamb chops

Orzo

Plum tomatoes

Red onion slices
(from the salad bar)

Pitted kalamata olives or
other black olives

Fresh mint

Crumbled feta cheese

Baklava

from your pantry

Garlic

Olive oil

Salt and pepper

Extra virgin olive oil

serves 4

beforeyoustart

Bring the water to a boil in a large
saucepan, covered, over high heat to
cook the orzo.

step **1** cook the **herbed rib lamb chops**

step **2** cook the **orzo**

step **3** make the **tomato, olive, and feta salsa**

step **4** **serve**

luckyforyou Some supermarkets have a
section of the meat case set
aside for specialty cuts. Check it out before automatically
assuming your market won't have something like double-
cut, or Frenched, lamb chops.

"Lamb chops are lovely to serve to company because they are special and easy to prepare."

—minutemeals' Chef Miriam

step 1

cook the **herbed rib lamb chops**

- 2 garlic cloves
- 1 tablespoon finely chopped fresh rosemary or 1 teaspoon dried, crumbled
- 2 tablespoons fresh lemon juice
- 2 tablespoons olive oil
- 8 rib lamb chops, 1 inch thick and Frenched
- Salt and pepper to taste
- 4 small sprigs rosemary

1. Mince the garlic. Finely chop enough rosemary to measure 1 tablespoon.

2. In a small bowl, combine the garlic, rosemary, lemon juice, and olive oil. Rub the mixture on both sides of the chops. Season with salt and pepper.

3. Arrange the chops on the rack of the broiler pan. Broil 2 inches from the heat for 4 to 5 minutes per side for medium-rare; 6 to 7 minutes per side for barely pink. Remove to a plate and keep warm, loosely covered.

step 2

cook the **orzo**

- 2 quarts water
- Salt to taste
- 1 1/3 cups orzo
- 2 tablespoons extra virgin olive oil

Pour the water into a large saucepan, salt lightly, and cover. Bring to a boil over high heat. Add the orzo, stir, and boil, uncovered, for 9 to 11 minutes, or until *al dente*. Drain well, return to the pot, and toss with the olive oil. Keep warm, covered.

step 3

make the **tomato, olive, and feta salsa**

- 6 plum tomatoes
- 1/2 cup red onion slices
- 1/2 cup pitted kalamata or other black olives
- 3 tablespoons minced fresh mint
- 1/2 cup crumbled feta cheese
- 2 tablespoons olive oil
- 2 tablespoons fresh lemon juice

1. Dice the tomatoes and onion slices. Coarsely chop the olives. Chop enough fresh mint to measure 3 tablespoons. Place all in a medium bowl.

2. Add the feta, olive oil, and lemon juice. Toss to combine well.

step 4

serve

1. Have serving plates ready. Place a serving of orzo on each plate. Top with 2 lamb chops. Spoon some of the salsa over each chop. Garnish each plate with a rosemary sprig and serve.

2. When ready for dessert, place a piece of baklava on each dessert plate and serve.

Herbed Rib Lamb Chops
Single serving is 1/4 of the total recipe
CALORIES 505; PROTEIN 39g; CARBS 1g;
TOTAL FAT 38g; SAT FAT 16g; CHOLESTEROL 140mg;
SODIUM 126mg; FIBER 0g

hoisin-honey lamb kabobs

couscous with roasted garlic

warm spinach and clementine salad

vanilla frozen yogurt with fresh strawberries

menu gameplan

shopping list

Hoisin sauce

Lemon (for juice)

Lean lamb, cut into 1-inch cubes

4 metal skewers, each 12 inches long

Couscous with roasted garlic

Clementine or tangerine sections (from the salad bar), or whole fruit

Prewashed baby spinach

Sesame seeds

Strawberries

Vanilla frozen yogurt

from your pantry

Honey

Lite soy sauce

Canola oil

Balsamic vinegar

Salt

Freshly ground black pepper

serves 4

beforeyoustart

Preheat the barbecue grill or the broiler.

step	1	cook the **hoisin-honey lamb kabobs**
step	2	prepare the **couscous with roasted garlic**
step	3	assemble the **spinach and clementine salad**
step	4	**serve**

luckyforyou

There are all kinds of meats cut for kabobs in the super-market. And some markets sell kabobs already threaded on skewers, completely set for the grill. If that's the case in your market, buy the already made kabobs and brush with hoisin-honey sauce. You've just reduced the time needed to make the kabob recipe by at least half!

"Grilling is my favorite way to cook lamb because it brings out the flavor. The hoisin sauce lends a sweetness that I find irresistible."

—minutemeals' Chef Nancy

step 1

cook the **hoisin-honey lamb kabobs**

2 tablespoons hoisin sauce

Juice of 1/2 medium lemon

1 teaspoon honey

1 teaspoon lite soy sauce

1 pound lean lamb, cut into 1-inch cubes

4 metal skewers, each 12 inches long

1. Preheat the barbecue grill or the broiler.

2. In a medium bowl, stir together the hoisin sauce, lemon juice, honey, and soy sauce. Add the lamb and toss to coat.

3. Thread the lamb on the skewers. If grilling, place the skewers on the rack and grill, turning them when the meat is browned, for about 3 minutes per side for medium-rare. If using the broiler, cook about 3 inches from the heat for 7 to 10 minutes, turning once or twice.

step 2

prepare the **couscous with roasted garlic**

1 box (5.8 ounces) couscous with roasted garlic

Prepare the couscous according to the directions on the package. Cover until serving time.

step 3

assemble the **spinach and clementine salad**

1 cup clementine or tangerine sections or 3 medium-sized fruit

1 bag (10 ounces) prewashed baby spinach

1 tablespoon canola oil

2 tablespoons balsamic vinegar

1/8 teaspoon salt

4 teaspoons sesame seeds

Freshly ground black pepper to taste

1. If using whole clementines, peel them, remove any strings, and divide into sections. Place the spinach in a serving bowl.

2. In a medium skillet, heat the canola oil over medium heat. Add the clementine sections and cook, stirring, until tender, about 1 minute. Add the balsamic vinegar and salt and toss. Pour the warm clementines and balsamic over the spinach, toss to combine, and sprinkle with the sesame seeds and fresh pepper. Place the bowl, with 4 salad plates, on the table.

step 4

serve

1. Divide the couscous equally among 4 dinner plates, then place a lamb kabob on top.

2. If possible, serve the salad while it is still warm.

3. When ready for dessert, rinse enough strawberries for 4 servings and hull them. Scoop the frozen yogurt into dessert bowls, garnish the yogurt with the whole berries, and serve.

Hoisin-Honey Lamb Kabobs
Single serving is 1/4 of the total recipe
CALORIES 249; PROTEIN 22g; CARBS 6g;
TOTAL FAT 15g; SAT FAT 7g; CHOLESTEROL 74mg;
SODIUM 246mg; FIBER 0g

lamb-topped eggplant

couscous with chickpeas and green beans

orange sorbet and marzipan cookies

menu gameplan

serves 4

step 1 cook the **lamb-topped eggplant**

step 2 make the **couscous with chickpeas and green beans**

step 3 **serve**

shopping list

Baby eggplant

Red onion

Lean ground lamb

Chickpeas

Plain couscous

Cooked green beans (from the salad bar)

Orange sorbet

Marzipan cookies

from your pantry

Garlic

Canola oil

Tomato paste

Dried oregano

Ground cumin

Ground cloves

Sugar

Salt

headsup

Ground lamb is only one of the options for meat in this dish. Want to make this even lower in calorie? Substitute lean ground turkey breast for the lamb. Want to minimize the lamb taste? Use beef, with little if any lamb added.

"What makes this dish so Mediterranean-tasting and successful are all the seasonings: the oregano, cumin, and cloves with the lamb and eggplant."

—minutemeals' Chef Paul

step 1

cook the **lamb-topped eggplant**

4 baby eggplant (1¼ pounds)

1 small red onion

1 teaspoon chopped garlic (1 large garlic clove)

1 tablespoon canola oil

¾ pound lean ground lamb (or beef)

2 tablespoons tomato paste

¾ teaspoon dried oregano

¾ teaspoon ground cumin

¼ teaspoon ground cloves

1 teaspoon sugar

¾ teaspoon salt

1. Halve each eggplant and score the cut sides. Arrange, cut side down, in a shallow microwave-safe dish. Cover with plastic wrap and microwave on High for 8 minutes, or until fork-tender.

2. Meanwhile, chop the onion and the garlic.

3. In a medium nonstick skillet, heat the canola oil over medium heat until hot. Add the chopped onion and garlic and cook, stirring, for 4 minutes. Stir in the lamb, tomato paste, oregano, cumin, cloves, sugar, and salt until blended. Cook for 5 minutes, stirring and breaking up the meat, until the liquid has evaporated and the lamb is cooked through. Keep warm.

step 2

make the **couscous with chickpeas and green beans**

1½ cups water

1 can (7¾ ounces) chickpeas, drained

½ teaspoon salt

1 cup plain couscous

1 cup cooked green beans

1. Pour the water into a medium saucepan, covered, and bring to a boil over high heat.

2. Drain and rinse the chickpeas.

3. Pour the boiling water into a heatproof serving bowl and add the salt and chickpeas. Stir in the couscous, cover, and let stand for 5 minutes. Fluff with a fork and stir in the green beans. Keep warm, covered.

step 3

serve

1. Transfer the couscous to a bowl and place on the table.

2. On each of 4 dinner plates, place 2 eggplant halves, cut side up. Spoon some of the lamb mixture over the top and serve.

3. When ready for dessert, scoop the orange sorbet into dessert bowls and serve with the marzipan cookies.

Lamb-Topped Eggplant
Single serving is ¼ of the total recipe
CALORIES 324; PROTEIN 16g; CARBS 13g; TOTAL FAT 24g; SAT FAT 9g; CHOLESTEROL 62mg; SODIUM 556mg; FIBER 4g

microwave pork and broccoli
with asian sauce
sesame noodles
fresh pineapple and almond cookies

menu gameplan

serves 4

step 1 — cook the **pork and broccoli in asian sauce**

step 2 — plate the **sesame noodles**

step 3 — **serve**

shopping list

Gingerroot

Lean pork loin cut for stir-fry

Pineapple slices (from the produce department)

Almond cookies

from the salad bar

Chopped scallions

Broccoli florets (or from the produce department)

Sesame noodles

from your pantry

Lite soy sauce

Rice or white vinegar

Orange juice

Brown sugar

Garlic

Toasted sesame oil

Cornstarch

headsup Toasted sesame oil is an important ingredient in Chinese cooking. It is nutty brown in color, with a powerful sesame taste. Available in bottles in Asian markets and some supermarkets, it should not be confused with cold-pressed sesame oil that is clear and sold in health food stores. The two are not interchangeable. Store toasted sesame oil that has been opened in the refrigerator.

"If you're buying store-bought prepared sesame noodles anyway, why not add to the meal with sesame-marinated tofu? It's loaded with protein."

—minutemeals' Chef Miriam

step 1

cook the **pork and broccoli in asian sauce**

For the Asian sauce

3 tablespoons grated fresh ginger

1 cup lite soy sauce

1/2 cup rice or white vinegar

1/2 cup orange juice

3 tablespoons brown sugar

For the pork and broccoli

1 garlic clove

1 teaspoon toasted sesame oil

3/4 pound lean pork loin cut for stir-fry (the strips should be 1/4 inch thick and 2 inches long)

2 teaspoons cornstarch

1/2 cup Asian sauce (see above)

1/3 cup chopped scallions

2 cups broccoli florets

1. Make the Asian sauce: Grate enough ginger to measure 3 tablespoons. Place the ginger and the remaining sauce ingredients in a jar with a lid, cover, and shake well to combine. Store in the refrigerator for up to 1 month. Makes 2 1/2 cups.

2. Make the pork and broccoli: Mince the garlic. In a microwave-safe 9-inch pie plate, place the garlic, drizzle with the sesame oil, and microwave on High for 30 seconds to develop flavor.

3. Add the pork strips to the plate and stir to coat with the seasoned garlic; move the strips to the outer rim of the plate. Cover and microwave on High for 2 minutes. Remove cover.

4. Stir the cornstarch into the 1/2 cup Asian sauce until blended.

5. Add the sauce mixture and scallions to the pork, stirring to combine. Arrange the broccoli florets around the rim of the plate. Cover and microwave on High for 2 minutes.

6. Move the broccoli florets to the center of the plate. Cover and microwave on High for 2 minutes more, or until the broccoli is crisp-tender.

step 2

plate the **sesame noodles**

Sesame noodles for 4

Put the noodles in a shallow bowl and place the bowl on the table.

step 3

serve

1. Place the pork and broccoli on the table and serve with the noodle salad, with chopsticks, if desired.

2. When ready for dessert, serve the pineapple well chilled in dessert bowls with the almond cookies as an accompaniment.

Microwave Pork and Broccoli with Asian Sauce
Single serving is 1/4 of the total recipe
CALORIES 297; PROTEIN 21g; CARBS 21g; TOTAL FAT 13g; SAT FAT 4g; CHOLESTEROL 51mg; SODIUM 1065mg; FIBER 0g

⭐ broiled herbed pork chops

mashed potatoes with cabbage and scallions

old-fashioned apple pie with cheddar cheese

menu gameplan

shopping list

Center-cut loin pork chops

Dried grilling herb mix

Savoy cabbage, cored and sliced (from the produce department)

Scallions

Prepared mashed potatoes (from refrigerated section of the produce department)

Apple pie

Cheddar cheese

from your pantry

Vegetable oil

Salt and pepper

Butter

Milk

serves 4

beforeyoustart

Preheat the broiler.

step 1 prepare the **broiled herbed pork chops**

step 2 make the **mashed potatoes with cabbage and scallions**

step 3 warm the **apple pie with cheddar cheese,** if desired

step 4 **serve**

luckyforyou

In most supermarkets, pork chops are sold in family packs and are cheaper when sold like that in volume. Buy the family packs, divide the chops into more manageable serving sizes, wrap for the freezer, and freeze them. You will be saving money and planning for a rainy day when your refrigerator is almost empty.

"There's always the temptation to buy thin pork chops, but overcook them and they're unbelievably tough. The thickness of the chops keeps them moist."

—minutemeals' Chef Miriam

step 1

prepare the **broiled herbed pork chops**

4 center-cut loin pork chops (about 8 ounces each, at least 1 inch thick)

2 tablespoons vegetable oil

2 tablespoons dried grilling herb mix

Salt and pepper to taste

1. Preheat the broiler.

2. Brush the pork chops on both sides with vegetable oil, then sprinkle with the herb mix and salt and pepper.

3. Place the chops on the broiler pan and broil almost 4 inches from the heat for 6 minutes. Turn and broil 5 to 7 minutes, depending upon thickness, until cooked through. Remove to a serving platter and keep warm, loosely covered.

step 2

make the **mashed potatoes with cabbage and scallions**

1/4 pound cored and sliced Savoy cabbage

2 tablespoons butter

Salt and pepper to taste

1/4 cup thinly sliced scallions

1 package (20 ounces) prepared mashed potatoes

1/4 cup milk

1. Slice the cabbage into thin strips (you should have 3 cups).

2. In a large nonstick skillet, melt the butter over medium heat. Add the cabbage and season with salt and pepper. Toss, reduce the heat to medium-low, and cover. Cook until wilted, about 5 minutes. Stir in the scallions and cook for 5 minutes.

3. Meanwhile, in a medium saucepan, combine the mashed potatoes and milk. Heat over low heat, stirring occasionally, for 7 minutes, or until piping hot.

4. Stir the cabbage and scallions into the potatoes until combined. Keep warm, covered.

step 3

warm the **apple pie with cheddar cheese,** if desired

1 high-standing double-crust apple pie

1 small wedge sharp Cheddar cheese

Heat the apple pie, if desired, in a low (300°F) oven while you have dinner.

step 4

serve

1. Place a pork chop on each of 4 dinner plates and place the plates on the table.

2. Transfer the mashed potatoes to a bowl and serve.

3. When ready for dessert, transfer the apple pie to a large plate, slice, plate, and serve with the Cheddar.

Broiled Herbed Pork Chops
Single serving is 1/4 of the total recipe
CALORIES 434; PROTEIN 42g; CARBS 2g; TOTAL FAT 29; SAT FAT 9g; CHOLESTEROL 117mg; SODIUM 847mg; FIBER 0g

☆ cheese-stuffed pork chops

glazed baby carrots
greens vinaigrette
pears with caramel sauce

menu
gameplan

shopping list

Oil-cured sun-dried tomatoes

Scallion

Boneless loin pork chops, trimmed

Swiss or fontina cheese

Baby carrots

Lemon juice (optional)

Prewashed mixed spring or baby greens

Pecans

Pears

Caramel sauce

from your pantry

Bread crumbs

Grainy mustard

Olive oil

Honey

Butter

Ground cinnamon

Ground allspice (optional)

Vinaigrette dressing, store-bought or homemade

serves 4

step **1** stuff and cook the **cheese-stuffed pork chops**

step **2** while the chops are cooking, prepare the **glazed baby carrots**

step **3** assemble the **greens vinaigrette**

step **4** prepare the **pears with caramel sauce**

step **5** **serve**

heads**up**
Pork is done when it reaches an internal temperature of 150° to 160°F on a meat thermometer. Many homemakers, though, do not own a meat thermometer and because of that worry about how to judge for doneness. Should it be even slightly pink in the center? We say barely. If the juices run clear, the pork is cooked. If in doubt, cut into the meat in the thickest part. Better still, invest in a meat thermometer.

"I've always liked foods with fillings. There's an element of surprise to them. These chops have that."

—minutemeals' Chef Paul

stuff and cook the **cheese-stuffed pork chops**

1 tablespoon chopped oil-cured sun-dried tomatoes

1 scallion

4 boneless loin pork chops, each about 1/2 inch thick (about 1 1/2 pounds in all), trimmed

3/4 cup shredded Swiss or fontina cheese (1 small wedge)

2 tablespoons dried bread crumbs

1 tablespoon grainy mustard

1 tablespoon olive oil

1. Chop enough sun-dried tomatoes, drained, to measure 1 tablespoon; chop the scallion. With the blade of a sharp knife, cut a pocket horizontally in each of the 4 pork chops, cutting from the bone side to the fat side. Do not cut all the way through. Shred enough cheese to measure 3/4 cup.

2. In a small bowl, combine the cheese, tomatoes, bread crumbs, mustard, and scallion. Spoon some of the stuffing into the pocket in each chop and secure the opening with a wooden toothpick. Press down on the chop to even the filling.

3. In a large nonstick skillet, heat the olive oil over medium-low heat until hot. Add the chops without crowding, cover, and cook for 5 minutes. Turn the chops, cover, and cook for 5 minutes more. Turn again and cook, uncovered, for 2 minutes, or until cooked through and the juices run clear when pricked with a fork.

while the chops are cooking, prepare the **glazed baby carrots**

1 bag (16 ounces) baby carrots

2 tablespoons honey

1 tablespoon butter

1/4 teaspoon ground cinnamon, or to taste

1/8 teaspoon ground allspice (optional)

1 teaspoon lemon juice (optional)

1. Place the carrots in a medium saucepan. Add water to cover, place lid on pan, and bring to a boil over high heat. Boil for 8 minutes, or just until tender. Drain well.

2. Return the carrots to the pan and add the honey, butter, cinnamon, and allspice and lemon juice, if using; cook, tossing gently, for 2 minutes, or until glazed. Keep warm, covered.

assemble the **greens vinaigrette**

1 bag (5 ounces) prewashed mixed spring or baby greens

1/4 cup vinaigrette dressing

Place the greens in a salad bowl, add the vinaigrette, and toss gently to taste. Place the bowl on the table.

prepare the **pears with caramel sauce**

3 tablespoons pecans

2 ripe pears, such as Bartlett or Bosc

1/4 cup jarred caramel sauce, at room temperature

1. In a toaster oven at 350°F, toast the pecans for 5 minutes, stirring once, or until fragrant. Remove, cool, and chop.

2. Core each pear and slice. Divide the slices among 4 dessert plates and drizzle with the caramel sauce. Set aside until serving time.

serve

1. Add the lemon juice, if using, to the carrots and toss.

2. Place a pork chop on each of 4 dinner plates and add a serving of carrots alongside.

3. When ready for dessert, sprinkle each serving of pears with chopped pecans. Serve additional caramel sauce, if desired.

Cheese-Stuffed Pork Chops
Single serving is 1/4 of the total recipe
CALORIES 401; PROTEIN 37g; CARBS 3g;
TOTAL FAT 26g; SAT FAT 11g; CHOLESTEROL 112mg;
SODIUM 818mg; FIBER 0g

pork medallions
in savory apricot sauce
zucchini with red peppers and dill
corn muffins
melon with berry sorbet

menu gameplan

serves 4

step 1 cook the **pork medallions in savory apricot sauce**

step 2 heat the **corn muffins**

step 3 steam the **zucchini with red peppers and dill**

step 4 **serve**

shopping list

Pork tenderloin

Fresh parsley (optional)

Lemons

Apricot preserves

Dry white wine

Corn muffins

Zucchini

Fresh dill

Berry sorbet

from the salad bar

Red pepper slices

Cantaloupe or honeydew melon chunks (or from the produce department)

from your pantry

Salt and pepper

Butter

Olive oil

Dijon mustard

Curry powder

headsup
No white wine on hand for the apricot sauce? Substitute chicken broth; or use lemonade and reduce the lemon juice to 1 tablespoon.

"The pork makes a super party dish. You can slip out to the kitchen, cook it quickly, and no one will even know you were gone."

—minutemeals' Chef Ruth

step 1

cook the **pork medallions in savory apricot sauce**

For the pork

Pork tenderloin (1¼ pounds)

Salt and pepper to taste

1 tablespoon butter

1 tablespoon olive oil

Chopped parsley (optional)

Lemon slices for garnish (optional)

For the apricot sauce

½ cup apricot preserves

¼ cup Dijon mustard

⅓ cup dry white wine (or use chicken broth)

¼ teaspoon curry powder

2 tablespoons fresh lemon juice (½ large lemon)

1. Prepare the pork: Slice the pork tenderloin crosswise into 12 pieces, about 1 inch thick. Place each piece between 2 squares of waxed paper or plastic wrap. Pound with the bottom of a heavy skillet to flatten slightly. Sprinkle with salt and pepper.

2. Heat the butter and olive oil in a large nonstick skillet over medium heat until hot. Add the pork medallions in one layer and sauté them until golden brown on both sides, about 3 to 4 minutes. Remove to a platter and keep warm.

3. Make the apricot sauce: Add the apricot preserves, Dijon mustard, white wine, curry powder, and lemon juice to the skillet. Cook over medium heat, stirring occasionally, until slightly thickened, about 5 minutes. Add the pork medallions to the pan to reheat during last minute or two of cooking. Transfer to a platter and keep warm.

step 2

heat the **corn muffins**

4 to 6 premade corn muffins

In a toaster oven, warm the corn muffins until heated through.

step 3

steam the **zucchini with red peppers and dill**

1 small zucchini (6 to 8 ounces)

½ cup red pepper slices

1 tablespoon butter

2 teaspoons snipped fresh dill or ½ teaspoon dried

Salt and pepper to taste

1. Place a collapsible vegetable steamer basket in a large pot, add 1 inch water to pot, cover, and bring to a boil over high heat.

2. Meanwhile, trim the zucchini, then slice lengthwise into thin strips, ⅛ to ¼ inch thick. Coarsely chop the pepper slices. Add the zucchini and peppers to the steamer basket, cover, and steam for 3 to 4 minutes, until the zucchini is tender. Transfer to a serving bowl. Add the butter and toss. Snip about 2 teaspoons fresh dill over the vegetables or sprinkle with the dried dill, add salt and pepper to taste, and toss again. Place the bowl on the table.

step 4

serve

1. Transfer the corn muffins to a bread basket and place on the table.

2. Garnish the pork medallions with chopped parsley and fresh lemon slices, if desired, and serve at once with the steamed zucchini and red pepper.

3. When ready for dessert, serve the melon in wine glasses or goblets and top each serving with a scoop of your favorite berry sorbet.

Pork Medallions in Savory Apricot Sauce
Single serving is ¼ of the total recipe

CALORIES 400; PROTEIN 29g; CARBS 29g; TOTAL FAT 16g; SAT FAT 0g; CHOLESTEROL 8mg; SODIUM 168mg; FIBER 0g

roasted pork medallions
with balsamic-honey glaze

couscous with scallions

steamed broccoli

key lime pie

shopping list

Fresh rosemary

Pork tenderloin

Plain couscous

Fresh parsley

Key lime pie

from the salad bar

Chopped scallions

Broccoli florets
(or from the produce
department)

from your pantry

Garlic

Balsamic vinegar

Honey

Olive oil

Dijon mustard

Salt and pepper

Canola oil

Fat-free reduced-sodium
chicken broth

serves 4 to 6

beforeyoustart

Preheat the oven to 350°F to roast
the pork.

step 1 make the **pork medallions with balsamic-honey glaze**

step 2 meanwhile, make the **couscous with scallions**

step 3 prepare the **steamed broccoli**

step 4 **serve**

headsup

Be careful not to overcook pork tenderloin as it quickly dries out. These medallions are done when they are still barely pink in the center—which raises a point. At one time, only thoroughly cooked-through pork was considered fit for eating. Now, pork cooked until medium rare—about 150° to 160°F on a meat thermometer—is considered safe.

"It's really the glaze that provides most of the flavor here. It's made with balsamic vinegar, which is a marvelous ingredient."

—minutemeals' Chef Amanda

step 1

make the **pork medallions with balsamic-honey glaze**

For the balsamic-honey glaze

4 garlic cloves

1 tablespoon chopped fresh rosemary, plus rosemary branches for garnish

1/2 cup balsamic vinegar

3 tablespoons honey

2 tablespoons olive oil

1 tablespoon Dijon mustard

Salt and pepper to taste

For the pork

1 3/4 to 2 pounds pork tenderloin

Canola oil (for searing)

1. Preheat the oven to 350°F.

2. Make the glaze: Finely chop the garlic. Chop enough fresh rosemary to measure 1 tablespoon. Place both in a small bowl. Add the vinegar, honey, olive oil, mustard, and salt and pepper and stir to combine.

3. For the pork: Slice the tenderloin into 1-inch-thick medallions (rounds). Cover the bottom of a medium skillet with a light film of canola oil and heat over medium-high heat until hot. Add the pork slices in 1 layer, season with salt and pepper, and sear for 1 minute. Turn and sear for 1 minute, until lightly browned. Transfer the slices in one layer to a shallow baking dish.

4. Pour the glaze over the slices and turn them to coat.

5. Roast for 8 to 10 minutes, until cooked medium-rare. Remove from the oven and keep warm, loosely covered.

step 2

meanwhile, make the **couscous with scallions**

1 tablespoon canola oil

1 1/2 cups fat-free reduced-sodium chicken broth or water

1/2 cup chopped scallions

1 cup plain couscous

2 tablespoons chopped parsley (optional)

Salt and pepper to taste

1. In a medium saucepan, combine the oil and chicken broth or water and bring to a simmer. Stir in the scallions and couscous and cover the pan. Remove the pan from the heat and let stand for 5 minutes.

2. If desired, chop enough parsley to measure 2 tablespoons.

3. When all the liquid has been absorbed by the couscous, fluff it with a fork, and add the parsley, if using, and salt and pepper. Keep warm, covered.

step 3

prepare the **steamed broccoli**

1 to 1 1/2 pounds broccoli florets

Salt and pepper to taste

1. Place the broccoli florets in a vegetable steamer basket.

2. Pour about 3/4 inch water into a large saucepan. Place the steamer basket in the pan, bring the water to a simmer over medium-high heat, and cover. Steam for 5 minutes, or until the broccoli is crisp-tender. Transfer to a serving bowl and season with salt and pepper. Place the bowl on the table.

step 4

serve

1. Place the pork medallions on a platter and spoon the balsamic-honey glaze over them. Garnish the platter with the rosemary sprigs, if desired, and place the platter on the table.

2. Spoon a serving of the couscous onto 4 dinner plates to serve as a bed for the pork and glaze. Serve.

3. When ready for dessert, cut the pie into slices, plate, and serve.

Roasted Pork Medallions with Balsamic-Honey Glaze
Single serving is 1/4 of the total recipe
CALORIES 473; PROTEIN 46g; CARBS 22g;
TOTAL FAT 21g; SAT FAT 1g; CHOLESTEROL 0mg;
SODIUM 134mg; FIBER 0g

pork piccata

quick polenta

brussels sprouts
with parmesan

miniature cannoli

menu gameplan

shopping list

Yellow cornmeal

Frozen Brussels sprouts

Boneless pork chops

Lemon (for juice)

Capers

Miniature cannoli

from your pantry

Chicken stock cube

Salt and pepper

Olive oil

Grated Parmesan cheese

Plain dry unseasoned bread crumbs

Butter

serves 4

step **1** prepare the **quick polenta**

step **2** cook the **brussels sprouts with parmesan**

step **3** make the **pork piccata**

step **4** **serve**

headsup

When pan-frying meat, you will always have more success estimating doneness if the pieces are equally thick. Pound any thicker pork chops here with a meat mallet or the bottom of a heavy skillet to ensure even cooking.

"Pork Piccata is every bit as good as Veal Piccata, but it is significantly cheaper to make. I'd serve it to company anytime."

—minutemeals' Chef Sharon

step 1
prepare the **quick polenta**

- 1 quart water
- 1 cube chicken stock
- 1 cup yellow cornmeal
- Salt

1. Pour the water into a 2^1/2-quart saucepan, cover, and bring to a boil over high heat. Crumble the stock cube into the boiling water.

2. While stirring constantly with a whisk, sprinkle the cornmeal into the boiling water. Bring the mixture to a boil, lower the heat to medium, and cover. Cook, stirring occasionally, for 5 to 10 minutes, until thickened and creamy. Taste and add salt as desired. Remove the pan from the heat and keep warm, covered.

step 2
cook the **brussels sprouts with parmesan**

- 1 box (10 ounces) frozen Brussels sprouts
- 1 tablespoon olive oil, or more to taste
- 2 tablespoons grated Parmesan cheese

In a medium saucepan, cook the sprouts according to the directions on the package. Drain and keep warm, covered.

step 3
make the **pork piccata**

- ^{3}/4 cup plain dry unseasoned bread crumbs
- 8 thin boneless pork chops (about 2 ounces each, for total weight of 1 pound)
- Salt and pepper to taste
- 2 tablespoons butter
- 2 tablespoons olive oil
- 1 lemon
- 4 tablespoons drained capers

1. Spread the bread crumbs on a plate. Dredge the pork chops, 1 at a time, in the crumbs to lightly coat. Season the chops on both sides with salt and pepper.

2. Place 1 tablespoon of the butter and 1 tablespoon of the olive oil in each of 2 medium nonstick skillets and heat over medium heat until hot. Place 4 chops in each skillet, without overlapping, and cook for 3 to 4 minutes on each side, until golden. Do not overcook.

3. Halve the lemon and squeeze the juice into the skillets over the chops. Add 2 tablespoons capers to each pan, stir to combine, and cook just until heated through. Remove the pan from the heat.

step 4
serve

1. Add the olive oil to the sprouts, turn to coat, and transfer to a serving bowl. Sprinkle with the Parmesan and place the bowl on the table.

2. Spoon a serving of polenta onto each of 4 dinner plates. Grind fresh black pepper on top. Place 2 pork chops on each plate and spoon some of the sauce and capers over each serving.

3. When ready for dessert, arrange the cannoli on a platter and place on the table with dessert plates.

Pork Piccata
Single serving is ^{1}/4 of the total recipe
CALORIES 336; PROTEIN 22g; CARBS 8g;
TOTAL FAT 24g; SAT FAT 5g; CHOLESTEROL 74mg;
SODIUM 734g; FIBER 1g

spinach-stuffed pork "ravioli"
with marinara sauce

french potato salad

sliced peaches with brown sugar and sour cream

menu gameplan

serves 4

step	1	plate the **french potato salad**
step	2	make the **pork "ravioli" with marinara sauce**
step	3	**serve**

shopping list

French potato salad
(from the deli counter)

Frozen chopped spinach

Boneless pork loin,
trimmed and sliced

Marinara sauce

Peaches

Sour cream

from your pantry

Eggs

Grated or shredded
Parmesan cheese

Fine dry bread crumbs

Salt and pepper

All-purpose flour

Olive oil

Brown sugar

headsup If you want to keep your hands relatively free of crumb mixture while you dip the pork packets, designate your left hand as "wet" and right hand as "dry." Use the right hand for the flour and bread crumbs, the left for the egg.

"These fun and surprising 'ravioli' are a real conversation piece. They make a tasty meat-with-vegetable entree in one."

—minutemeals' Chef Nancy

step 1

plate the **french potato salad**

> 1 pound store-bought French potato salad, or more as desired

Spoon the potato salad into a serving bowl and place on the table.

step 2

make the **pork "ravioli" with marinara sauce**

> 1 package (10 ounces) frozen chopped spinach
>
> 3 large eggs
>
> 2 tablespoons grated or shredded Parmesan cheese
>
> 1 tablespoon plus 1/2 to 3/4 cup fine dry bread crumbs
>
> Salt and pepper to taste
>
> 8 slices trimmed boneless pork loin, each 1/4 inch thick (1 1/4 to 1 1/2 pounds)
>
> 1 cup all-purpose flour
>
> 1/4 cup olive oil
>
> 2 cups marinara sauce

1. Thaw the spinach in the microwave oven, then squeeze it of as much liquid as possible.

2. In a medium bowl, beat 1 of the eggs lightly. Add the spinach, Parmesan, and 1 tablespoon of the bread crumbs, season with salt and pepper, and combine well.

3. Place 4 of the pork slices between 2 large sheets of plastic wrap. Pound the meat with a rolling pin or the bottom of a heavy skillet until it is one half its original thickness—but take care not to make holes in it. Repeat with remaining pork.

4. Remove the top piece of plastic wrap and place 1/4 of the spinach mixture on each slice; top with remaining pork slices. Press the edges to seal the "ravioli." Insert 1 toothpick at each end of each packet to close.

5. In a shallow bowl, beat the remaining 2 eggs with 1 teaspoon water. Spread the flour on a plate; spread the remaining 3/4 cup bread crumbs on another plate. Dip the pork packets, 1 at a time, into the flour, then into the beaten eggs, then into the crumbs, patting them on.

6. In a large heavy skillet, heat the olive oil over medium-high heat until hot but not smoking. Add the pork packets and sauté for 4 to 5 minutes, or until golden. With a spatula, turn and cook for 4 to 5 minutes, or until cooked through and the juices run clear when tested with a fork.

7. While the pork cooks, in a medium saucepan, heat the marinara sauce over medium-low heat until hot.

step 3

serve

1. Pour the marinara sauce into a serving bowl.

2. Place the "ravoli" on a serving platter, remove the toothpicks, and take the platter and sauce to the table.

3. When ready to for dessert, rinse the peaches, then slice enough for 4 servings. Sprinkle with brown sugar and top each with a dollop of sour cream. Serve.

Spinach-Stuffed Pork "Ravioli"
with Marinara Sauce
Single serving is 1/4 of the total recipe
CALORIES 713; PROTEIN 39g; CARBS 32g;
TOTAL FAT 47g; SAT FAT 5g; CHOLESTEROL 164mg;
SODIUM 978mg; FIBER 5g

grilled sausages

creamy cheese polenta

mixed greens vinaigrette

fresh apricots, dried figs, and almonds

serves 4

shopping list

Turkey sausages

Cornmeal for polenta (available in the bulk section at grocery and health food stores)

Pre-grated cheese such as Parmesan, Asiago, or Monterey Jack

Prewashed mixed spring or baby greens

Apricots

Dried figs

Almonds

from your pantry

Onion

Butter

Olive oil

Fat-free reduced-sodium chicken broth

Milk, low-fat or nonfat

Vinaigrette dressing, store-bought or homemade

Freshly ground black pepper

beforeyoustart

Preheat the barbecue grill or the broiler.

step 1 prepare the **grilled sausages**

step 2 make the **creamy cheese polenta**

step 3 toss the **mixed greens vinaigrette**

step 4 **serve**

headsup

If you decide to use regular sweet or hot Italian sausage, you will be adding almost another 300 calories per serving.

"Polenta and sausages make a lovely combination. It may seem informal, but I'd gladly serve this menu to company."

—minutemeals' Chef Connie

step 1

prepare the **grilled sausages**

8 turkey sausages

Arrange the sausages on the grill or broiler pan. Grill, turning them, for 12 to 15 minutes, until evenly browned and cooked through. Transfer to a platter and keep warm, covered.

step 2

make the **creamy cheese polenta**

1/2 cup chopped onion
(1 small onion)

1 tablespoon butter

1 tablespoon olive oil

1 can (14 1/2 ounces) fat-free reduced-sodium chicken broth plus water to measure 2 1/2 cups total

1 cup yellow cornmeal labeled polenta

1 cup low-fat or nonfat milk

1/4 to 1/2 cup pre-grated cheese such as Parmesan, Asiago, or Monterey Jack, plus additional for serving, if desired

1. Chop the onion to measure 1/2 cup.

2. In a 2 1/2-quart saucepan, melt the butter with olive oil over low heat. Add the onion and stir to coat. Cover and "sweat" the onion about 3 minutes, until softened.

3. Add the 2 1/2 cups diluted broth, raise the heat to high, and cover. Bring to a boil, then lower the heat to medium. Stirring constantly, slowly sprinkle in the cornmeal. (Sprinkling slowly helps to prevent lumps from forming.)

4. Stir in the milk. When the mixture begins to bubble, reduce the heat to low so that the polenta will simmer slowly. (It should bubble.) Cover and cook, stirring occasionally, for about 5 minutes, until thickened but still creamy. (Removing the lid will help the polenta thicken more.)

step 3

toss the **mixed greens vinaigrette**

1 bag (5 ounces) prewashed mixed spring or baby greens

1/4 cup vinaigrette dressing

Freshly ground black pepper to taste

Place the greens in a salad bowl, add the vinaigrette, and toss to coat. Add a few twists of fresh pepper. Divide among 4 salad plates and place the plates on the table.

step 4

serve

1. At serving time, stir the grated cheese into the hot polenta until well combined. Divide the polenta among 4 plates or large rimmed bowls. Add 2 grilled sausages to each serving. Serve at once as the polenta will thicken as it cools. Serve with additional cheese, if desired.

2. When ready for dessert, arrange the apricots, figs, and almonds on a large tray and serve, with small plates or napkins.

Grilled Sausages on Creamy Cheese Polenta
Single serving is 1/4 of the total recipe

CALORIES 520; PROTEIN 21g; CARBS 14g; TOTAL FAT 45g; SAT FAT 12g; CHOLESTEROL 80mg; SODIUM 882mg; FIBER 0g

canadian bacon and jack cheese sandwiches

homemade coleslaw
roasted pepper salad
frozen fruit popsicles

menu gameplan

shopping list

Shredded cabbage

Fresh dill

Nonfat sour cream

Horseradish

Jarred roasted red peppers

Capers

Canadian bacon

Pre-shredded Monterey Jack cheese

Fruit Popsicles

from the salad bar

Grated carrots (or from the produce department)

Red onion slices

Tomato slices

from your pantry

Reduced-fat mayonnaise

Rice vinegar

Salt and pepper

Vinaigrette dressing, store-bought or homemade

Hearty whole-grain bread

Whole-grain mustard

serves 4

beforeyoustart

Place the broiler rack 2 inches from the heat and preheat the broiler to toast the sandwiches.

step **1** make the **homeade coleslaw**

step **2** assemble the **roasted red pepper salad**

step **3** make the **canadian bacon and jack cheese sandwiches**

step **4** **serve**

luckyforyou Ready-to-use ingredients from the salad bar make assembling these sandwiches a breeze. As does buying already sliced Canadian bacon—it's tricky to slice under the best of circumstances and if you're in a hurry it's even harder.

"Canadian bacon is precooked, which makes it a great ingredient for sandwiches, salads, or stews. It's closer to ham than classic bacon."

—minutemeals' Chef Hillary

step 1
make the **homemade coleslaw**

1 bag (10 ounces) shredded cabbage

1/2 cup grated carrots

2 tablespoons snipped fresh dill or 1 teaspoon dried

1/4 cup nonfat sour cream

1/4 cup reduced-fat mayonnaise

2 tablespoons rice vinegar

1 tablespoon drained bottled horseradish

Salt and pepper to taste

1. In a large bowl, combine the cabbage and carrots. Snip enough fresh dill to measure 2 tablespoons.

2. In a bowl, combine the sour cream, mayonnaise, vinegar, dill, horseradish, and salt and pepper. Stir to blend. Pour the dressing over the cabbage, toss well, and place in the refrigerator until ready to serve.

step 2
assemble the **roasted red pepper salad**

2 jars (12 ounces each) roasted red peppers, drained

1/2 cup red onion slices

2 tablespoons vinaigrette dressing

2 tablespoons drained capers

Salt and pepper to taste

1. Drain the roasted peppers. Cut into thin strips and place in a wide shallow serving bowl.

2. Add the onion slices, vinaigrette, capers, and salt and pepper. Toss to coat. Place the bowl on the table.

step 3
make the **canadian bacon and jack cheese sandwiches**

8 slices hearty whole-grain bread

Whole-grain mustard

8 slices Canadian bacon

8 tomato slices

2 cups pre-shredded Monterey Jack cheese

1. Place the broiler rack 2 inches from the heat and preheat the broiler. Place the bread in a single layer on the broiler rack. Broil until golden brown, about 30 seconds. Turn and broil for 30 seconds longer. Remove.

2. Spread 4 of the slices with mustard. Top the remaining 4 slices with 2 slices each of bacon and tomato and shredded cheese. Return these 4 slices to the oven and broil until the cheese has melted, about 1 to 2 minutes.

3. Top each of the melted cheese slices with a mustard-coated slice. Place on individual plates.

step 4
serve

1. Cut the sandwiches in half and serve with the coleslaw and roasted pepper salad.

2. If the Popsicles are frozen rock-solid, be sure to remove them from the freezer to thaw slightly before serving.

Canadian Bacon and Jack Cheese Sandwiches
Single serving is 1/4 of the total recipe
CALORIES 463; PROTEIN 31g; CARBS 38g;
TOTAL FAT 24g; SAT FAT 13g; CHOLESTEROL 73mg;
SODIUM 985mg; FIBER 6g

minute

20-minute gourmet

fish and shellfish menus

meals

menus

flounder
with olive-caper tapenade
fresh pasta with tomato sauce
crisp cucumber salad
spumoni with almond biscotti

menu
gameplan

serves 4

beforeyoustart

Preheat the oven to 350°F. Bring the water to a boil in a large pot, covered, over high heat to cook the pasta.

step 1 — make the **tomato sauce;** cook the **pasta**

step 2 — plate the **crisp cucumber salad**

step 3 — bake the **flounder with olive-caper tapenade**

step 4 — **serve**

shopping list

Tomatoes

Fresh basil

Fresh pasta, such as fettuccine or linguine

Thin cucumber slices (from the salad bar)

Flounder fillets

Lemon (for juice)

Shallot

Pitted kalamata olives

Capers

Spumoni

Almond biscotti

from your pantry

Garlic

Olive oil

Salt and pepper

Rice vinegar

luckyforyou

Fresh pasta, which cooks in a fraction of the time dried pasta does, can be frozen. We suggest keeping a package or two on hand as a standard freezer staple. There is no need to defrost it before cooking. Simply add it frozen to the boiling water. Whether you are using it frozen or fresh, it will save you considerable cooking time.

"A minimum number of ingredients contribute the maximum amount of flavor here—just my kind of recipe!"

—minutemeals' Chef Amanda

step 1

make the **tomato sauce;** cook the **pasta**

For the sauce

1 garlic clove

4 ripe tomatoes, roughly chopped, or 2 cans (14 ounces each) diced tomatoes, drained

2 tablespoons chopped fresh basil

1 tablespoon olive oil

Salt and pepper to taste

For the pasta

4 quarts water

Salt to taste

12 ounces fresh pasta, such as fettuccine or linguine

1. Make the tomato sauce: Finely chop the garlic. Rinse, then roughly chop the fresh tomatoes. Chop enough basil to measure 2 tablespoons.

2. In a large nonstick skillet, heat the olive oil and garlic over medium heat, stirring. Add the tomatoes and cook over medium-high heat, stirring occasionally, for 5 minutes. Stir in the basil and season with salt and pepper. Remove from the heat and keep warm, covered.

3. Cook the pasta: Pour the water into a large pot, salt lightly, and cover. Bring to a boil over high heat. Add the pasta, stir to separate the strands, and boil for 2 minutes, or until cooked *al dente*. Drain well.

4. Transfer the pasta to a serving bowl, add the tomato sauce, and toss. Keep warm, loosely covered.

step 2

plate the **crisp cucumber salad**

Thin cucumber slices for 4

Rice vinegar to taste

Arrange the cucumber slices, overlapping them, on a platter and sprinkle with the vinegar. Refrigerate until serving time.

step 3

bake the **flounder with olive-caper tapenade**

4 flounder fillets (5 ounces each)

1 lemon

1 1/2 tablespoons olive oil

Salt and pepper to taste

1 shallot

2 garlic cloves

10 pitted kalamata olives

3 tablespoons drained capers

1. Preheat the oven to 350°F.

2. Rinse the flounder fillets and pat dry.

3. In a baking dish, arrange the fillets in a single layer. Squeeze the juice of 1/2 lemon over them. Drizzle with 1/2 tablespoon of the olive oil and season with salt and pepper. Bake for 4 to 8 minutes, until the fish just flakes when tested with a fork. Remove from the oven.

4. Thinly slice the shallot. Finely chop the garlic. Chop the olives. Rinse the capers.

5. In a small skillet, heat the remaining 1 tablespoon olive oil over medium heat until hot. Add the shallot and cook, stirring, for 30 seconds, until softened. Add the garlic, capers, olives, and lemon juice to taste and cook, stirring, for 1 minute, or until heated through. Remove from the heat and keep warm, partially covered.

step 4

serve

1. Place a flounder fillet on each of 4 dinner plates. Spoon some of the tapenade sauce over each. Add a serving of the pasta to each plate.

2. Place the cucumber salad on the table with 4 salad plates.

3. When ready for dessert, place a cup of spumoni on each dessert plate and serve with the biscotti.

Flounder with Olive-Caper Tapenade
Single serving is 1/4 of the total recipe
CALORIES 213; PROTEIN 28g; CARBS 4g;
TOTAL FAT 10g; SAT FAT 0g; CHOLESTEROL 44mg;
SODIUM 500mg; FIBER 0g

crispy flounder fillets
with white-wine butter sauce

steamed broccoli

french rolls

chocolate pudding
with whipped cream

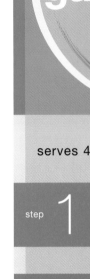

menu
gameplan

serves 4

step 1 steam the **broccoli**

step 2 cook the **crispy flounder fillets**

step 3 make the **white-wine butter sauce**

step 4 serve

shopping list

Broccoli florets
(from the salad bar or
produce department)

Flounder fillets

Shallots

Fresh tarragon

Dry white wine

French rolls

Prepared chocolate pudding

Instant whipped cream or
nondairy whipped topping

from your pantry

Salt and pepper

Eggs

All-purpose flour

Olive oil

Butter

Fat-free reduced-sodium
chicken broth

headsup

We're always in favor of prepping ahead when possible, but in the flounder recipe don't coat the fish with the flour/egg mixture too far in advance. The coating will become soggy and won't crisp up as it should when sautéed. Do have all the coating ingredients ready in advance, but wait to dredge the fillets and dip them until just before you plan to cook them.

"Butter sauces are easier to make than people think. You won't believe how successful you'll feel having made a butter sauce like this."

—minutemeals' Chef Hillary

step 1

steam the **broccoli**

1 pound broccoli florets

Place the broccoli florets in a vegetable steamer basket in a large pot with 2 inches of water. Cover the pot and bring the water to a boil over high heat. Steam until the florets are crisp-tender, about 5 minutes. Remove the pan from the heat and keep warm.

step 2

cook the **crispy flounder fillets**

1¹/2 pounds flounder fillets
(four 6-ounce pieces)

Salt and pepper to taste

3 large eggs

¹/2 cup all-purpose flour

2 tablespoons olive oil,
plus additional, if needed

1 tablespoon butter

1. Rinse the flounder fillets and pat dry. Season on both sides with salt and pepper.

2. Place the eggs in a bowl and beat lightly to combine; spread the flour on a large plate.

3. Dredge the fillets, 1 at a time, in the flour; dip in the eggwash, coating both sides well, then dredge in the flour again. Place in a single layer on a small baking sheet.

4. In a 12-inch nonstick skillet, heat the olive oil and butter over medium heat until the butter is melted. Arrange the fillets in a single layer in the skillet and cook for 3 minutes per side, or until lightly browned, adding a little more oil to the pan if necessary. (Depending upon the size of the fillets, you may need to cook them in 2 batches.) With a spatula, transfer 1 fillet to each of 4 dinner plates and cover loosely to keep warm while making the sauce.

step 3

make the **white-wine butter sauce**

2 large shallots

3 tablespoons butter

2¹/2 teaspoons chopped fresh tarragon or 1 teaspoon dried, plus 4 fresh sprigs for garnish (optional)

¹/4 cup dry white wine

¹/4 cup fat-free reduced-sodium chicken broth

Salt and pepper to taste

1. Finely chop the shallots. Cut the butter into small pieces. Chop enough fresh tarragon, if using, to measure 2¹/2 teaspoons.

2. Pour out most of the fat in the skillet used to cook the flounder, leaving just enough to film the surface. Add the shallots and cook over medium heat, stirring with a wooden spoon, for 30 seconds, or until softened. Add the wine and deglaze the pan, scraping the brown bits off the bottom, for 1 minute. Add the broth, increase the heat to medium-high, and boil the mixture for about 2 minutes, until reduced by half. Remove the pan from the heat.

3. Whisk in the butter, a few pieces at a time, until the sauce is creamy and lightly thickened. Stir in the chopped tarragon and season well with salt and pepper.

step 4

serve

1. Spoon some of the butter sauce over the flounder fillet on each plate and garnish with a fresh tarragon sprig, if desired. Serve the steamed broccoli on the same plate or transfer it to a bowl to pass separately.

2. Put bread on a napkin-lined bread basket, cover to keep warm, and place on the table.

3. When ready for dessert, garnish the chocolate pudding with whipped cream or nondairy whipped topping and serve.

Crispy Flounder Fillets with
White-Wine Butter Sauce
Single serving is ¹/4 of the total recipe
CALORIES 449; PROTEIN 40g; CARBS 15g;
TOTAL FAT 26g; SAT FAT 8g; CHOLESTEROL 243mg;
SODIUM 206mg; FIBER 0g

red snapper
with fresh vegetable packages

herbed rice
orange and black olive salad
dried dates with walnut halves

shopping list

Jasmine rice

Fresh basil leaves

Fresh parsley

Red snapper fillets

Pitted black olives, preferably imported

Dried apricots

Dried dates

Walnut halves

from the salad bar

Yellow pepper strips

Red pepper strips

Diced tomatoes

Orange slices

Red onion slices

from your pantry

Butter

Salt and pepper

Dried Italian herb blend (or a combination of dried basil and oregano)

Extra virgin olive oil

Red wine vinegar

Ground cumin

Sugar

serves 4

beforeyoustart

Place a rack in the middle of the oven and preheat the oven to 450°F to cook the fish.

| step | 1 | cook the **herbed rice** |

| step | 2 | assemble the **fresh vegetable packages**; cook the **red snapper** |

| step | 3 | plate the **orange and black olive salad** |

| step | 4 | **serve** |

 There is a very simple way to fast-forward the prepping of the fish packages. Instead of cutting aluminum foil into 4 individual squares yourself, why not buy the sheets already cut? Look for a package of Reynolds Wrapper Pop-Up Sheets in the supermarket. (Because they are made of regular, not heavy-duty, foil, you will need to use 2 sheets per package.)

"Cooking 'en papillote' is great for entertaining. You can assemble the packages beforehand and hold them in the refrigerator until it's time to cook."

—minutemeals' Chef Anne

step 1

cook the **herbed rice**

1 1/2 cups jasmine rice

1/2 cup fresh basil leaves

1 bunch fresh parsley

2 tablespoons butter

1. Cook the jasmine rice in a medium saucepan in the amount of water and for the time suggested on the package. Drain, if necessary, and return to the pan.

2. While the rice is cooking, rinse the parsley, then pick off enough parsley and basil leaves to measure 1/2 cup. Combine the leaves and finely chop.

3. Add the butter and chopped herbs to the rice, and stir to combine. Keep warm, covered.

step 2

assemble the **fresh vegetable packages**; cook the **red snapper**

1/2 cup yellow pepper strips

1/2 cup red pepper strips

1/2 cup diced tomatoes

4 red snapper fillets (about 6 ounces each)

Salt and pepper to taste

1 teaspoon dried Italian herb blend (or a combination of dried basil and oregano)

4 tablespoons extra virgin olive oil

1. Place a rack in the center of the oven and preheat the oven to 450°F. Cut out 4 12-inch squares of heavy-duty aluminum foil.

2. In a bowl, combine the yellow and red pepper strips and tomatoes. Place 1/4 of the mixture in the middle of the lower half of each foil square.

3. Rinse the snapper fillets and pat dry. Season on both sides with salt and pepper and 1/4 teaspoon each of the herb blend. Place 1 fillet on top of the vegetables on each foil square. Drizzle 1 tablespoon of the olive oil over each fillet. Crimp the edges of the foil airtight to form 4 well-sealed packages. Place on a baking sheet. Bake on the middle rack for 10 minutes.

step 3

plate the **orange and black olive salad**

2 cups orange slices, or 2 whole oranges

1/2 cup red onion slices

10 pitted black olives, preferably imported

1 1/2 tablespoons extra virgin olive oil

2 to 3 teaspoons red wine vinegar

Pinch of ground cumin

Pinch of sugar

Salt and pepper to taste

1. Arrange the orange slices on a serving platter. Scatter the red onion and black olives on top.

2. In a small bowl, stir together the olive oil, vinegar, cumin, sugar, and add salt and pepper to taste. Drizzle over the salad. Place on the table with 4 salad plates.

step 4

serve

1. Place 1 foil package on each of 4 dinner plates. Using scissors and averting your face to avoid the steam that escapes, cut open the foil.

2. Spoon a serving of basil rice alongside. Serve with the orange and black olive salad.

3. When ready for dessert, place the dried fruits and walnuts on a decorative plate and serve as is.

Red Snapper with Fresh Vegetable Packages
Single serving is 1/4 of the total recipe
CALORIES 265; PROTEIN 30g; CARBS 3g;
TOTAL FAT 15g; SAT FAT 2g; CHOLESTEROL 84mg;
SODIUM 171mg; FIBER 1g

microwave mako shark steaks
with honey-ginger sauce

scallion rice

bean sprouts with snow peas

fresh fruit kabobs with berry sauce and wafer cookies

shopping list

Frozen raspberries

Strawberry jam

Lemon

Wafer cookies (optional)

Ginger

Mako shark steaks

Snow peas

from the salad bar

Chopped scallions

Pineapple chunks
(or from the produce
department or canned)

Hulled whole strawberries
(or from the produce
department)

Honeydew melon chunks
(or from the produce
department)

from your pantry

Instant rice

Sugar (optional)

Honey

Teriyaki sauce

Bean sprouts

serves 2

beforeyoustart

Thaw the frozen raspberries for the dessert sauce.

step 1 prepare the **scallion rice**

step 2 prepare the **berry sauce and fruit kabobs**

step 3 microwave the **mako shark steaks** and **vegetables**

step 4 **serve**

headsup

If your market does not have shark steaks, substitute another firm-fleshed fish here, such as halibut or cod fillets. It is worth keeping your eye out for shark, though, because it is flavorful, with a meaty steak-like texture.

"Mako shark reminds me of swordfish, only with a stronger flavor. Ginger and honey complement it nicely. The microwave is great for cooking fish and vegetables."

—minutemeals' Chef Miriam

step 1

prepare the **scallion rice**

1 cup instant rice

1/4 cup chopped scallions

Prepare the rice according to the directions on the package. When done, stir in the scallions, cover, and keep warm.

step 2

prepare the **berry sauce and fruit kabobs**

For the berry sauce

1/2 bag (16 ounces) frozen raspberries, thawed

1/4 cup strawberry jam, or to taste

1/4 cup water

Fresh lemon juice to taste

Sugar, if needed

For the fruit kabobs

Pineapple chunks for 2

Hulled whole strawberries for 2

Honeydew melon chunks for 2

2 wooden or metal skewers

Wafer cookies, for serving

1. Prepare the berry sauce: In a food processor, process the raspberries, jam, and water until blended. Strain the sauce through a sieve into a bowl and add lemon juice and sugar, if desired. Let stand at room temperature.

2. Make the fruit kabobs: Make kabobs with the cut-up fruit, alternating the pieces on the skewers. Place the kabobs on individual plates and refrigerate until serving time.

step 3

microwave the **mako shark steaks** and **vegetables**

For the fish

2 teaspoons grated fresh ginger

2 mako shark steaks (5 to 6 ounces each)

2 tablespoons honey

2 teaspoons teriyaki sauce

For the vegetables

2 cups fresh bean sprouts

1/2 cup stringed snow peas

1. Grate enough ginger to measure 2 teaspoons.

2. Prepare the fish: Rinse the shark steaks and pat dry. Arrange on a microwave-safe dish in a single layer with the thickest part of the steak on the outside of the dish.

3. In a small bowl, combine the honey, teriyaki sauce, and ginger. Spoon over the shark steaks.

4. Prepare the vegetables: Rinse the bean sprouts and snow peas. Pat dry with paper towels. Combine in a microwave-safe bowl.

5. Microwave the shark steaks and the vegetables at the same time on High for 4 to 5 minutes, or until the fish is done when tested with a fork. Remove and place on the table.

step 4

serve

1. Spoon a portion of the scallion rice and vegetables onto each dinner plate. Top with a shark steak. Spoon the pan juices over the top.

2. When ready for dessert, serve the kabobs on plates and pass the raspberry sauce for spooning over them. Serve with wafer cookies.

Microwave Mako Shark Steaks
with Honey-Ginger Sauce
Single serving is 1/2 of the total recipe
CALORIES 227; PROTEIN 32g; CARBS 22g;
TOTAL FAT 2g; SAT FAT 0g; CHOLESTEROL 80mg;
SODIUM 347mg; FIBER 2g

oven-fried fish sandwiches
with bacon

tartar sauce

cucumber, tomato, and chickpea salad

eskimo pies

menu gameplan

shopping list

Haddock, orange roughy, or turbot fillets

Bacon

Kaiser or whole-grain rolls

Bibb lettuce leaves (from the salad bar)

Ripe tomatoes

Cucumbers

Chickpeas

Eskimo Pies

from your pantry

Olive oil

All-purpose flour

Salt and pepper

Egg

Italian-style or seasoned bread crumbs

Tartar sauce (optional)

Vinaigrette dressing, store-bought or homemade

serves 4

beforeyoustart

Preheat the oven to 450°F to oven-fry the sandwiches.

step 1 make the **oven-fried fish sandwiches with bacon**

step 2 assemble the **cucumber, tomato, and chickpea salad**

step 3 serve

luckyforyou

The salad is meant to be easy—3 main ingredients and bottled dressing. If you don't have chickpeas, use white cannellini beans. If you don't have beans, use drained marinated artichoke hearts. Use what you have on hand. See what's on the shelf and improvise.

"Oven-frying is a great technique. You can have the wonderful crispy coating without all the calories and fat of deep-frying."

—minutemeals' Chef Miriam

step 1

make the **oven-fried fish sandwiches with bacon**

2 tablespoons olive oil

1/2 cup all-purpose flour

Salt and pepper to taste

1 egg

1 tablespoon water

1 1/2 cups Italian-style or seasoned bread crumbs

4 haddock, orange roughy, or turbot fillets (about 6 ounces each)

4 bacon slices

4 Kaiser or whole-grain rolls

Tartar sauce (optional)

4 large Bibb lettuce leaves

1. Preheat the oven to 450°F. Grease a jelly-roll pan with 1 tablespoon of the olive oil.

2. Spread the flour on a large plate and season with salt and pepper. Break the egg into a wide shallow bowl, add the water, and beat lightly. Spread the bread crumbs on a small baking sheet.

3. Rinse the fish fillets and pat dry. Dredge the fillets, 1 at a time, in the seasoned flour. Then dip into the egg, coating both sides, and dredge in the bread crumbs, pressing them on with your fingers. Place the fillets as they are breaded on the greased jelly-roll pan. Drizzle with the remaining tablespoon olive oil. Bake for 10 to 12 minutes, or until the fish flakes easily when tested with a fork.

4. While the fillets are baking, place 2 paper towels on top of each other on a microwave-safe plate. Lay the bacon slices on top, being careful that they do not overlap. Cover loosely with another sheet of paper towel. Microwave on High for 3 1/2 minutes for crisp bacon. Let stand for about 5 minutes to crisp.

5. Halve each of the rolls horizontally. Spread the cut sides with tartar sauce, if desired. Place a lettuce leaf on each bottom half and top with bacon, a fish fillet, and a roll top. Cut in half, if you like. Place each sandwich on a serving plate.

step 2

assemble the **cucumber, tomato, and chickpea salad**

2 ripe medium tomatoes

2 or 3 small cucumbers

1 can (15 ounces) chickpeas

2 to 3 tablespoons vinaigrette dressing

Cut the tomatoes into 1/4-inch chunks. Peel the cucumbers, if you like, and cut into 1/4-inch chunks. Drain the chickpeas, rinse, and drain again. Combine all in a salad bowl. Add the vinaigrette and toss to coat. Place the bowl on the table.

step 3

serve

1. Serve the sandwiches hot, with additional tartar sauce at the table, if desired. Serve with the salad.

2. When ready for dessert, serve the Eskimo Pies directly from the freezer.

Oven-Fried Fish Sandwiches with Bacon
Single serving is 1/4 of the total recipe
CALORIES 504; PROTEIN 45g; CARBS 39g; TOTAL FAT 19g; SAT FAT 4g; CHOLESTEROL 174mg; SODIUM 840mg; FIBER 2g

creamy glazed salmon fillets

green beans with browned-in-butter pine nuts

crispy breadsticks

lime ice with seasonal berries

menu
gameplan

shopping list

Fresh chives or parsley

Horseradish

Lemon juice

Lemons

Salmon fillets

Frozen French-style green beans

Pine nuts *(pignoli)*

Breadsticks

Lime ice

Seasonal berries

from your pantry

Olive oil or nonstick vegetable cooking spray

Mayonnaise

Dijon mustard

Salt and pepper

Butter

serves 4

beforeyoustart

Preheat the oven to 450°F to roast the salmon.

step **1** roast the **creamy glazed salmon fillets**

step **2** cook the **green beans with browned-in-butter pine nuts**

step **3** heat the **breadsticks**

step **4** **serve**

headsup

Looking for a way to cut the calories here? Use light mayonnaise, not low-fat or nonfat, and pass on browning the pine nuts in butter. Toast them in the oven or stovetop in a small skillet instead. And if you don't have pine nuts, use slivered almonds. You probably won't be saving yourself many calories, but you will be saving yourself shopping time.

"Don't overcook the salmon—use the 'Canadian rule' for doneness: about 10 minutes of cooking time per inch of fish at its thickest point."

—minutemeals' Chef Ruth

step 1

roast the **creamy glazed salmon fillets**

Olive oil or nonstick vegetable cooking spray

2 tablespoons chopped fresh chives or parsley

1/4 cup mayonnaise, regular or light

1 tablespoon prepared horseradish

2 teaspoons Dijon mustard

1 teaspoon fresh lemon juice, plus 1 whole lemon, for serving

Salt and pepper to taste

4 salmon fillets, skin on (about 6 ounces each)

1. Preheat the oven to 450°F. Line the broiler pan with foil. Lightly mist the foil with olive oil or nonstick vegetable cooking spray.

2. Chop enough chives or fresh parsley to measure 2 tablespoons and put in a small bowl. Add the mayonnaise, horseradish, mustard, lemon juice, and salt and pepper and stir to combine.

3. Arrange the 4 salmon fillets on the foil-covered broiler pan, skin side down. Roast for 6 to 8 minutes. Spread the mayonnaise glaze over the fillets. Turn the oven to broil. Place the broiler pan 6 inches from the heat. Broil the fillets for 2 minutes, until the glaze is golden brown and bubbly.

step 2

cook the **green beans with browned-in-butter pine nuts**

1 package (about 16 ounces) frozen French-style green beans or small whole green beans

2 tablespoons butter

1/4 cup pine nuts

Salt and pepper to taste

1. In a large saucepan, cook the green beans according to the directions on the package, just until crisp-tender. Drain and return to the pan.

2. Meanwhile, in a small heavy skillet, heat the butter until bubbling. Add the pine nuts and cook over medium heat, stirring often, until lightly toasted and the butter is a rich golden brown. Add to the beans, season with salt and pepper, and toss to combine. Keep warm, covered.

step 3

heat the **breadsticks**

1 package premade breadsticks

Heat the breadsticks in a toaster oven at the temperature and for the time suggested on the package. Transfer to a napkin-lined bread basket, cover to keep warm, and place on the table.

step 4

serve

1. If desired, remove the lime ice from the freezer to soften slightly while you have dinner.

2. Arrange the green beans on each side of 4 dinner plates; place a salmon fillet in the center. Slice the lemon and garnish each serving with 1 wedge.

3. When ready for dessert, scoop the lime ice into small bowls and garnish each with fresh berries of choice. Serve, with any remaining berries, if desired.

Creamy Glazed Salmon Fillets
Single serving is 1/4 of the total recipe
CALORIES 259; PROTEIN 35g; CARBS 1g;
TOTAL FAT 12g; SAT FAT 1g; CHOLESTEROL 132mg;
SODIUM 222mg; FIBER 0g

grilled sesame-crusted salmon

lemon mustard sauce

sesame noodle salad

cucumber salad

vanilla ice cream with maple syrup and sliced peaches

menu gameplan

serves 4

shopping list

Salmon steaks

Sesame seeds

Lemon (for zest and juice)

Nonfat plain yogurt

Horseradish

Vanilla ice cream

Peaches, fresh or sliced canned

from the salad bar

Sesame noodle salad

Cucumber salad

from your pantry

Olive oil

Salt and pepper

Low-fat mayonnaise

Dijon mustard

Maple syrup

step	1	cook the **grilled sesame-crusted salmon**
step	2	make the **lemon mustard sauce**
step	3	plate the **sesame noodle and cucumber salads**
step	4	**serve**

luckyforyou More and more markets have freshly prepared, ready-to-serve salads to go. If sesame noodles aren't sold where you shop, choose another pasta salad, like tortellini vinaigrette. Simplify even more, if you like: Instead of cucumber salad, slice up several ripe tomatoes and sprinkle with nothing more than coarse salt and a drizzling of olive oil.

"This is a great summertime meal. When it's hot, I limit myself to cooking only one dish. It works!"

—minutemeals' Chef Miriam

step 1

cook the **grilled sesame-crusted salmon**

4 salmon steaks (about 1 1/2 pounds total weight), each about 1 inch thick

2 tablespoons olive oil

1/2 teaspoon salt

1/4 teaspoon pepper

2 tablespoons sesame seeds

1. Brush the salmon steaks on both sides with 1 tablespoon of the olive oil. Season with the salt and pepper. Press the sesame seeds onto both sides of each fish steak.

2. Heat the remaining 1 tablespoon olive oil in a large nonstick skillet over medium-high heat until hot. Add the salmon steaks and cook for 5 to 6 minutes on each side, or until the fish flakes when tested with a fork.

step 2

make the **lemon mustard sauce**

1/2 teaspoon lemon zest plus 1 tablespoon fresh lemon juice (1 lemon)

1/2 cup low-fat mayonnaise

1/2 cup nonfat plain yogurt

1 to 2 tablespoons Dijon mustard

1 tablespoon drained prepared horseradish

1/4 teaspoon salt

1/8 teaspoon pepper

1. Grate enough lemon zest to measure 1/2 teaspoon. Squeeze enough fresh lemon juice to measure 1 tablespoon.

2. While the salmon steaks are cooking, combine all the sauce ingredients, starting with only 2 teaspoons lemon juice, in a small servingbowl. Taste and add the remaining lemon juice, if desired. Place the bowl on the table. (Makes about 1 1/4 cups.)

step 3

plate the **sesame noodle salad** and **cucumber salad**

Sesame noodle salad for 4

Cucumber salad for 4

Place the noodle salad and cucumber salad in separate bowls and place on the table.

step 4

serve

1. Transfer 1 salmon steak to each of 4 dinner plates. Pass the lemon mustard sauce for spooning over the steaks.

2. When ready for dessert, scoop vanilla ice cream into small bowls, slice the peaches over each serving, and drizzle maple syrup to taste over all. Serve.

Grilled Sesame-Crusted Salmon
Single serving is 1/4 of the total recipe
CALORIES 311; PROTEIN 36g; CARBS 1g;
TOTAL FAT 17g; SAT FAT 1g; CHOLESTEROL 128mg;
SODIUM 418mg; FIBER 1g

Nutrient Analysis includes 2 tablespoons lemon mustard sauce.

poached salmon
with salsa cruda

orzo

sautéed arugula

cantaloupe with
vanilla frozen yogurt

shopping list

Tomatoes

Lemons

Orzo

Salmon fillets

Arugula (prewashed and
stemmed, if available)

Cantaloupe chunks
(from the salad bar or produce
department)

Vanilla frozen yogurt

from your pantry

Garlic

Extra virgin olive oil

Ground cumin

Hot pepper sauce

Salt and pepper

serves 4

beforeyoustart

Bring the water to a boil in a large pot,
covered, over high heat to cook the orzo.

step 1 make the **salsa cruda**

step 2 cook the **orzo**

step 3 poach the **salmon**

step 4 sauté the **arugula**

step 5 **serve**

luckyforyou You can make this minute
meal even quicker: Buy a
container of "fresh" salsa and skip Step 1. Salsa comes in
mild, medium, and hot and can be found in the refrigerated
section of the produce department in most supermarkets.

"Poaching is one of the easiest ways to cook fish and has an added benefit built in: It keeps the fish moist."

—minutemeals' Chef Hillary

step 1

make the **salsa cruda**

2 large ripe tomatoes
(or 3/4 cup canned diced
tomatoes, drained)

1 large garlic clove

Juice of 1 large lemon
(2 tablespoons)

1 1/2 tablespoons extra virgin
olive oil

1/2 teaspoon ground cumin

1/2 teaspoon hot pepper sauce

Salt and pepper to taste

1. Chop the fresh tomatoes in a food processor or by hand. If using a processor, quarter the tomatoes first, add them to the machine, and pulse several times to chop coarse. Be careful not to puree. Transfer to a bowl.

2. Mince the garlic. Add the garlic and the remaining ingredients to the tomatoes and toss to combine. Let stand for the flavors to develop while you make the rest of the meal.

step 2

cook the **orzo**

1 quart water

Salt to taste

1 cup orzo (rice-shaped pasta)

Pour the water into a medium saucepan, salt lightly, and cover. Bring to a boil over high heat. Add the orzo and cook 5 to 7 minutes, or until *al dente*. Drain in a colander, return to the pan, and keep warm, covered.

step 3

poach the **salmon**

For the poaching liquid

1 lemon

6 cups water

1 tablespoon extra virgin
olive oil

1 teaspoon salt

1/4 teaspoon pepper

For the salmon

4 salmon fillets without skin
(6 ounces each)

1. Thinly slice the lemon.

2. Put all the ingredients for the poaching liquid in a 12-inch high-sided skillet. Cover and bring to a boil over high heat. Reduce the heat to medium and simmer for 5 minutes to blend the flavors.

3. Add the salmon fillets to the poaching liquid and reduce the heat to low. Cover and poach for 5 to 7 minutes, or until just opaque in the thickest part. With a spatula, remove the fillets and pat dry with paper towels.

step 4

sauté the **arugula**

1 tablespoon extra virgin
olive oil

2 large bunches arugula,
prewashed and stemmed,
if available

Salt and pepper to taste

1. Heat the olive oil in a large nonstick skillet over medium heat until hot. Add the arugula, toss to coat, and sauté, tossing, until wilted, about 2 minutes. Season well with salt and pepper. Transfer to a serving bowl.

2. (If you cannot buy ready-to-cook arugula, remove the tough stems. Fill a clean sink with plenty of cold water and swirl the leaves in the water. Lift out, drain in a colander, and spin or pat dry.)

step 5

serve

1. Divide the orzo evenly among 4 dinner plates, spooning it in the center of each. Top with a salmon fillet. Spoon salsa over the top and surround with arugula.

2. When ready for dessert, divide the cantaloupe chunks among dessert bowls, add a scoop of frozen yogurt to each, and serve.

Poached Samon with Salsa Cruda
Single serving is 1/4 of the total recipe
CALORIES 273; PROTEIN 35g; CARBS 5g;
TOTAL FAT 12g; SAT FAT 1g; CHOLESTEROL 127g;
SODIUM 94mg; FIBER 1g

salmon with balsamic-orange sauce

steamed sugar snap peas

greens vinaigrette

french bread

sliced plums and nectarines
with lemon yogurt

menu
gameplan

serves 4

beforeyoustart

Preheat the oven to 400°F to roast
the salmon.

step	1	cook the **salmon with balsamic-orange sauce**
step	2	assemble the **greens vinaigrette**
step	3	steam the **sugar snap peas**
step	4	**serve**

shopping list

Salmon fillets

Fresh mint

Fresh basil

Fresh parsley

Prewashed salad greens
of choice

Lemon (for juice)

Sugar snap peas

French bread

Nectarines

Plums

Lemon yogurt

from your pantry

Olive oil

Salt and pepper

Onion

Orange juice

Balsamic vinegar

Dijon mustard

Canola oil

Brown sugar

 In most cases—not all, but
in most—dried herbs can be
used in place of fresh. Not in this salmon recipe, however.
You want the lovely fragrance that only fresh herbs can
supply. If investing in whole bunches of herbs is impractical
for you, look for smaller packages of just the leaves.
And, of course, you can always grow your own.

"I use balsamic vinegar often in my cooking because it adds depth and flavor to a dish, without adding fat or calories."

—minutemeals' Chef Amanda

step 1

cook the **salmon with balsamic-orange sauce**

1 tablespoon olive oil

4 salmon fillets, with skin (about 5 ounces each)

Salt and pepper to taste

1 small onion

1 tablespoon chopped fresh mint

1 tablespoon chopped fresh basil

1 tablespoon chopped fresh parsley

1/2 cup orange juice, preferably fresh

1/4 cup balsamic vinegar

1. Preheat the oven to 400°F.

2. In a large nonstick ovenproof skillet, with an ovenproof handle, heat the olive oil over medium-high heat. Add the salmon fillets in one layer, skin side down, season with salt and pepper, and cook 3 minutes. Transfer the skillet to the oven and roast 6 to 8 minutes, or until the fillets just flake when tested with a fork.

3. Finely chop the onion. Chop enough fresh mint, basil, and parsley to measure 1 tablespoon each. Put the onion and herbs in a medium skillet. Add the orange juice and vinegar and bring to a boil over medium-high heat. Boil gently for 5 minutes, until reduced slightly. Remove the pan from the heat.

step 2

assemble the **greens vinaigrette**

8 ounces mixed prewashed salad greens of choice

2 to 3 tablespoons lemon juice (1 lemon)

1 tablespoon Dijon mustard

1/4 cup olive or canola oil

Salt and pepper to taste

1. Put the salad greens in a large salad bowl.

2. Squeeze 2 tablespoons lemon juice into a small bowl and add the mustard. Whisk to combine. Add the oil slowly, whisking, until blended. Season with salt and pepper. Taste and add the remaining tablespoon lemon juice, if desired. Pour the dressing over the salad and toss. Place the bowl on the table.

step 3

steam the **sugar snap peas**

1 pound sugar snap peas

Place the sugar snap peas in a steamer basket. Cover the bottom of a large saucepan with about 1 inch water, cover, and bring to a boil over high heat. Place the basket in the pan and cover. Steam for 2 minutes, or until the peas are crisp-tender. Remove from the heat.

step 4

serve

1. Place 1 salmon fillet on each of 4 dinner plates and spoon the balsamic-orange sauce over the top. Spoon a serving of sugar snap peas alongside. Serve.

2. Put the French bread on a cutting board and place the board on the table.

3. When ready for dessert, serve the nectarines and plums rinse and serve whole, to be sliced at the table. Serve brown sugar and lemon yogurt as toppings.

Salmon with Balsamic-Orange Sauce
Single serving is 1/4 of the total recipe
CALORIES 243; PROTEIN 29g; CARBS 9g;
TOTAL FAT 9g; SAT FAT 1g; CHOLESTEROL 106mg;
SODIUM 76mg; FIBER 0g

sole fillets
with sun-dried tomato butter

baby peas with endive

goat cheese salad

croissants

red and green grapes

shopping list

Frozen baby peas

Belgian endive leaves

Prewashed mixed spring or baby greens

Goat cheese

Sun-dried tomatoes packed in oil

Sole fillets

Croissants

Red and green grapes (from the salad bar or produce department)

from your pantry

Butter

Vinaigrette dressing, store-bought or homemade

Vegetable cooking spray

Dried basil

Salt and pepper

Grated Parmesan cheese

menu gameplan

serves 4

beforeyoustart

Preheat the broiler.

step 1 cook the **baby peas with endive**

step 2 assemble the **goat cheese salad**

step 3 broil the **sole fillets with sun-dried tomato butter**

step 4 serve

luckyforyou If investing in a head of endive for just 6 leaves to cook with the peas seems a little extravagant for you, use the remainder of the head, sliced thin, in the goat cheese salad.

"Flavored butters are a breeze to make and can be frozen in individual servings. Just remove from the freezer to use."

—minutemeals' Chef Miriam

step 1

cook the **baby peas with endive**

1 package (10 ounces) frozen baby peas

6 Belgian endive leaves

1 tablespoon butter

1. Cook the peas in a medium saucepan according to the directions on the package. Drain and return to the pan.

2. Meanwhile, shred the 6 endive leaves crosswise. Stir the endive and the butter into the peas and place over very low heat just until the butter is melted and the endive is slightly wilted.

step 2

assemble the **goat cheese salad**

1 bag (5 ounces) prewashed mixed spring or baby greens

1 log (3 ounces) goat cheese

2 to 3 tablespoons vinaigrette dressing

1. Divide the greens among 4 salad plates.

2. Slice the log of goat cheese into 4 rounds and place 1 on each salad. Drizzle each salad with dressing. Place the plates on the table.

step 3

broil the **sole fillets with sun-dried tomato butter**

Vegetable cooking spray

3 tablespoons butter

1 tablespoon drained oil-packed sun-dried tomatoes

Pinch of dried basil

4 large fresh sole fillets (1¼ pounds total weight)

Salt and pepper to taste

4 tablespoons grated Parmesan cheese

1. Preheat the broiler. Coat a jelly-roll pan with nonstick vegetable cooking spray.

2. Place the butter in a small bowl and mash. Finely chop the sun-dried tomatoes, add them to the butter, and mash/stir until thoroughly combined. Stir in the basil.

3. Rinse the sole fillets and pat dry. Season both sides with salt and pepper and place on the jelly-roll pan. Broil about 4 inches from the heat for 3 to 5 minutes, or until the fish flakes when tested with a fork.

4. With a spatula, transfer the fillets to individual dinner plates, top with a nugget of the tomato butter, and a dusting, about 1 tablespoon, of the Parmesan.

step 4

serve

1. Spoon a serving of the peas and endive on each dinner plate and serve at once.

2. Place croissants in a bread basket on the table.

3. When ready for dessert, place the grapes in a large bowl and place on the table to be eaten from the bowl.

Sole Fillets with Sun-Dried Tomato Butter
Single serving is ¼ of the total recipe

CALORIES 241; PROTEIN 31g; CARBS 1g;
TOTAL FAT 12g; SAT FAT 7g; CHOLESTEROL 30mg;
SODIUM 364mg; FIBER 0g

broiled sole
with potatoes and artichokes

cucumber and beet salad

french rolls

fudge ripple ice cream

shopping list

Pre-scrubbed baby red potatoes (from the produce department)

Artichoke bottoms

Lemon

Sole fillets

Prewashed European-style salad greens

Herbed vinaigrette dressing, store-bought or homemade

French rolls

Fudge ripple ice cream

from the salad bar

Cucumber slices

Pickled beets

from your pantry

Butter

Salt and pepper

Dried thyme

serves 4

beforeyoustart

Preheat the broiler.

step 1 cook the **vegetables; broil the sole**

step 2 while the fillets are cooking, assemble the **cucumber and beet salad**

step 3 serve

luckyforyou Pre-scrubbed potatoes are available in airtight bags in the produce department of many supermarkets. They are ready to use and a tremendous convenience item for the busy cook.

"Fish and potatoes are frequently paired, but here the addition of artichokes makes for a more interesting and colorful entree."

—minutemeals' Chef Joanne

step 1

cook the **vegetables; broil the sole**

1 pound pre-scrubbed baby red potatoes

1 can (7 1/2 ounces drained weight) artichoke bottoms

1 lemon

3 tablespoons butter

Salt and pepper to taste

4 sole fillets (1 1/4 pounds total weight)

1 teaspoon dried thyme

1. Preheat the broiler.

2. With a sharp knife, halve the potatoes. Drain the artichoke bottoms and cut into 1/2-inch pieces. Cut the lemon into 4 wedges.

3. In a large nonstick skillet, melt 2 tablespoons of the butter over medium-high heat. Add the potatoes and artichoke bottoms and 1/2 teaspoon salt. Toss to coat, cover, and cook, tossing occasionally, until the potatoes are golden and tender, about 15 minutes.

4. Rinse the sole fillets and pat dry. Season with thyme and salt and pepper on both sides. Place in a single layer on a heavy baking sheet and dot with the remaining tablespoon butter. Broil about 4 inches from the heat for 4 to 6 minutes, or until the fish flakes easily when tested with a fork. With a spatula, transfer the fillets to a platter.

step 2

while the fillets are cooking, assemble the **cucumber and beet salad**

1 bag (5 ounces) prewashed European-style salad greens

1 cup cucumber slices

1/2 cup pickled beets

Herbed vinaigrette dressing

Divide the salad greens among 4 salad plates. Top each with 1/4 of the cucumbers and beets. Drizzle with dressing to taste and place the salads on the table.

step 3

serve

1. Spoon the potatoes and artichokes around the sole and add the lemon wedges to the platter. Serve at once, with the French rolls.

2. When ready for dessert, scoop the ice cream into dessert bowls or goblets and serve.

Broiled Sole with Potatoes and Artichokes
Single serving is 1/4 of the total recipe
CALORIES 287; PROTEIN 27g; CARBS 22g;
TOTAL FAT 10g; SAT FAT 5g; CHOLESTEROL 23mg;
SODIUM 248mg; FIBER 3g

grilled swordfish
with lemon-rosemary butter

couscous with pimiento

steamed asparagus

lattice-top peach pie

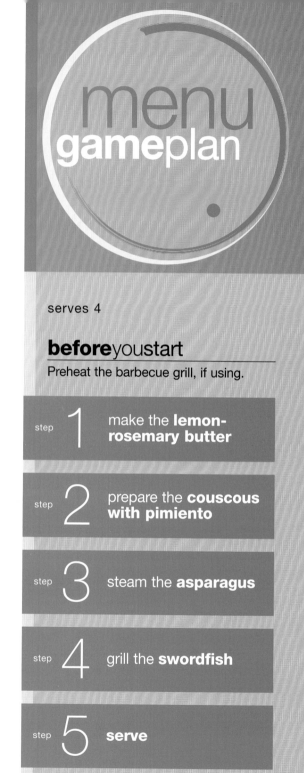

shopping list

Fresh rosemary leaves

Lemon (for juice)

Plain couscous

Pimiento

Asparagus

Swordfish steaks

Lattice-top peach pie

from your pantry

Butter

Salt and pepper

Fat-free reduced-sodium chicken broth

Olive oil

serves 4

beforeyoustart

Preheat the barbecue grill, if using.

step 1 make the **lemon-rosemary butter**

step 2 prepare the **couscous with pimiento**

step 3 steam the **asparagus**

step 4 grill the **swordfish**

step 5 **serve**

headsup

There is fresh swordfish and frozen and the prices are not the same, the fresh being considerably more expensive. Try both and see which best suits your taste.

"This is a birthday-dinner menu. Swordfish is special and so is asparagus—the flavors are fresh, the colors are lovely."

—minutemeals' Chef Hillary

step 1

make the **lemon-rosemary butter**

1½ teaspoons fresh rosemary leaves

3 tablespoons fresh lemon juice (1 large lemon)

3 tablespoons butter, softened

Salt and pepper to taste

1. Strip enough leaves from a branch of rosemary to measure 1½ teaspoons. Coarsely chop and place in a small bowl.

2. Squeeze 3 tablespoons fresh lemon juice into the bowl and add the butter. Mash with the back of a spoon until completely combined, almost fluffy. Season with salt and pepper.

step 2

prepare the **couscous with pimiento**

2 cups fat-free reduced-sodium chicken broth

1½ cups plain couscous

3 tablespoons drained chopped pimiento

Salt and pepper to taste

Bring the chicken broth to a boil, covered, in a 1-quart saucepan over high heat. Stir in the couscous, pimiento, and salt and pepper. Cover and remove the pan from the heat. Let stand for 5 minutes.

step 3

steam the **asparagus**

1 pound pencil-thin asparagus

Salt and pepper to taste

1. Snap off the end of each stalk of asparagus where it naturally breaks. Put the stalks in a steamer basket.

2. Put 1 inch of water in a saucepan large enough to hold the steamer basket. Place the basket in the pan, cover, and bring the water to a boil over high heat. Steam for 3 minutes, or until the stalks are crisp-tender when tested with a fork. Transfer the asparagus to a plate, season with salt and pepper, and keep warm, loosely covered.

step 4

grill the **swordfish**

4 thin-to-medium-thick swordfish steaks (6 ounces each)

1 tablespoon olive oil

Salt and pepper to taste

1. Preheat the barbecue grill or a grill pan over high heat until hot.

2. Rinse the swordfish steak and pat dry. Brush on both sides with the olive oil and season with salt and pepper. Grill 3 to 5 minutes on each side, or until opaque when tested with a fork.

step 5

serve

1. Transfer each of the swordfish steaks to a large dinner plate. Immediately top each with 1 tablespoon of the lemon-rosemary butter and let it melt over the top.

2. Fluff the couscous with a fork. Divide the couscous among the plates and add a serving of asparagus to each. Serve at once.

3. When ready for dessert, cut the pie into slices, plate, and serve.

Grilled Swordfish with
Lemon-Rosemary Butter
Single serving is ¼ of the total recipe
CALORIES 317; PROTEIN 34g; CARBS 1g;
TOTAL FAT 19g; SAT FAT 2g; CHOLESTEROL 89mg;
SODIUM 153mg; FIBER 0g

tuna steaks
with green peppercorn vinaigrette

greens with parmesan shavings

soft garlic breadsticks

raspberries with mascarpone

menu
gameplan

serves 4

beforeyoustart

Preheat the oven to 400°F to heat the breadsticks. Preheat the barbecue grill, if using.

| step | 1 | make the **vinaigrette;** assemble the **greens** |

| step | 2 | heat the **soft garlic breadsticks** |

| step | 3 | grill the **tuna steaks** |

| step | 4 | **serve** |

shopping list

Green peppercorns packed in brine

Fresh thyme

Belgian endives

Prewashed Italian-style salad mix

Wedge of Parmigiano-Reggiano cheese

Boboli soft breadsticks flavored with garlic

Tuna steaks

Raspberries

Mascarpone

from your pantry

Garlic

Red wine vinegar

Olive oil

Salt and pepper

headsup

When buying tuna, make certain it is bright red in color and slightly translucent, with no brown spots or strong odor. It should feel firm to the touch. Trim any dark meat from the steaks before cooking since this can often have a fishy taste.

"I like grilled tuna still really pink in the middle. If you like your tuna well cooked, this isn't the recipe for you. Try swordfish instead."

—minutemeals' Chef Hillary

step 1

make the **vinaigrette**; assemble the **greens**

For the vinaigrette

2 tablespoons drained green peppercorns in brine

1 teaspoon chopped fresh thyme or 1/4 teaspoon dried

1 garlic clove

2 to 3 tablespoons red wine vinegar

1/2 cup olive oil

Salt and pepper to taste

For the salad

2 Belgian endives

1 bag (12 ounces) prewashed Italian-style salad mix

1 wedge (2 ounces) Parmigiano-Reggiano cheese

1. Rinse, drain, and chop the green peppercorns. Chop enough fresh thyme to measure 1 teaspoon. Smash the garlic with the flat side of a large knife.

2. Make the vinaigrette: In a medium bowl, combine the peppercorns, thyme, and 2 tablespoons of the vinegar. Whisk in the olive oil until well blended. Add the garlic. Season with salt and pepper and the remaining 1 tablespoon vinegar, if desired.

3. Assemble the salad: Slice the endives. Put the salad mix and endive in a large salad bowl.

4. Place the cheese on a cutting surface. With a vegetable peeler, cut the cheese so that it comes off the wedge in wide shavings. Reserve.

step 2

heat the **soft garlic breadsticks**

1 package Boboli soft breadsticks flavored with garlic

1. Preheat the oven to 400°F.

2. Place the breadsticks on a small baking sheet and heat for about 5 minutes, until toasty and fragrant. Transfer to a napkin-lined bread basket, cover to keep warm, and put the basket on the table.

step 3

grill the **tuna steaks**

4 tuna steaks, about 1/2 inch thick (6 ounces each)

1 tablespoon olive oil

Salt and pepper to taste

1. Preheat the barbecue grill or heat a grill pan over high heat until hot.

2. Rinse the tuna steaks and pat dry. Brush on both sides with the olive oil and season with salt and pepper.

3. Grill the tuna 2 minutes on each side for medium-rare, or longer if desired. Remove to a serving platter and keep warm, loosely covered.

step 4

serve

1. Add the reserved cheese shavings to the salad and toss with 2 tablespoons of the peppercorn vinaigrette. Divide the salad among 4 dinner plates.

2. Top each serving with a grilled tuna steak, then drizzle it with some of the remaining vinaigrette. Serve with the warm breadsticks.

3. When ready for dessert, rinse the raspberries lightly and shake dry. Serve in small bowls, with the mascarpone passed at the table as a topping.

Tuna Steaks with Green Peppercorn Vinaigrette
Single serving is 1/4 of the total recipe
CALORIES 315; PROTEIN 40g; CARBS 1g; TOTAL FAT 17g; SAT FAT 1g; CHOLESTEROL 78mg; SODIUM 276mg; FIBER 0g
Nutrient Analysis includes 1/4 cup vinaigrette for entire recipe.

spicy grilled tuna steaks

mango salsa

cauliflower and broccoli florets

vanilla ice cream with dark cherries and chocolate sauce

menu gameplan

serves 4

step 1 make the **spice rub;** marinate the **tuna steaks**

step 2 make the **mango salsa**

step 3 steam the **cauliflower and broccoli florets**

step 4 grill the **tuna steaks**

step 5 **serve**

shopping list

Tuna steaks

Mangoes

Red onion

Jalapeño pepper

Cilantro

Red or green pepper

Limes (for juice)

Cauliflower and broccoli florets (packaged, from the produce department)

Vanilla ice cream

Canned dark cherries packed in syrup

from your pantry

Ground cumin

Dried oregano

Coarsely ground black pepper

Chili powder

Salt and pepper

Garlic powder

Ground ginger

Cayenne pepper

Olive oil

Sugar

Chocolate sauce

headsup

A ripe mango should smell fragrant and sweet and yield to the touch when pressed. Unlike other fruits—pineapple, for example—color is not necessarily an indicator of ripeness. If you want to ripen mangoes at home, store them at room temperature out of the sun, turning them occasionally.

"The rub is spicy, but you can ratchet the heat level down. Use less black pepper, less chili powder, and only 1/4 teaspoon cayenne."

—minutemeals' Chef Linda

step 1

make the **spice rub**; marinate the **tuna steaks**

1 tablespoon ground cumin

2 teaspoons dried oregano

1 teaspoon coarsely ground black pepper

1 teaspoon chili powder

3/4 teaspoon salt

1/2 teaspoon garlic powder

1/2 teaspoon ground ginger

1/4 to 1/2 teaspoon cayenne pepper

2 tablespoons olive oil

4 tuna steaks, about 1 inch thick (6 ounces each)

1. In a small bowl, stir together the cumin, oregano, black pepper, chili powder, salt, garlic powder, ginger, and cayenne. Add the olive oil and stir until blended.

2. Spread the spice rub on both sides of the tuna steaks. Reserve the steaks on a plate until ready to cook.

step 2

make the **mango salsa**

2 ripe mangoes

1/4 cup chopped red onion (1 small red onion)

1 small jalapeño pepper

3 tablespoons chopped fresh cilantro

1 red or green pepper

1/4 cup fresh lime juice (3 medium limes)

Salt and pepper to taste

Sugar to taste

1. With a vegetable peeler, peel the 2 mangoes, cut the fruit off the pit, and chop into 1-inch pieces. Chop enough red onion to measure 1/4 cup. Seed and mince the 1 jalapeño pepper. Chop enough cilantro to measure 3 tablespoons. Coarsely chop the pepper. Squeeze enough lime juice to measure 1/4 cup.

2. In a bowl, combine the mango, red onion, jalapeño, cilantro, and pepper. Sprinkle the lime juice over the mixture and toss. Season with salt, pepper, and sugar and toss. Place the bowl on the table.

step 3

steam the **cauliflower and broccoli florets**

1 package (12 ounces) combined cauliflower and broccoli florets

Juice of 1/2 lime

Place the florets in a steamer basket. Fill a pan large enough to hold the steamer basket with 1 inch water. Cover and bring to a boil over high heat. Add the steamer basket, cover the pan, and steam about 5 to 7 minutes or until the florets are crisp-tender. Remove to a bowl and keep warm, covered.

step 4

grill the **tuna steaks**

1. Heat a grill pan over medium-high heat until hot. Oil the pan lightly.

2. Add the tuna steaks and grill about 2 minutes, or until the steaks can be turned without sticking. Turn and grill the second side for 2 minutes. At this point, the tuna will be rare. Cook longer for greater doneness, if desired, but do not overcook or the tuna will dry out. Remove from the heat.

step 5

serve

1. Place a tuna steak on each of 4 dinner plates. Pass the salsa to serve on or alongside the tuna.

2. Before serving, sprinkle the fresh lime over the florets and serve.

3. When ready for dessert, scoop the ice cream into small bowls, top with a spoonful or two of dark cherries, and drizzle chocolate sauce over all. Serve.

Spicy Grilled Tuna Steaks
Single serving is 1/4 of the total recipe
CALORIES 384; PROTEIN 42g; CARBS 27g; TOTAL FAT 15g; SAT FAT 0g; CHOLESTEROL 77mg; SODIUM 607mg; FIBER 4g
Nutrient Analysis includes mango salsa.

crab and roasted pepper salad
with corn bread croutons
nectarines in minted balsamic honey
fudge brownies

shopping list

Prebaked corn bread

Nectarines

Fresh mint

Lemons (for juice)

Jarred roasted red peppers

Fresh lump crab meat or surimi

Prewashed baby spinach leaves or mixed spring or baby greens

Fudge brownies

from your pantry

Honey

Balsamic vinegar

Extra virgin olive oil

Maple syrup

Lite soy sauce

Salt and pepper

serves 4

beforeyoustart

Preheat the oven to 375°F to toast the croutons.

step 1 make the **corn bread croutons**

step 2 prepare the **nectarines in minted balsamic honey**

step 3 make the **crab salad with corn bread croutons**

step 4 serve

heads up

You can purchase fresh lump crab meat in one-pound plastic containers at most fish markets and from many gourmet food shops. It is already cooked and partially picked over for pieces of shell and cartilage. Very special—a treat— it makes for an unforgettable summertime meal. For a less expensive alternative, you can use surimi, a mixture of processed Pacific pollock and seasonings made to look like crab, but neither the flavor nor the texture will be the same. Smoked flaked whitefish or chub could also be substituted.

"This is a memorable crab salad. The maple syrup complements the crab beautifully. It's an elegant but simple dish, and for adults only."

—minutemeals' Chef Nancy

step 1

make the **corn bread croutons**

1 small loaf prebaked corn bread (or use corn muffins)

1. Preheat the oven to 375°F.

2. Cut enough of the corn bread into ¹/₂-inch cubes to measure about 2 cups of cubes. Place on a baking sheet and toast, turning 2 or 3 times, about 10 minutes, until golden. Remove and let cool.

step 2

while the croutons are baking, prepare the **nectarines in minted balsamic honey**

5 large ripe nectarines

1 to 2 tablespoons snipped fresh mint leaves

2 tablespoons honey

1 tablespoon balsamic vinegar

1. Pit and slice the nectarines. Place in a serving bowl. With kitchen scissors, snip about 2 tablespoons mint leaves over the nectarines. Toss.

2. In a small bowl, mix the honey and vinegar together with a fork. Pour over the nectarines and toss gently to combine. Cover the bowl and refrigerate until serving time.

step 3

make the **crab salad with corn bread croutons**

For the lemon maple dressing

¹/₄ cup fresh lemon juice (2 extra-large lemons)

¹/₃ cup extra virgin olive oil

1 tablespoon maple syrup

1 tablespoon lite soy sauce

Salt and pepper to taste

For the salad

1 jar (7 ounces) roasted red peppers

1 pound fresh lump crab meat or surimi

5 ounces prewashed baby spinach leaves or mixed spring or baby greens

1. Make the lemon maple dressing: Squeeze enough lemon juice to measure ¹/₄ cup juice. In a small bowl, with a fork, mix the lemon juice, olive oil, maple syrup, and soy sauce together with a fork. Season with salt and pepper.

2. For the salad: Drain the roasted red peppers and slice. Pick over crab and remove any pieces of cartilage or shell. Or, break the surimi into flakes, if necessary. Put the crab in a bowl and toss with 3 tablespoons of the dressing and the roasted peppers.

3. Line a serving platter with the spinach leaves or salad greens. Mound the crab salad on top. Scatter the corn bread croutons over the salad.

step 4

serve

1. Spoon the remaining dressing over the salad just before serving.

2. Place the chilled minted nectarines on the table to serve as an accompaniment.

3. When ready for dessert, cut the brownies into large pieces and serve.

Crab and Roasted Pepper Salad with Corn Bread Croutons
Single serving is ¹/₄ of the total recipe
CALORIES 449; PROTEIN 28g; CARBS 32g; TOTAL FAT 25g; SAT FAT 3g; CHOLESTEROL 83mg; SODIUM 877mg; FIBER 2g

moules marinière
(mussels steamed in white wine)

greens with artichokes and cherry tomatoes
garlic toasts
lemon meringue pie

menu
gameplan

shopping list

Mussels, small farm-raised, if available

Dry vermouth or dry white wine

Italian bread

Artichoke hearts marinated in oil

Prewashed mixed spring or baby greens

Lemon meringue pie

from the salad bar

Cherry tomatoes

Chopped scallions

from your pantry

Garlic

Dried Italian herb blend

Butter

Freshly ground black pepper

Olive oil

serves 4

beforeyoustart

Preheat the oven to 400°F to bake the garlic toasts.

step 1   steam the **mussels**

step 2   make the **garlic toasts**

step 3   assemble the **greens with artichokes and cherry tomatoes**

step 4   **serve**

luckyforyou

You can skip the whole step of making your own garlic toasts and use ready-to-heat garlic bread.

"If you're using white wine for cooking the mussels, go with a French Chablis. Then enjoy the rest of the bottle with the meal."

—minutemeals' Chef Hillary

step 1

steam the **mussels**

4 to 5 pounds small mussels, farm-raised if available

2 large garlic cloves

1 cup dry vermouth or dry white wine

1 teaspoon dried Italian herb blend

1. Scrub the mussels under cool running water and remove the beards.

2. Coarsely chop the garlic and place in a large pot with a tight-fitting lid. Add the vermouth and herb blend. Add the mussels and cover tightly. Steam over medium-high heat, shaking the pot once or twice, until the shells open and the mussels are cooked, about 5 to 7 minutes. Remove the pot from the heat and let stand, covered.

step 2

make the **garlic toasts**

1 long loaf Italian bread

2 garlic cloves

4 tablespoons (1/2 stick) butter

Freshly ground black pepper

1. Preheat the oven to 400°F. Slice the loaf of Italian bread in half horizontally, and place on a baking sheet.

2. Crush the garlic cloves in a garlic press or mince them as finely as

possible. Cut the butter into 4 pieces. In a small saucepan, melt the butter with the garlic and pepper over low heat. Use a pastry brush to brush the cut surfaces of the bread with the garlic butter. Bake for 5 minutes, until warm. Remove to a bread board and keep warm.

step 3

assemble the **greens with artichokes and cherry tomatoes**

1/2 cup cherry tomatoes

1/4 cup chopped scallions

1 jar (6 1/2 ounces) marinated artichoke hearts

1 bag (5 ounces) mixed spring or baby greens

Olive oil, as needed

1. Rinse the cherry tomatoes, pat dry, and halve. Place in a bowl with the scallions.

2. Drain the marinated artichokes hearts, reserving the oil, and chop coarse. Add the artichokes to the bowl with enough of the reserved oil to just coat the ingredients. Toss gently.

3. Place the greens on a serving platter, toss with a little olive oil, then spoon the tomato and artichoke salad on top. Place on the table with 4 salad plates.

step 4

serve

1. Cut the garlic bread into generous slices, place on a bread board, and place on the table.

2. Ladle the mussels into soup bowls. Serve immediately with the garlic toasts and the salad.

3. When ready for dessert, cut the pie into slices, plate, and serve.

Moules Marinière
Single serving is 1/4 of the total recipe
CALORIES 424; PROTEIN 54g; CARBS 18g; TOTAL FAT 10g; SAT FAT 2g; CHOLESTEROL 127mg; SODIUM 1300mg; FIBER 0g

mussels mexicano

avocado and olive salad
warm sourdough rolls
rich chocolate cake

shopping list

Sourdough rolls

Mussels, small farm-raised,
if available

Mexican- or chili-style
diced tomatoes

Dry white wine or white
vermouth

Avocados

Lime (for juice)

Red onion slices
(from the salad bar)

Pitted small ripe olives

Prewashed mixed spring or
baby greens

Rich chocolate cake

from your pantry

Freshly ground black pepper

Salt and pepper

Olive oil

serves 4

step **1** heat the **sourdough rolls**

step **2** clean and steam the **mussels mexicano**

step **3** make the **avocado and olive salad**

step **4** **serve**

 Store mussels in a bowl
covered with a wet paper
towel in the refrigerator. Never store them in plain water
because it will kill them. Clean them shortly before they
are to be cooked. A quick brushing under a stream of
cool water should do the trick. Discard any mussel with a
cracked, broken, or partially opened shell before cooking.
Any mussel that has not opened after cooking should
also be discarded.

"Farm-raised mussels are a decided convenience to the busy cook because they require no heavy scrubbing."

—minutemeals' Chef Ruth

step 1
heat the **sourdough rolls**

4 crusty sourdough rolls,
or more, as desired

Warm the rolls in a toaster oven at the temperature and for the time recommended on the package. Transfer to a napkin-lined basket, cover to keep warm, and place the basket on the table.

step 2
clean and steam the **mussels mexicano**

4 pounds small mussels, farm-raised if available

1 can (14 1/2 ounces) Mexican- or chili-style diced tomatoes

1 cup dry white wine or white vermouth

Freshly ground black pepper to taste

1. Scrub the mussels and remove the beards under cold running water. Reserve in a large colander.

2. Pour the tomatoes and wine into a large pot or 4- or 5-quart kettle with a tight-fitting lid. Season with freshly ground black pepper and stir to combine. Bring to a simmer over medium-high heat.

3. Add the mussels. Cover tightly and steam over high heat, shaking the kettle once or twice, until the mussels open, about 8 minutes. Remove from the heat.

step 3
make the **avocado and olive salad**

3 ripe avocados

3 tablespoons fresh lime juice (1 large lime)

1/2 cup thin red onion slices

1/2 cup pitted small ripe olives

Salt and pepper to taste

1 bag (5 ounces) prewashed mixed spring or baby greens

Olive oil, for drizzling (optional)

1. Peel and pit the avocados, cut into large chunks, and place in a bowl. Sprinkle with the lime juice. Add the red onion and olives. Season with salt and pepper and toss lightly to combine.

2. Line a serving platter with the salad greens. Drizzle lightly with olive oil, if desired. Spoon the avocado mixture over the greens. Chill until serving time.

step 4
serve

1. With a slotted spoon, remove the mussels to individual serving bowls, discarding any that have not opened. Spoon the tomato broth in the kettle over the mussels, being careful not to include the last of the broth in case there is a little sand in it.

2. Serve the mussels with the warm sourdough rolls. Serve the salad on individual plates, either with the mussels or as a second course.

3. When ready for dessert, cut the cake into thin slices, place on dessert plates, and serve.

Mussels Mexicano
Single serving is 1/4 of the total recipe
CALORIES 456; PROTEIN 55g; CARBS 23g; TOTAL FAT 10g; SAT FAT 2g; CHOLESTEROL 127mg; SODIUM 1610mg; FIBER 2g

emerald prawns

jasmine rice
cucumber salad
peppermint stick ice cream

shopping list

Jasmine rice

Cucumber

Red or orange pepper strips
(from the salad bar)

Fresh basil

Fresh cilantro

Fresh parsley

Large shrimp, peeled and
deveined

Bean paste, hot or sweet

Peppermint stick ice cream

from your pantry

Rice vinegar

Toasted sesame oil

Garlic

Peanut or corn oil

serves 4

step **1** cook the **jasmine rice**

step **2** prepare the **cucumber salad**

step **3** make the **emerald prawns**

step **4** **serve**

 If you have a mini chopper,
use it to chop the basil,
cilantro, parsley, and garlic. You will be saving yourself a
considerable amount of time. If you don't have one of
these handy small countertop machines, consider buying
one. It cuts down a lot on chopping time.

"Every time I make this dish, it's a hit. It tastes great, looks beautiful, and is quick to make."

—minutemeals' Chef Connie

cook the **jasmine rice**

1 cup jasmine rice

Cook the jasmine rice in a medium saucepan in the amount of water and for the time suggested on the package. Keep warm, covered.

prepare the **cucumber salad**

1 large seedless cucumber (or paper-thin cucumber slices for 4, from the salad bar)

6 to 8 red or orange pepper strips

Rice vinegar to taste

Toasted sesame oil to taste

1. Rinse the cucumber and pat dry. With a sharp knife, slice the cucumber into paper-thin rounds. Arrange the slices, overlapping them, in concentric circles on a round serving plate.

2. Chop the pepper strips. Scatter the chopped pepper over the cucumber slices, then drizzle the salad with rice vinegar and a few drops of sesame oil. Place the plate on the table.

make the **emerald prawns**

1/4 cup fresh basil sprigs

1/4 cup fresh cilantro sprigs

1/4 cup fresh parsley sprigs

3 or 4 large garlic cloves

2 tablespoons peanut or corn oil

1 1/4 pounds peeled and deveined large shrimp, patted dry

1 tablespoon hot or sweet bean paste

1. Stem enough basil, cilantro, and parsley sprigs to measure 1/4 cup each. Combine the herbs on a cutting board and with a large knife, finely chop. Mince the garlic (you should have about 1 tablespoon).

2. In a wok or 12-inch heavy skillet, heat the peanut or corn oil and minced garlic over low heat, stirring, until softened. Do not let the garlic brown.

3. Increase the heat to medium and add the shrimp. Cook, stir-frying, until the shrimp turn pink, about 2 to 3 minutes. Add the bean paste and minced fresh herbs and cook, tossing, until well combined. Remove the pan from the heat.

serve

1. Fluff the jasmine rice with a fork, then divide among 4 large soup bowls. Top each portion with emerald prawns. Serve at once, with chopsticks, if desired.

2. When ready for dessert, scoop the ice cream into small bowls and serve.

Emerald Prawns
Single serving is 1/4 of the total recipe
CALORIES 416; PROTEIN 34g; CARBS 43g; TOTAL FAT 11g; SAT FAT 1g; CHOLESTEROL 215mg; SODIUM 211mg; FIBER 2g
Nutrient Analysis includes rice.

fish-house broiled scallops
with garlic and herbs
tomato juice with lemon
sautéed fresh spinach
chocolate sorbet
with almond cookie thins

shopping list

Lemon

Tomato juice, preferably low sodium

Sea scallops

Prewashed baby spinach leaves

Peeled hard-cooked egg (from the salad bar, optional)

Chocolate sorbet

Almond cookie thins

from your pantry

Garlic

Olive oil

Dried tarragon

Salt and pepper

Plain dry bread crumbs

Grated Parmesan cheese

Butter

menu
gameplan

serves 4

beforeyoustart

Preheat the broiler.

step 1   pour the **tomato juice**

step 2   make the **fish-house broiled scallops with garlic and herbs**

step 3   sauté the **spinach**

step 4   **serve**

luckyforyou Baby spinach leaves are ready-to-use. If there is no baby spinach in the market when you plan to make this menu, don't even entertain the idea of cleaning two bags of regular spinach. There isn't time. Substitute 2 packages of frozen chopped spinach instead and be sure to drain it very well after cooking.

"I put sea scallops in the same category as lobster. They are a treat. Broiling is a wonderful way to cook them."

—minutemeals' Chef Miriam

step 1

pour the **tomato juice**

1 lemon

1 bottle (32 ounces) tomato juice, preferably low sodium

1. Cut the lemon into 4 wedges.

2. Divide the tomato juice among 4 small glasses and chill while you prepare the meal.

step 2

make the **fish-house broiled scallops with garlic and herbs**

1 to 1¼ pounds sea scallops

2 large garlic cloves

2 tablespoons olive oil

1 teaspoon dried tarragon, crumbled

Salt and pepper to taste

3 tablespoons plain dry bread crumbs

2 tablespoons grated Parmesan cheese, preferably fresh grated

1 tablespoon butter

1. Place the broiler rack as close to the heat as possible and preheat the broiler.

2. Remove the tough muscle at the side of the scallops. Rinse the scallops in a bowl of water; lift from the water and dry on paper towels. Cut very large scallops in half crosswise. They should all be about the same size for even cooking. Arrange on a jelly-roll pan.

3. Mince the garlic and scatter over the scallops. Add the olive oil, tarragon, and salt and pepper to the scallops and toss to coat. Arrange the scallops in 1 layer.

4. Broil as close to the heat as possible, for 4 to 6 minutes, turning once, until just starting to become opaque in the center.

5. Meanwhile, in a cup, mix the bread crumbs and Parmesan. Sprinkle over the scallops, dot with small bits of the butter, and broil 30 seconds to 1 minute longer, just until the crumbs are lightly browned. Remove and keep warm, loosely covered.

step 3

sauté the **spinach**

2 garlic cloves

1 tablespoon olive oil

2 to 3 packages (5 ounces each) prewashed baby spinach leaves

Salt and pepper to taste

Peeled hard-cooked egg (optional)

1. Smash the garlic with the flat side of a large knife.

2. In a large nonstick skillet or Dutch oven, combine the oil and garlic cloves. Cook over medium heat, turning the garlic several times, until it begins to sizzle and turns golden.

3. In batches, add the spinach, tossing each batch to coat with the oil. Cook just until all of it is wilted, about 1 to 2 minutes.

4. Remove from the heat and season with salt and pepper. If desired, chop the hard-cooked egg and sprinkle over the hot spinach. Serve at once.

step 4

serve

1. Garnish each serving of tomato juice with a lemon wedge and place on the table.

2. Divide the broiled scallops among 4 dinner plates and add a serving of the spinach to each. Place the plates on the table.

3. When ready for dessert, serve the sorbet in small bowls and garnish each with an almond thin.

Fish-House Broiled Scallops with Garlic and Herbs
Single serving is ¼ of the total recipe
CALORIES 241; PROTEIN 26g; CARBS 5g;
TOTAL FAT 12g; SAT FAT 3g; CHOLESTEROL 60mg;
SODIUM 327mg; FIBER 0g

scallops provençale

white rice with
herbes de provence

spinach salad with
mandarin oranges

french bread

key lime pie

menu
gameplan

serves 4

step 1 cook the **white rice with herbes de provence**

step 2 cook the **scallops provençale**

step 3 assemble the **spinach salad with mandarin oranges**

step 4 **serve**

shopping list

Chopped tomatoes

Fresh thyme or parsley

Sea scallops

Dry white wine

Mandarin oranges

Prewashed baby spinach leaves

Poppyseed salad dressing

French bread

Key lime pie

from your pantry

Long-grain white rice

Dried herbes de Provence

Butter

Garlic

All-purpose flour

Salt and pepper

Olive oil

luckyforyou Garlic comes peeled and chopped in jars in the produce department. Try it and see how it works.

"Fresh thyme adds a wonderful French flair to these scallops. Though it can sometimes be difficult to find, it's worth the search."

—minutemeals' Chef Joanne

cook the **white rice with herbes de provence**

2 1/2 cups water

1 1/4 cups long-grain white rice

1/2 teaspoon dried herbes de Provence

1 tablespoon butter

In a large saucepan, combine the water, rice, and herb and bring to a boil over high heat. Cover, reduce the heat to low, and simmer for 12 to 15 minutes, until the rice is tender and all the water has been absorbed. Stir in the butter and keep warm, covered.

cook the **scallops provençale**

2 garlic cloves

1 can (14 1/2 ounces) chopped tomatoes

1 teaspoon fresh thyme leaves or 2 tablespoons finely chopped fresh parsley

1 1/2 pounds sea scallops

1/2 cup all-purpose flour

Salt and pepper to taste

2 tablespoons butter

2 tablespoons olive oil

3 tablespoons dry white wine

1. Crush the garlic in a garlic press. Drain the tomatoes. Chop the fresh herb of choice.

2. Rinse the scallops and remove the muscle, if necessary. Pat dry.

3. Place the flour in a plastic food-storage bag and season with salt and pepper. Add the scallops to the flour in batches and shake to coat. Remove to a large plate or baking sheet.

4. In a large nonstick skillet, melt the butter with 1 tablespoon of the olive oil over medium-high heat. Add 1/2 of the scallops in a single layer, without crowding, and sear them for about 2 minutes per side, until lightly browned. Remove to a plate. If necessary, add the remaining tablespoon olive oil to the skillet and sear the remaining scallops in the same manner. Return the first batch of scallops to the skillet.

5. Add the garlic, tomatoes, wine, and herb to the skillet, stir to combine well, and cook just until the sauce is hot and the scallops are heated through. Remove from the heat and season with salt and pepper.

make the **spinach salad with mandarin oranges**

1 can (6 ounces) mandarin oranges

1 bag (5 ounces) prewashed baby spinach leaves

Bottled poppyseed dressing to taste

1. Drain the oranges.

2. Place the spinach in a salad bowl, top with oranges, and add dressing to taste. Toss to coat. Place the salad bowl on the table.

serve

1. Transfer the herbed rice to a serving bowl.

2. Serve the scallops from the skillet. Serve French bread as an accompaniment to soak up the flavorful sauce.

3. When ready for dessert, cut the pie into slices and serve on dessert plates.

Scallops Provençale
Single serving is 1/4 of the total recipe
CALORIES 331; PROTEIN 31g; CARBS 17g;
TOTAL FAT 15g; SAT FAT 1g; CHOLESTEROL 71mg;
SODIUM 692mg; FIBER 1g

paella in a flash

cucumber and ripe olive salad
warm crusty rolls
fresh cherries and chocolate wafers

shopping list

Diced tomatoes

Chorizo or pepperoni

Large shrimp, peeled and deveined

Prewashed European-blend mixed lettuce

Assorted ripe olives (from the deli counter)

French or sourdough rolls

Cherries

Chocolate wafers

Cucumber slices (from the salad bar)

from your pantry

Boil-in-bags rice

Garlic

Dried red pepper flakes

Olive oil

Paprika

Turmeric

Salt and pepper

Vinaigrette dressing, store-bought or homemade

menu gameplan

serves 4

step 1 prepare the **rice**

step 2 make the **paella in a flash**

step 3 assemble the **cucumber and ripe olive salad**

step 4 heat the **rolls**

step 5 **serve**

luckyforyou

Certain brands of boil-in-bags rice can stand for 30 minutes in the water in which it was prepared, which means you can get a jump-start on the preparation of this menu. Do that. Make the rice ahead, then concentrate on the paella. You've just saved yourself some valuable time!

"Paella is a party dish if ever there was one. And this way of preparing it really does make it ready 'in a flash.'"

—minutemeals' Chef Miriam

prepare the **rice**

2 boil-in-bags rice

Prepare the rice according to the directions on the package. Keep warm until ready to serve.

step 2

make the **paella in a flash**

4 large garlic cloves

1 can (14 ounces) diced tomatoes

1/4 to 1/2 teaspoon dried red pepper flakes

2 tablespoons olive oil

4 ounces sliced dry chorizo or a package of sliced pepperoni

1 pound peeled and deveined large shrimp, patted dry

1 teaspoon paprika

1/2 teaspoon turmeric

Salt and pepper to taste

1. Smash the garlic cloves with the flat side of a large knife. Drain the tomatoes and reserve.

2. In a large deep nonstick skillet, cook the garlic and red pepper flakes in the olive oil over medium-high heat, stirring, just until the garlic begins to turn golden, about 2 minutes.

3. Stir in the chorizo or pepperoni and cook, tossing, until heated through, 2 to 3 minutes.

4. Add the shrimp. Sprinkle with the paprika, turmeric, a little salt and a good bit of pepper. Cook, tossing with 2 spoons, until the shrimp turn pink and are opaque in the thickest part, 2 to 3 minutes.

5. Add the tomatoes and bring just to a simmer. Remove from the heat. Taste for seasoning. Remove the garlic cloves, if you like.

step 3

assemble the **cucumber and ripe olive salad**

1 bag (5 ounces) prewashed European-blend mixed lettuce

1 cup cucumber slices

3/4 cup assorted ripe olives

1/4 cup vinaigrette dressing

Divide the lettuce among 4 salad plates. Top with cucumber slices and olives. Drizzle with dressing. Place the salads on the table.

step 4

heat the **rolls**

4 French or sourdough rolls

Heat the rolls in a toaster oven according to the directions on the package. Wrap in a napkin-lined basket, cover to keep warm, and place on the table.

step 5

serve

1. Put the rice in a large, deep bowl. Spoon the paella over the top and serve.

2. When ready for dessert, rinse the cherries lightly, shake to dry, and place in a basket. Serve with chocolate wafers.

Paella in a Flash
Single serving is 1/4 of the total recipe
CALORIES 347; PROTEIN 31g; CARBS 10g;
TOTAL FAT 20g; SAT FAT 4g; CHOLESTEROL 197mg;
SODIUM 730mg; FIBER 1g

shrimp and broccoli stir-fry

chinese noodles

fresh fruit salad with lime and candied ginger

menu gameplan

shopping list

Chinese egg noodles, fresh or dried

Scallions

Gingerroot

Large shrimp, peeled and deveined

Precut fresh fruit platter

Limes (for juice)

Candied ginger

from the salad bar

Broccoli florets (or from the produce department)

Red pepper slices

from your pantry

Canola oil

Fat-free reduced-sodium chicken broth

Lite soy sauce

Cornstarch

Garlic

Salt and pepper

Dried red pepper flakes

Toasted sesame oil

serves 4

beforeyoustart

Bring the water to a boil in a large pot, covered, over high heat to cook the noodles.

step **1** cook the **chinese noodles**

step **2** make the **shrimp and broccoli stir-fry**

step **3** **serve**

headsup

Chinese noodles come fresh and dried. The fresh are ideally suited for a minutemeal because they are so quick to cook. Look for them in the produce department where Asian ingredients are sold. Failing finding the fresh, use thin dried egg noodles, sold in 16-ounce packages. You could also used fresh or dried angel hair pasta.

"Stir-frying is a wonderful way to cook. I use a wok, but if you don't have one, a large skillet will work just fine."

—minutemeals' Chef Amanda

cook the **chinese noodles**

3 quarts water

1 pound Chinese egg noodles, fresh or dried

1 teaspoon canola oil (optional)

Pour the water into a large pot, cover, and bring to a boil over high heat. Add the noodles, stir to separate, and cook them according to the directions on the package, until just firm to the bite. Drain well, return to the pot, and toss with the oil to prevent sticking, if desired. Keep warm, covered.

make the **shrimp and broccoli stir-fry**

3 cups small broccoli florets

1/2 cup fat-free reduced-sodium chicken broth

2 tablespoons lite soy sauce

1 teaspoon cornstarch

3 scallions

2 garlic cloves

1 tablespoon grated fresh ginger (1 knob [about 3/4 inch long] gingerroot)

2 tablespoons canola oil

1 pound peeled and deveined large shrimp, patted dry

Salt and pepper

1 cup thin red pepper slices

1/2 teaspoon dried red pepper flakes

1 teaspoon toasted sesame oil

1. Arrange the broccoli florets in a microwave-safe dish and add the water. Microwave on High for about 6 minutes, or until just crisp-tender. Let stand until ready to use.

2. In a cup, stir together the chicken broth, soy sauce, and cornstarch until blended. Reserve.

3. Cut the scallions on the diagonal into 1-inch pieces. Finely chop the garlic. Grate enough fresh ginger to measure 1 tablespoon.

4. In a wok or large skillet, heat 1 tablespoon of the canola oil over medium-high heat until hot. Add the shrimp and stir-fry for 2 minutes, or until pink. Season with salt and pepper and remove to a plate with a slotted spoon.

5. Add the remaining 1 tablespoon canola oil to the wok and heat until hot. Add the scallions, garlic, ginger, and red pepper slices and stir-fry for 30 seconds, until fragrant.

6. Stir the broth mixture, add it to the wok with the pepper flakes, shrimp, and broccoli and cook, tossing, for 2 minutes, or until thickened and bubbly and all the ingredients are heated through. Remove from the heat. Add the sesame oil and toss well to combine.

serve

1. Transfer the shrimp and broccoli stir-fry to a platter. Place on the table.

2. Arrange a serving of noodles on each of 4 dinner plates to serve as a bed for the stir-fry.

3. When ready for dessert, sprinkle fresh lime over the fruit platter. Put the candied ginger in a bowl to serve as an accompaniment with the fruit.

Shrimp and Broccoli Stir-Fry
Single serving is 1/4 of the total recipe
CALORIES 389; PROTEIN 31g; CARBS 50g;
TOTAL FAT 6g; SAT FAT 1g; CHOLESTEROL 173mg;
SODIUM 493mg; FIBER 5g
Nutrient Analysis includes a serving of noodles.

microwave shrimp creole

new potatoes with scallions
green salad with blue cheese
banana splits à la minute

menu
gameplan

shopping list

Prewashed mixed spring or baby greens

Crumbled blue cheese

New potatoes (ready-to-cook, if available)

Reduced-fat sour cream

Stewed tomatoes

Large shrimp, cooked, peeled, and deveined

Lemon (for juice)

Ripe bananas

Ice cream flavors of choice

Instant whipped cream

Marachino cherries

from the salad bar

Chopped scallions

Onion slices

Green pepper slices

Celery sticks (or from the produce department)

from your pantry

Olive oil

White wine vinegar

Salt and pepper

Garlic

Cornstarch

Creole seasoning

Tabasco sauce

Chocolate sauce

serves 4

step **1** assemble the **green salad with blue cheese**

step **2** make the **new potatoes with scallions**

step **3** make the **microwave shrimp creole**

step **4** **serve**

There are ready-to-cook new potatoes sold in airtight bags in the produce section of most supermarkets. Scrubbed and trimmed and set to go, they are a tremendous help to the busy cook.

"I used a traditional Creole seasoning blend in this shrimp dish, which explains why it is so flavorful in only 20 minutes."

—minutemeals' Chef Miriam

step 1

assemble the **green salad with blue cheese**

1 bag (5 ounces) prewashed mixed spring or baby greens

1/4 cup crumbled blue cheese

Olive oil to taste

White wine vinegar to taste

Place the salad greens n a salad bowl, add the blue cheese and olive and vinegar to taste, and toss to combine. Place the bowl on the table.

step 2

make the **new potatoes with scallions**

1 1/2 pounds ready-to-cook new potatoes

Salt and pepper to taste

1/3 cup chopped scallions

4 teaspoons reduced-fat sour cream, for serving

1. Put the potatoes in a medium saucepan and add water to cover. Bring to a boil over high heat. Reduce the heat to medium and cook for 10 to 12 minutes, or until fork-tender. Drain and transfer to a serving dish. Add salt and pepper.

2. While the potatoes are cooking, finely chop the scallion greens. Sprinkle them over the hot potatoes, toss, and cover to keep warm.

step 3

make the **microwave shrimp creole**

2 garlic cloves

1 cup onion slices

1 cup green pepper slices

1/2 cup celery sticks

2 to 3 teaspoons Creole seasoning, or to taste

Salt and pepper to taste

1 tablespoon olive oil

3 tablespoons water

1 tablespoon cornstarch

1 can (14 1/2 ounces) stewed tomatoes, undrained

1 pound cooked, peeled, and deveined large shrimp, patted dry

3 scallions

Fresh lemon juice to taste

Tabasco sauce (optional)

1. Slice the garlic and put it in a food processor. Add the onion slices, pepper slices, and celery, and pulse until coarsely chopped. Scrape the mixture into a 2 1/2-quart microwave-safe casserole with lid.

2. Add the Creole seasoning, salt and pepper, and olive oil; stir to combine. Cover and microwave on High, stirring once, for 5 minutes.

3. In a cup, stir together the water and cornstarch.

4. Add the tomatoes, including the liquid, and the cornstarch mixture to the vegetables. Cover and microwave on High, stirring once, for 5 minutes.

5. Add the shrimp and stir to combine. Cover and microwave on High, stirring once, for 3 to 4 minutes, or until the shrimp are heated through and the sauce is flavorful.

6. While the casserole is cooking, slice the whole scallions. Remove the casserole from the microwave and add lemon juice and Tabasco, if desired. Sprinkle the scallions over all.

step 4

serve

1. Place the shrimp Creole on the table with the scallion potatoes. Serve the sour cream in a small bowl for spooning on the potatoes while they are warm, if desired.

2. When ready for dessert, make banana splits: Halve each banana lengthwise and put in a bowl. Top with ice creams of choice, chocolate sauce, whipped cream (and don't forget the cherry). Serve.

Microwave Shrimp Creole
Single serving is 1/4 of the total recipe
CALORIES 195; PROTEIN 25g; CARBS 12g;
TOTAL FAT 6g; SAT FAT 1g; CHOLESTEROL 221mg;
SODIUM 549mg; FIBER 2g

☆ shrimp scampi

saffron rice
sautéed lemon spinach
icy mandarin oranges and chocolate-covered cookies

menu gameplan

serves 4

beforeyoustart
Place the dessert bowls and cans of mandarin oranges in the freezer until serving time.

step **1** cook the **saffron rice**

step **2** while the rice is cooking, make the **shrimp scampi**

step **3** sauté the **lemon spinach**

step **4** serve

shopping list

Saffron threads or ground turmeric

Fresh parsley

Large shrimp, peeled and deveined

Lemons (for juice and zest)

Prewashed spinach

Mandarin oranges

Chocolate cookies

from your pantry

Salt and pepper

Long-grain rice

Garlic

Butter

Extra virgin olive oil

Brandy

luckyforyou
Shrimp comes in a variety of sizes and states of readiness for cooking. If you want to shave time off shopping for this menu, consider stocking frozen peeled and deveined shrimp, frequently sold in 2-pound bags in many supermarkets, as a freezer staple. Not only are they on hand when you need them, they sometimes are cheaper than the same-size ones sold on ice in the fish case.

"This is a wonderful menu for company. The garlic sauce for the shrimp, though, stops conversation—it smells so delicious."

—minutemeals' Chef Connie

step 1

cook the **saffron rice**

1/2 teaspoon saffron threads or
1/4 teaspoon ground turmeric

1/2 teaspoon salt

1 cup long-grain rice

1. In a small bowl, break up the saffron threads with a small spoon.

2. In a medium saucepan, bring 2 cups water to a boil over high heat. Add 1 tablespoon of the boiling water to the pulverized saffron and set aside.

3. Add the salt to the water, then stir in the rice. Cover, lower the heat, and simmer 15 to 18 minutes, until the water is absorbed. When the rice is tender, with a fork, stir in the saffron water and combine gently to avoid breaking up the rice. Keep warm.

step 2

while the rice is cooking, make the **shrimp scampi**

6 to 8 garlic cloves

2 tablespoons chopped
fresh parsley

2 tablespoons butter

2 tablespoons extra virgin olive oil

1 1/4 pounds peeled and
deveined large shrimp,
patted dry

2 tablespoons brandy

2 tablespoons fresh lemon juice
(1/2 large lemon)

Salt and pepper to taste

1. Finely chop the garlic. Chop enough parsley to measure 2 tablespoons.

2. In a large nonstick skillet, melt the butter with the olive oil over medium-high heat. Reduce the heat to low and add the minced garlic; cook, stirring, until fragrant. Do not let it brown. Add the shrimp, raise the heat to medium, and cook, stirring, until they turn pink. Add the brandy, lemon juice, and salt and pepper. Stir to combine, remove the pan from the heat, and stir in the parsley. Cover and keep warm.

step 3

sauté the **lemon spinach**

1/2 teaspoon lemon zest
(1 large lemon)

2 teaspoons olive oil

1 pound prewashed spinach

Salt and pepper to taste

1. Grate enough lemon zest to measure 1/2 teaspoon.

2. In a large nonstick high-sided skillet, heat the olive oil over medium-high heat. In 2 batches, add the spinach and toss to coat with the oil. Cook, stirring, about 1 minute, just until the spinach is wilted. Transfer to a bowl. (Avoid over-cooking the spinach—it will lose all of its volume and become watery.) Add the lemon zest, season with salt and pepper, and toss to combine.

step 4

serve

1. Divide the saffron rice among 4 dinner plates and either serve the shrimp, with plenty of the garlic sauce, on the rice or alongside. Serve with the lemon spinach.

2. When ready for dessert, divide the mandarin orange sections, along with some of their juice, among the chilled bowls. Serve at once with chocolate cookies.

Shrimp Scampi
Single serving is 1/4 of the total recipe
CALORIES 281; PROTEIN 29g; CARBS 4g;
TOTAL FAT 16g; SAT FAT 1g; CHOLESTEROL 230mg;
SODIUM 254mg; FIBER 0g

spicy shrimp in garlic broth

couscous

tomato and red onion salad

strawberries and blueberries with orange sorbet

shopping list

Lager beer or dry white wine

Fresh oregano

Large shrimp, peeled and deveined

Lemon juice

Couscous, plain or flavored

Strawberries

Blueberries

Orange sorbet

from the salad bar

Tomato slices

Red onion slices

Chopped scallions

from your pantry

Garlic

Olive oil

Fat-free reduced-sodium chicken broth

Worcestershire sauce

Dried red pepper flakes

Salt and pepper

Balsamic vinegar (optional)

Grand Marnier (optional)

serves 4

beforeyoustart

Bring the chicken broth or water to a boil in a saucepan over high heat.

step **1** make the **spicy shrimp in garlic broth**

step **2** prepare the **couscous**

step **3** assemble the **tomato and red onion salad**

step **4** prepare the **strawberries and blueberries with orange sorbet**

step **5** **serve**

 Peeled and deveined shrimp are available fresh or frozen. If you are using the frozen variety, there is no need to defrost them before adding them to the pan.

"I love this menu. It's filled with marvelous ingredients, all of which are light. You eat well, and leave the table satisfied, not stuffed."

—minutemeals' Chef Miriam

step 1

make the **spicy shrimp in garlic broth**

2 garlic cloves

1 tablespoon olive oil

3/4 cup lager beer or dry white wine

3/4 cup fat-free reduced-sodium chicken broth

1 teaspoon Worcestershire sauce

1/4 teaspoon dried red pepper flakes, or to taste

1 1/2 teaspoons minced fresh oregano or 1/2 teaspoon dried

1 pound peeled and deveined large shrimp, patted dry

Salt to taste

Fresh lemon juice to taste

1. Crush the garlic cloves with the flat side of a large knife.

2. In a large skillet, cook the garlic in the olive oil over medium heat, stirring, until golden. Add the beer or wine, chicken broth, Worcestershire sauce, and pepper flakes. Cover the skillet and simmer for 5 minutes.

3. Meanwhile, mince enough fresh oregano to measure 1 1/2 teaspoons.

4. Add the shrimp, oregano, and salt to taste to the skillet and stir to combine. Cover and simmer, stirring occasionally, for 3 minutes, or until the shrimp are pink and just firm to the touch. Season with the lemon juice. Remove the pan from the heat.

step 2

prepare the **couscous**

1 can (14 1/2 ounces) fat-free reduced-sodium chicken broth or 1 3/4 cups water

1 tablespoon olive oil

1 box (5.7 ounces) plain or flavored couscous

In a medium saucepan, bring the chicken broth or water and olive oil to a boil, covered. Stir in the couscous. Cover and remove the pan from the heat. Let stand for 5 minutes, until the liquid is absorbed.

step 3

assemble the **tomato and red onion salad**

Tomato slices for 4

Salt and fresh pepper to taste

Red onion slices for 4

About 1/4 cup chopped scallions

Olive oil for drizzling

Balsamic vinegar (optional)

On a platter, arrange the tomato slices, overlapping slightly. Season with salt and fresh ground pepper to taste. Scatter the red onion slices on top and sprinkle with the scallions. Drizzle with olive oil and a little vinegar, if desired. Place the platter on the table, with 4 salad plates.

step 4

prepare the **strawberries and blueberries with orange sorbet**

1/2 pint strawberries

1/2 pint blueberries

Grand Marnier to taste (optional)

1 pint orange sorbet

1. Rinse the strawberries, hull, and quarter. Place in a bowl.

2. Rinse the blueberries, pick them over, and add to the strawberries. Sprinkle with Grand Marnier or another orange-flavored liqueur, if desired.

step 5

serve

1. Place a mound of the hot couscous in 4 large pasta bowls, and top with some of the shrimp, and spoon some of the broth over all.

2. Serve the salad with the shrimp.

3. When ready for dessert, scoop orange sorbet into each bowl and top with the mixed berries.

Spicy Shrimp in Garlic Broth
Single serving is 1/4 of the total recipe
CALORIES 376; PROTEIN 29g; CARBS 33g;
TOTAL FAT 10g; SAT FAT 1g; CHOLESTEROL 173mg;
SODIUM 201mg; FIBER 2g

Nutrient Analysis includes a serving of couscous.

sweet-and-sour shrimp

in pineapple shells

sugar snap pea salad

crusty dinner rolls

butter pecan ice cream
with pecan cookies

menu gameplan

shopping list

Pineapples

Apricot preserves

Jumbo shrimp, peeled and deveined

Sugar snap peas

Prewashed Asian-style salad greens

Soy or sesame vinaigrette

Butter pecan ice cream

Pecan cookies

from the salad bar

Green pepper slices

Chopped scallions

from your pantry

Cider vinegar

Lite soy sauce

Butter

Ground ginger

serves 4

beforeyoustart

Preheat the oven to 300°F.

step **1** cook the **sweet-and-sour shrimp in pineapple shells**

step **2** assemble the **sugar snap pea salad**

step **3** **serve**

headsup Ripe fresh pineapple has the sweetest taste and best texture. In another words, it's what you want. Plan ahead and start looking for a ripe pineapple in the market a few days ahead of making this menu. The fruit should have a deep, rich aroma and yield slightly when pressed on the bottom. If a whole fruit is not an option, use the precut fresh pineapple, available on ice in most produce sections, instead. Or, try canned pineapple, another reliable substitute. About serving the shrimp on the pineapple shells, well, that will have to wait until another time.

"Here is a main dish that is Chinese inspired but requires almost none of the chopping that deters many a harried cook."

—minutemeals' Chef Joanne

make the **sweet-and-sour shrimp in pineapple shells**

2 small (1¹/₂ to 2 pounds) fresh ripe pineapples, halved lengthwise through frond or 1 large (3¹/₂ to 4 pounds) pineapple, quartered through frond

1 cup green pepper slices

¹/₂ cup apricot preserves

1 tablespoon cider vinegar

1 tablespoon lite soy sauce

1 teaspoon ground ginger

2 tablespoons butter

1 pound peeled and deveined jumbo shrimp, patted dry

¹/₂ cup chopped scallions

1. Preheat the oven to 300°F. With a curved grapefruit knife or a small serrated knife, cut the pineapple flesh from the pineapple shell, leaving a ¹/₂-inch-thick shell and the fronds still attached. Place the shells with the fronds attached on a rimmed baking sheet and warm in the oven until ready to serve.

2. Remove and discard the cores from the pieces of pineapple. Cut the cored pineapple pieces into ³/₄-inch pieces. Reserve 2 cups of pieces; wrap and refrigerate any extra pieces for another use. Coarsely chop the green pepper.

3. In a measuring cup, combine the apricot preserves, cider vinegar, soy sauce, and ginger, stirring well.

4. In a large nonstick skillet, melt the butter over medium-high heat. Add the shrimp, green pepper, and scallions. Cook, stirring, for 4 to 5 minutes, or until the shrimp are cooked through. Stir in the reserved pineapple chunks and toss for 1 minute.

5. Pour the apricot sauce over the shrimp mixture and cook, stirring, until the sauce bubbles and the pineapple is heated. Remove the pan from the heat.

assemble the **sugar snap pea salad**

1¹/₂ cups (about 6 ounces) stringed sugar snap peas

1 bag (5 ounces) prewashed Asian-style salad greens

Soy or sesame vinaigrette

1. Rinse the sugar snap peas and pat dry.

2. Divide the salad greens among 4 chilled salad plates. Top with the sugar snap peas and drizzle with the dressing of choice. Place the salads on the table.

serve

1. Remove the ice cream from the freezer to soften in time for dessert. Put the cookies on a serving plate.

2. Transfer the pineapple shells to 4 dinner plates, draining any juice that has collected into the shrimp mixture. Stir the shrimp mixture and, with a slotted spoon, divide among the pineapple shells. Transfer any sauce remaining in the skillet to a small bowl. Place the plates and sauce on the table.

3. When ready for dessert, serve the ice cream in small bowls with the cookies.

Sweet-and-Sour Shrimp in Pineapple Shells
Single serving is ¹/₄ of the total recipe

CALORIES 415; PROTEIN 25g; CARBS 58g; TOTAL FAT 9g; SAT FAT 0g; CHOLESTEROL 187mg; SODIUM 306mg; FIBER 4g

minute

20-minute gourmet

pasta and grain menus

meals

menus

capellini
with ham and asparagus
roasted red pepper and red onion salad
amaretto ice cream with amaretti cookies

shopping list

Fresh parsley (optional)

Fresh thyme

Jarred roasted red peppers

Capellini

Asparagus

Cooked ham, such as Westphalian, prosciutto, or Black Forest

Sun-dried tomato paste

Amaretto ice cream

Amaretti cookies

from the salad bar

Red onion slices

Prewashed romaine leaves

from your pantry

Extra virgin olive oil

Balsamic vinegar

Salt and pepper

Grated Parmesan cheese

Fat-free reduced-sodium chicken broth

serves 4

beforeyoustart

Bring the water to a boil in a large pot, covered, over high heat to cook the pasta.

step 1 make the **roasted red pepper and red onion salad**

step 2 cook the **pasta;** make the **sauce**

step 3 **serve**

 Ham, a cut of meat from a hog's hind leg, is processed in many ways. Their individual flavors can be attributed to a number of factors. Westphalian ham is produced from pigs raised on acorns and is cured before being smoked over beechnut wood and juniper branches. Prosciutto comes from pigs fed on chestnuts and whey (the by-product of cheese-making). The leg is seasoned, salt-cured, and then air-dried. Prosciutto and Westphalian ham are available in the deli section of large supermarkets or at specialty markets.

> *"Ham and asparagus make a wonderful combination. The beauty of a pairing like this is that, unlike a lot of other pasta dishes, it's light."*
>
> —minutemeals' Chef Hillary

step 1

make the **roasted red pepper and red onion salad**

1/3 cup chopped fresh parsley (optional)

1/2 teaspoon chopped fresh thyme or 1/4 teaspoon dried

1 jar (12 ounces) roasted red peppers

1/2 cup thin red onion slices

1 tablespoon extra virgin olive oil

2 teaspoons balsamic vinegar

Salt and pepper to taste

4 large prewashed romaine leaves

1. If using parsley, chop enough to measure 1/3 cup. Chop enough fresh thyme to measure 1/2 teaspoon. Drain the roasted red peppers and cut them into thin strips.

2. In a medium bowl, combine the parsley, if using, the sliced peppers, red onion, thyme, olive oil, and vinegar, and season with salt and pepper. Toss well.

3. Place 1 romaine leaf on each of 4 salad plates. Top with the salad, dividing it equally. Place the salads on the table.

step 2

cook the **pasta;** make the **sauce**

For the pasta

4 quarts water

Salt to taste

1 pound fresh capellini

1 bunch (1 pound) thin asparagus

1/2 cup grated Parmesan cheese

For the sauce

1/2 pound cooked ham, such as Westphalian, prosciutto, or Black Forest, in 1 piece

4 to 6 tablespoons olive oil

2 tablespoons sun-dried tomato paste

2 cups fat-free reduced-sodium chicken broth

1. Cook the pasta: Pour the water into a large pot, salt lightly, and cover. Bring to a boil over high heat.

2. While the water is heating, trim 1 inch off the ends of the asparagus stalks. Cut the stalks into 1-inch lengths.

3. Add the capellini to the boiling water, stir to separate the strands, and cook about 2 minutes. Add the asparagus, bring the water back to a boil, and boil about 1 to 2 minutes, depending upon the thickness of the stalks, until the asparagus is crisp-tender and the capellini is cooked

al dente. Drain in a colander. Return the pasta and asparagus to the pot and keep warm, covered.

4. Make the sauce: Cut the ham into 1/4-inch cubes.

5. In a 12-inch nonstick skillet, heat the olive oil over high heat. Add the ham and cook, stirring constantly, for 2 minutes. Add the tomato paste and stir to coat the ham. Stir in the chicken broth, bring the mixture to a boil, and simmer for 5 minutes, until slightly thickened.

6. Pour the sauce over the capellini and asparagus, and toss well to combine.

step 3

serve

1. Divide the pasta evenly among 4 pasta bowls. Sprinkle with the grated Parmesan and serve immediately.

2. When ready for dessert, scoop the ice cream into dessert bowls, garnish with 2 amaretti cookies per serving, and serve.

Capellini with Ham and Asparagus
Single serving is 1/4 of the total recipe

CALORIES 742; PROTEIN 33g; CARBS 90g; TOTAL FAT 27g; SAT FAT 5g; CHOLESTEROL 36mg; SODIUM 974mg; FIBER 3g

⭐ fettuccine alfredo

roasted peppers, marinated artichokes, and olives

semolina bread

sliced oranges with grand marnier and chocolate cookies

menu gameplan

shopping list

Navel oranges

Grand Marnier

Black and green olives

Parmesan cheese in a wedge

Semolina bread

Fettuccine, fresh or dried

Evaporated skimmed milk

Nonfat sour cream

Chocolate cookies

from the salad bar

Roasted peppers

Marinated artichokes

from your pantry

Olive oil

Salt

Freshly ground black pepper

Grated Parmesan cheese

Butter

serves 4

beforeyoustart

Bring the water to a boil in a large pot, covered, over high heat to cook the fettuccine.

step 1 prepare the **sliced oranges with grand marnier**

step 2 plate the **roasted peppers, marinated artichokes, and olives**

step 3 make the **fettuccine alfredo**

step 4 serve

luckyforyou

We've suggested purchasing the ingredients for the antipasto platter from the salad bar at your market. There is, of course, another option that is much less time-consuming. You won't even have to leave the house! Just keep a jar or two of roasted peppers, marinated artichoke hearts, and olives as standard pantry items. Then, it is just a matter of opening the jars and plating.

"The evaporated skimmed milk and nonfat sour cream in this Alfredo sauce makes it lower in fat, but rich-tasting. There's still lots of Parmesan."

—minutemeals' Chef Miriam

step 1

prepare the **sliced oranges with grand marnier**

4 large navel oranges

Grand Marnier to taste

On a rimmed cutting board, cut a small piece of the skin off the bottom of each orange. Holding the orange upright and starting at the top, cut the skin off each orange. Cut the oranges crosswise into thin slices. Arrange, overlapping the slices, on a shallow platter and drizzle with Grand Marnier or another orange-flavored liqueur. Refrigerate until serving time.

step 2

plate the **roasted peppers, marinated artichokes, and olives**

Roasted peppers for 4

Marinated artichokes for 4

Black and green olives

1 wedge of Parmesan cheese

Olive oil for drizzling

Freshly ground black pepper

1. On a serving platter, arrange the roasted peppers, artichokes, and olives. With a vegetable peeler, shave thin slices of the Parmesan and lay them across the top of the vegetables. Place the platter on the table with 4 salad plates, a small bottle of olive oil, and a pepper mill.

2. Place the semolina bread on a bread board and place on the table.

step 3

make the **fettuccine alfredo**

For the pasta

4 quarts water

Salt to taste

12 ounces fettuccine, fresh or dried

For the sauce

1 cup evaporated skimmed milk

1/2 cup nonfat sour cream

1 cup grated Parmesan cheese, plus additional for serving

2 tablespoons butter

Freshly ground pepper to taste

1. Cook the pasta: Pour the water into a large pot, salt lightly, and cover. Bring to a boil over high heat. Add the fettuccine, stir to separate the strands, and cook according to the directions on the package until just *al dente*. Drain well in a colander and return to the pot.

2. Make the sauce: In a medium saucepan, heat the evaporated skimmed milk until hot. Remove the pan from the heat and stir in the sour cream and the Parmesan until thoroughly combined. Add the butter, place the pan over low heat, and cook, stirring, until the butter is melted and the sauce has thickened slightly.

3. Pour the sauce over the pasta, toss to coat the strands, then add a generous amount of fresh black pepper to taste. Toss to combine.

Variations: Add 1 cup cooked green peas, or 2 cups chopped smoked turkey or ham, or one 4-ounce can mushrooms, drained, after tossing. Heat the sauce for an additional minute or two before combining with the pasta.

step 4

serve

1. Serve the fettuccine in pasta bowls, with additional Parmesan for serving at the table.

2. Serve the semolina bread with both the antipasto platter and the fettuccine.

3. When ready for dessert, arrange the cookies on a serving plate and place on the table. Serve the chilled oranges in dessert bowls with any juice that has collected in the serving bowl spooned over the top.

Fettuccine Alfredo
Single serving is 1/4 of the total recipe
CALORIES 532; PROTEIN 29g; CARBS 62g;
TOTAL FAT 17g; SAT FAT 6g; CHOLESTEROL 42mg;
SODIUM 571mg; FIBER 9g

ziti
with fresh herbs, smoked mozzarella, and prosciutto
sliced vine-ripened tomatoes
sourdough baguette
lemon ice

shopping list

Ziti

Smoked mozzarella

Prosciutto

Fresh chives

Fresh parsley

Fresh tarragon

Vine-ripened tomatoes

Sourdough baguette

Lemon ice

from your pantry

Extra virgin olive oil

Butter

Salt and pepper

Coarse salt

serves 4

beforeyoustart

Bring the water to a boil in a large pot, covered, over high heat to cook the ziti. Preheat oven to 400°F to heat the bread.

step **1** cook the **ziti;** make the **smoked mozzarella** and **prosciutto**

step **2** prepare the **sliced vine-ripened tomatoes**

step **3** heat the **sourdough baguette**

step **4** **serve**

 Smoked mozzarella, which used to be a specialty item, is available at most large supermarkets in the foreign cheese selection. If you cannot find smoked mozzarella, substitute regular mozzarella.

"This pasta dish is so versatile. Serve it hot or at room temperature, or as a salad or as a casserole."

—minutemeals' Chef Hillary

step 1

cook the **ziti**; make the **smoked mozzarella** and **prosciutto**

For the pasta

4 quarts water

Salt to taste

1 pound ziti

For the sauce

8 ounces smoked mozzarella

4 ounces prosciutto, in 1 piece

2 tablespoons chopped fresh chives

2 tablespoons chopped fresh parsley

1 tablespoon chopped fresh tarragon

3 tablespoons extra virgin olive oil

2 tablespoons butter

Salt and pepper to taste

1. Cook the pasta: Pour the water into a large pot, salt lightly, and cover. Bring to a boil over high heat. Add the ziti, stir to separate, and cook according to the directions on the package for *al dente*. Drain well, return to the pot, and keep warm, covered.

2. Make the sauce: Dice the smoked mozzarella and prosciutto.

3. Snip enough chives to measure 2 tablespoons; chop enough parsley to measure 2 tablespoons and enough fresh tarragon to measure 1 tablespoon. Place the herbs in a large serving bowl with the olive oil and butter.

step 2

prepare the **sliced vine-ripened tomatoes**

4 medium-to-large vine-ripened tomatoes

Coarse salt to taste

Rinse the tomatoes and cut them into thin slices. Arrange the slices on a serving platter and sprinkle with coarse salt. Place the platter on the table.

step 3

heat the **sourdough baguette**

1 sourdough baguette

1/3 cup extra virgin olive oil

1. Preheat the oven to 400°F. Place the baguette in the oven for 4 to 5 minutes, or until heated.

2. Meanwhile, pour the olive oil into a small shallow bowl and place on the table.

step 4

serve

1. Add the ziti to the serving bowl with the butter, oil, and fresh herbs and toss until well coated. Add the prosciutto and mozzarella and toss until distributed. Season with salt and freshly ground black pepper and toss one final time.

2. Divide the pasta evenly among 4 pasta bowls and place on the table.

3. Transfer the bread to a cutting board and place on the table. To serve, cut or tear into pieces. The olive oil serves as a "dip" for the bread.

4. When ready for dessert, scoop the lemon ice into dessert bowls and serve.

Ziti with Fresh Herbs, Smoked Mozzarella, and Prosciutto
Single serving is 1/4 of the total recipe
CALORIES 833; PROTEIN 33g; CARBS 84g;
TOTAL FAT 40g; SAT FAT 8g; CHOLESTEROL 55mg;
SODIUM 882mg; FIBER 2g

fettuccine
with smoked salmon and dill

romaine with red onion and orange salad
semolina bread
chocolate-covered strawberries

shopping list

Fresh spinach fettuccine

Fresh egg fettuccine

Shallot

Tomato

Fresh dill

Sliced smoked salmon

Capers (optional)

Dry white wine

Heavy cream

Frozen peas

Semolina bread

Prewashed torn hearts of romaine

Honey-Dijon vinaigrette, store-bought or homemade

Chocolate-covered strawberries

from the salad bar

Orange segments

Red onion slices

from your pantry

Salt and pepper

Canola oil

serves 6

beforeyoustart
Bring the water to a boil in a large pot over high heat to cook the pasta. Preheat the oven to 350°F to heat the bread.

step 1 cook the **fettuccine;** prepare the **smoked salmon and dill sauce**

step 2 heat the **semolina bread**

step 3 assemble the **romaine with red onion and orange salad**

step 4 **serve**

headsup
When adding smoked fish to a hot dish, do so at the end of the cooking time. That keeps the integrity of the fish intact. Otherwise the fish gets overcooked, which changes its taste and texture.

"There's no complicated cooking and the ingredients are heavenly. You'll feel like a chef when you make this. Quite an accomplishment for only 20 minutes!"

—minutemeals' Chef Hillary

step 1

cook the **fettuccine**; prepare the **smoked salmon and dill sauce**

For the pasta

4 quarts water

Salt to taste

9 ounces fresh spinach fettuccine

9 ounces fresh egg fettuccine

For the sauce

1 large shallot

1 large tomato

1/3 cup chopped fresh dill or 1 tablespoon dried

12 ounces sliced smoked salmon

1 tablespoon canola oil

2 tablespoons drained capers (optional)

2/3 cup dry white wine

1 cup heavy cream

1 cup frozen peas, thawed

1. Cook the pasta: Pour the water into a large pot, salt lightly, and cover. Bring to a boil over high heat. Add the spinach and egg pasta, stir to separate the strands, and cook, stirring occasionally, for 3 to 5 minutes, or until *al dente*. Drain well in a colander.

2. Make the sauce: Mince the shallot. Rinse and chop the tomato. Snip enough fresh dill with kitchen scissors to measure 1/3 cup. Slice the smoked salmon into strips and set aside covered with a damp paper towel.

3. In a 12-inch nonstick deep skillet, heat the canola oil over high heat until hot. Add the minced shallot and cook, stirring, for 1 minute. Add the capers, if using, and the white wine and bring to a boil. Reduce the wine over high heat for 5 minutes. Add the heavy cream and reduce the mixture for 3 minutes, until the cream is slightly thickened. Remove the pan from heat and add the peas, chopped tomato, and snipped dill.

4. Add the drained hot pasta to the sauce and toss gently to coat. Cover the pan and keep the pasta warm.

step 2

heat the **semolina bread**

1 loaf semolina bread

Preheat the oven to 350°F. Place the bread in the oven and heat for about 5 minutes, or until warmed through. Transfer to a napkin-lined bread basket and place on the table.

step 3

assemble the **romaine with red onion and orange salad**

6 cups prewashed torn hearts of romaine

1 cup orange segments

1/2 cup red onion slices

1/4 cup honey-Dijon vinaigrette

Salt and pepper to taste

In a large salad bowl, combine the romaine, orange segments, onion slices, and vinaigrette. Toss gently to combine, season with salt and pepper, and place the salad bowl, with salad plates, on the table.

step 4

serve

1. At serving time, add the sliced smoked salmon to the pasta and toss gently to combine.

2. Divide the pasta evenly among pasta bowls. Divide the salad among the salad plates and serve with the warm bread.

3. When ready for dessert, arrange the strawberries on a serving plate and serve.

Fettuccine with Smoked Salmon and Dill
Single serving is 1/6 of the total recipe
CALORIES 591; PROTEIN 28g; CARBS 58g;
TOTAL FAT 25g; SAT FAT 11g; CHOLESTEROL 78mg;
SODIUM 776mg; FIBER 10g

fusilli and chicken
with pesto genovese
tomato and scallion salad
miniature fresh fruit tartlettes

shopping list

Fresh basil leaves

Grated Parmigiano-Reggiano cheese

Pine nuts *(pignoli)* or walnuts

Fusilli (corkscrew-shaped pasta)

Skinless boneless chicken breast, cut for stir-fry

Ripe tomatoes

Chopped scallions or red onion slices (from the salad bar)

Miniature fresh fruit tartlettes

from your pantry

Garlic

Salt

Olive oil

Butter

Rice vinegar

Freshly ground black pepper

serves 4

beforeyoustart

Bring the water to a boil in a large pot, covered, over high heat to cook the pasta.

step 1 make the **pesto genovese**

step 2 cook the **fusilli;** cook the **chicken**

step 3 assemble the **tomato and scallion salad**

step 4 **serve**

luckyforyou
You have two excellent options for reducing the prep time by about half: Pesto, Genoa's great basil and garlic sauce, can be bought ready to use. It can also be frozen. Then it is just a matter of thawing it overnight in the refrigerator. That makes this a 10-minute (or so) minutemeal.

"It wouldn't be summer without homemade pesto. The smell of all that fresh basil is just out of this world."

—minutemeals' Chef Linda

step 1

make the **pesto genovese**

2 cups loosely packed fresh basil leaves

2 garlic cloves

1/2 teaspoon salt

1/2 cup grated Parmigiano-Reggiano cheese

2 tablespoons pine nuts or walnuts

3/4 cup olive oil

1 tablespoon butter, at room temperature

1. Remove enough leaves from a bunch of basil to measure 2 cups loosely packed. Rinse and pat dry.

2. In a food processor or blender, combine the basil leaves, garlic, salt, grated cheese, and nuts. Process until chopped and combined. With the machine running, slowly pour in the olive oil. Blend, scraping down the sides of the bowl occasionally, until smooth and the color of the sauce is bright green, with darker flecks. Add the butter and blend until incorporated. Taste for salt and adjust if necessary. Makes about 1 1/2 cups.

step 2

cook the **fusilli**; cook the **chicken**

For the pasta

4 quarts water

Salt to taste

1 pound fusilli

For the chicken

1 tablespoon olive oil

1 pound skinless boneless chicken breast, cut for stir-fry

1 cup Pesto Genovese, or more to taste (see above)

Grated Parmigiano-Reggiano cheese for serving (optional)

1. Pour the water into a large pot, salt lightly, and cover. Bring to a boil over high heat. Add the fusilli, stir to separate, and cook about 8 minutes, or until *al dente*. Before draining, reserve 1 cup of the pasta cooking water. Drain well in a colander.

2. In a large nonstick skillet, heat the olive oil over medium-high heat until hot. Add the chicken strips, season with salt, and cook, turning frequently, about 5 minutes, or until cooked through. Remove the pan from the heat.

3. In a large serving bowl, combine the fusilli, chicken, and the 1 cup of the pesto. Add some of the reserved pasta cooking water, if desired, to make the pesto saucier.

step 3

assemble the **tomato and scallion salad**

2 large ripe tomatoes or 1 1/2 cups small cherry or grape tomatoes

1/2 cup chopped scallions or red onion slices

3 tablespoons rice vinegar

Salt and freshly ground black pepper

1. Rinse the tomatoes and pat dry. With a serrated knife, slice the 2 large tomatoes into thin rounds or halve the cherry or grape tomatoes. Arrange the tomatoes on a platter and sprinkle with the scallions or add the onion slices.

2. Sprinkle the rice vinegar over the salad, and season with salt and fresh pepper. Place the salad on the table.

step 4

serve

1. Place the fusilli and chicken on the table and serve with additional grated cheese and the remaining pesto, if desired.

2. When ready for dessert, place the tartlettes on a serving platter and serve with small dessert plates.

Fusilli and Chicken with Pesto Genovese
Single serving is 1/4 of the total recipe
CALORIES 860; PROTEIN 48g; CARBS 87g; TOTAL FAT 33g; SAT FAT 0g; CHOLESTEROL 84mg; SODIUM 446mg; FIBER 0g

linguine
with quick red clam sauce
bocconcini with arugula
garlic bread
miniature cannoli or italian cookies

menu gameplan

shopping list

Dried linguine

Whole peeled tomatoes

Fresh parsley

Whole or minced clams

Prewashed arugula, stemmed

Ready-to-heat garlic bread

Marinated bocconcini (bite-sized mozzarella balls)

Fresh basil (optional)

Miniature cannoli or Italian cookies

from your pantry

Salt

Freshly ground black pepper

Garlic

Olive oil

Dried red pepper flakes

serves 4 generously

beforeyoustart

Bring the water to a boil in a large pot, covered, over high heat to cook pasta. Preheat oven to 350°F to heat the bread.

step **1** cook the **linguine;** make the **quick red clam sauce**

step **2** heat the **garlic bread**

step **3** plate the **bocconcini with arugula**

step **4** **serve**

luckyforyou
In the fish department of some supermarkets, there are plastic containers of chopped fresh clams in juice, perfect for a clam sauce like this. Drain and use in place of the canned clams here for that special taste of the sea.

"It's quicker to use jarred or canned red clam sauce, but there's nothing like making your own and this one is so easy."

—minutemeals' Chef Katell

step 1

cook the **linguine;** make the **quick red clam sauce**

For the pasta

Salt to taste

1 pound dried linguine

For the sauce

1 can (35 ounces) whole peeled tomatoes

2 large garlic cloves

3 tablespoons chopped parsley, or more to taste

1 can (6.5 to 8 ounces) whole clams or minced clams

2 tablespoons olive oil

Dried red pepper flakes to taste

Salt and freshly ground black pepper to taste

1. Cook the pasta: Pour the water into a large pot, salt lightly, and cover. Bring the water to a boil over high heat. Add the linguine, stir to separate the strands, and cook, stirring, about 10 to 12 minutes, until *al dente*. Drain well in a colander and return to the pot. Keep warm, covered.

2. Make the sauce: Drain the tomatoes, reserving the juice. Chop the garlic. Chop at least 3 tablespoons parsley, or more to taste. Drain the clams, reserving at least 4 tablespoons of the juice.

3. In a large saucepan, heat the olive oil over medium heat until hot. Add the garlic and cook, stirring, until golden; do not let burn.

4. Add the drained tomatoes, breaking them up with the side of a wooden spoon. Stir in the 4 tablespoons clam juice. Bring the mixture to a simmer, then lower the heat to medium-low and cook, stirring occasionally, for 5 minutes, until heated through and combined. Stir in the clams and the chopped parsley and cook for 5 minutes.

5. Add red pepper flakes, salt, and lots of fresh pepper and taste for seasonings. Thin the sauce, if desired, with some of the reserved tomato juice. Remove the pan from the heat and keep warm, covered.

step 2

heat the **garlic bread**

1 loaf ready-to-heat garlic bread

Preheat the oven to 350°F. Heat the bread according to the directions on the package. Transfer to a napkin-lined bread basket and place the basket on the table; cover to keep warm.

step 3

plate the **bocconcini with arugula**

2 ounces prewashed stemmed arugula

1 container (enough for 4) marinated bocconcini

Extra virgin olive oil (optional)

Fresh basil (optional)

Freshly ground black pepper to taste

1. Line a shallow serving bowl with the arugula.

2. Top with the bocconcini and drizzle with a little olive oil, if desired.

3. Chop the basil, if using, and sprinkle it over the mozzarella balls. Grind fresh pepper over all. Place the salad bowl with salad plates on the table.

step 4

serve

1. Divide the hot linguine among 4 pasta bowls and ladle clam sauce over each. Serve at once.

2. When ready for dessert, place the pastries on a platter and serve with small dessert plates.

Linguine with Quick Red Clam Sauce
Single serving is ¹/₄ of the total recipe

CALORIES 638; PROTEIN 31g; CARBS 102g; TOTAL FAT 10g; SAT FAT 1g; CHOLESTEROL 33mg; SODIUM 117mg; FIBER 4g

macaroni and cheese
with broccoli and corn

green salad with herb vinaigrette

rainbow sherbet and sugar cookies

shopping list

Broccoli florets (from the salad bar or produce department)

Boxed macaroni and cheese

Frozen corn

Grated Cheddar cheese

Prewashed mixed salad greens

Herbed vinaigrette dressing, store-bought or homemade

Rainbow sherbet

Sugar cookies

from your pantry

Salt

Butter (for casserole)

Milk

serves 4

beforeyoustart

Bring the water to a boil in a large saucepan, covered, over high heat to cook the macaroni. Preheat the broiler.

step **1** make the **macaroni and cheese with broccoli and corn**

step **2** assemble the **green salad with herb vinaigrette**

step **3** **serve**

luckyforyou Broccoli also comes chopped frozen. When you don't have the time to chop fresh florets, use frozen instead.

"Macaroni and cheese is comfort food. And when you add vegetables, as in this version, it's a one-pot meal. It makes a perfect Sunday night supper."

—minutemeals' Chef Miriam

step 1

make the **macaroni and cheese with broccoli and corn**

2 cup loosely packed broccoli florets

2 quarts water, plus 3 cups

Salt to taste

1 box (14 ounces) macaroni and cheese

1 cup frozen corn

1/4 cup milk

1/2 cup grated Cheddar cheese

1. Preheat the broiler. Butter a 2-quart casserole.

2. Coarsely chop the broccoli florets.

3. Pour the 2 quarts water into a 3-quart saucepan, salt lightly, and cover. Bring to a boil, over high heat. Add the macaroni, stir to separate, and cook for 8 to 10 minutes, or until cooked to taste. When the macaroni is almost done, add the corn and cook until warmed through. Drain in a colander and transfer it to a medium bowl.

4. In another saucepan, bring the 3 cups water, covered, to a boil over high heat. Add the chopped broccoli and cook for 3 minutes, or until crisp. Drain and add to the macaroni mixture.

5. In a small saucepan, combine the packet of cheese sauce with the milk and heat over low heat, stirring, until smooth. Add to the macaroni and stir to combine.

6. Pour the macaroni mixture into the prepared casserole. Sprinkle the Cheddar over the top. Broil for 4 to 5 minutes, or until the cheese is melted and golden brown.

step 2

assemble the **green salad with herb vinaigrette**

1 bag (5 ounces) prewashed mixed salad greens of choice

1/4 cup herbed vinaigrette dressing

Put the greens in a salad bowl, add the dressing, and toss. Put the bowl on the table.

step 3

serve

1. Place the casserole on the table.

2. When ready for dessert, scoop the sherbet into dessert bowls and serve with the sugar cookies.

Macaroni and Cheese with Broccoli and Corn
Single serving is 1/4 of the total recipe
CALORIES 456; PROTEIN 16g; CARBS 51g;
TOTAL FAT 21g; SAT FAT 7g; CHOLESTEROL 27mg;
SODIUM 719mg; FIBER 2g

rosy macaroni and cheese

carrot and celery sticks

whole-grain rolls

fresh fruit popsicles

menu
gameplan

shopping list

Elbow macaroni

Crushed tomatoes

Carrot and celery sticks
(from the salad bar or the
produce department)

Whole-grain rolls

Fresh fruit Popsicles

from your pantry

Butter

All-purpose flour

Lowfat (1%) milk

Grated Parmesan cheese

Pepper

serves 6

beforeyoustart

Bring the water to a boil in a large
saucepan, covered, over high heat to
cook the macaroni.

step 1 cook the **macaroni;**
make the **sauce**

step 2 plate the **vegetable
sticks**

step 3 **serve**

luckyforyou The rosy macaroni is the
only dish that has to be
cooked in the entire menu. Make the sauce ahead and
you will be way ahead of the time curve for prepping
this meal.

"Kids like this rendition of an old favorite. I like to make this fun—try substituting shaped pasta, like dinosaurs, for a new twist."

—minutemeals' Chef Miriam

step 1

cook the **macaroni**; make the **sauce**

For the pasta

3 quarts water

12 ounces elbow macaroni

For the sauce

3 tablespoons butter

1/4 cup all-purpose flour

2 cups lowfat (1%) milk

1 cup grated Parmesan cheese, plus additional for serving, if desired

1 can (15 ounces) crushed tomatoes

1/4 teaspoon pepper

1. Make the pasta: Pour the water into a large pot, cover, and bring to a boil over high heat. Add the macaroni, stir to separate, and cook according to the package directions, until *al dente*. Drain in a colander.

2. Make the sauce: In a large saucepan, melt the butter over medium heat. Stir in the flour and cook, stirring, for 3 minutes. Add the milk and bring to a simmer. Cook, stirring, for 3 minutes, or until thickened. Stir in the Parmesan, crushed tomatoes, and pepper and combine well. Simmer, stirring occasionally, for 5 minutes.

3. Add the macaroni to the tomato-cheese sauce and stir to combine. Cook, stirring, for 2 to 3 minutes, until heated through. Remove from the heat and keep warm, covered.

step 2

plate the **vegetable sticks**

Carrot and celery sticks for 6

Arrange the carrot and celery sticks on a plate and place on the table.

step 3

serve

1. Put the rolls in a bread basket and place on the table.

2. Serve the macaroni in pasta bowls, with additional Parmesan, if desired.

3. When ready for dessert, serve the Popsicles directly from the freezer.

Rosy Macaroni and Cheese
Single serving is 1/6 of the total recipe
CALORIES 398; PROTEIN 18g; CARBS 61g; TOTAL FAT 9g; SAT FAT 4g; CHOLESTEROL 24mg; SODIUM 538mg; FIBER 1g

microwave cheese manicotti
with marinara sauce

mixed green salad

olive bread

lime sherbet with raspberries

serves 4

shopping list

Manicotti shells

Ricotta cheese

Grated lite mozzarella

Prewashed mixed spring or baby greens

Packaged croutons

Italian olive bread

Lime sherbet

Frozen raspberries

from your pantry

Salt and pepper

Olive oil

Garlic

Egg

Dried oregano

Dried thyme

Marinara sauce

Salad dressing of choice, store-bought or homemade

Grated Parmesan cheese

beforeyoustart

Bring the water to a boil in a large pot, covered, over high heat to cook the manicotti shells. Remove the raspberries from the freezer to thaw.

| step | 1 | cook the **manicotti shells;** fill and bake the **manicotti** |

| step | 2 | assemble the **mixed green salad** |

| step | 3 | **serve** |

luckyforyou

Marinara sauce, jarred or fresh refrigerated, is available in an amazing variety: with garlic, with mushrooms, with sun-dried tomatoes, with pesto added, to name just a few. We keep several different kinds on our kitchen pantry shelves as a matter of course, and think you should, too.

"This is a magic menu—it makes both kids and adults happy. One bite and you know it's a find."

—minutemeals' Chef Hillary

step 1

cook the **manicotti shells;** fill and bake the **manicotti**

For the manicotti shells

4 quarts water

Salt to taste

8 manicotti shells

2 tablespoons olive oil

For the filling

2 garlic cloves

3 cups ricotta cheese

1 cup grated lite mozzarella

1 large egg

1/2 teaspoon dried oregano

1/2 teaspoon dried thyme

Salt and pepper to taste

2 cups jarred marinara sauce

1. Cook the manicotti shells: Pour the water into a large pot, salt lightly, and cover. Bring to a boil over high heat. Add the manicotti shells, stir to distribute, and boil about 6 minutes, or until just *al dente*. Drain in a colander, rinse under running cold water, and drain again. Return the shells to the pot and toss with the olive oil.

2. Make the filling: Finely chop the garlic. In a medium bowl, combine the ricotta, 3/4 cup of the mozzarella, and egg, and blend together well. Stir in the garlic, oregano, thyme, and salt and pepper until combined.

3. Heat the sauce: Microwave the marinara sauce in a microwave-safe measuring cup on High for 2 minutes, or until hot. Remove and keep warm.

4. Fill the shells: Using a spoon, fill each manicotti shell with ricotta filling and place in a single layer in a microwave-safe casserole. Pour the hot marinara sauce over the shells and sprinkle with the remaining 1/4 cup grated mozzarella. Cover the dish with plastic wrap and microwave on High for 5 to 7 minutes, or until heated through and bubbling.

step 2

assemble the **mixed green salad**

1 bag (5 ounces) prewashed mixed spring or baby greens

1/4 cup salad dressing of choice, store-bought or homemade

1/2 cup packaged croutons

2 tablespoons grated Parmesan cheese

Place the greens in a large salad bowl, add the dressing, and toss to coat. Sprinkle with the croutons and grated Parmesan. Place the bowl on the table.

step 3

serve

1. Place the casserole on the table. Serve 2 manicotti with a generous amount of sauce per person. Serve with the bread and salad on the side.

2. When ready for dessert, scoop lime sherbet into dessert bowls and garnish with the raspberries. If there is juice, spoon a little of it over each serving.

Microwave Cheese Manicotti
with Marinara Sauce
Single serving is 1/4 of the total recipe
CALORIES 619; PROTEIN 45g; CARBS 44g;
TOTAL FAT 29g; SAT FAT 6g; CHOLESTEROL 126mg;
SODIUM 1019mg; FIBER 3g

sesame noodles
shrimp with soy mayonnaise
steamed spinach
lemon ice with strawberries

menu
gameplan

shopping list
Fresh linguine

Sesame seeds

Red pepper strips
(from the salad bar)

Lemon

Large shrimp, cooked,
peeled, and deveined

Prewashed spinach leaves

Lemon ice

Strawberries

from your pantry
Butter

Toasted sesame oil

Reduced-fat mayonnaise

Lite soy sauce

Olive oil

Salt and pepper

serves 4

beforeyoustart
Bring the water to a boil in a large pot,
covered, over high to cook the linguine.
Rinse the strawberries.

step 1 make the **sesame noodles**

step 2 prepare the **shrimp with soy mayonnaise**

step 3 steam the **spinach**

step 4 **serve**

headsup
We have included 2 nutrient
analyses for this menu and
here's why: The shrimp constitute the protein in this meal
and therefore warranted analysis. We realized, however,
that some people will make the sesame noodles as a
stand-alone dish and will want to know its nutritional
content per serving as well. Interestingly, if you serve the
noodles with a serving of the shrimp with soy mayonnaise,
the per-serving increase is only 108 calories. And you can
cut back on that very simply. Omit the soy mayonnaise
completely and serve the shrimp on the sesame noodles.

step 1

make the **sesame noodles**

4 quarts water

1 pound fresh linguine

4 tablespoons (1/2 stick) butter

2 tablespoons sesame seeds

1 tablespoon toasted sesame oil

Red pepper strips, for garnish

1. Pour the water into a large pot, cover, and bring to a boil over high heat. Add the linguine, stir to separate the strands, and cook according to the directions on the package until *al dente*, about 3 to 5 minutes. Before draining, reserve 1/2 cup of the pasta cooking water. Drain well in a colander. Return the linguine to the pot and cover.

2. Meanwhile, in a small skillet, melt the butter over medium heat. Add the sesame seeds and sauté them, stirring, until golden. Stir in the sesame oil. Add the sesame butter to the linguine and toss well to combine. (Should you want a bit more sauce, add some of the reserved cooking water and toss.) Cover to keep warm.

step 2

prepare the **shrimp with soy mayonnaise**

1/4 cup reduced-fat mayonnaise

2 teaspoons lite soy sauce, or to taste

Fresh lemon juice to taste

1 pound cooked, peeled, and deveined large shrimp

1. In a small serving bowl, stir the mayonnaise and soy sauce together until combined. Season with fresh lemon juice. Place the bowl in the middle of a large serving platter.

2. Arrange the cooked shrimp around the edge of the platter. Place the platter on the table.

step 3

steam the **spinach**

1 bag (15 ounces) prewashed spinach leaves

Olive oil for drizzling

Salt and pepper to taste

Juice of 1/2 lemon

1. Rinse the prewashed spinach leaves one time in cold running water. Place the spinach leaves in a large saucepan with lid and cover the pan. Put the pan over high heat and steam the spinach in just the water remaining on the leaves. Steam for 3 to 5 minutes, until wilted.

2. Transfer the steamed spinach to a serving bowl and drizzle with olive oil to taste. Season with salt and pepper and toss to combine.

step 4

serve

1. Transfer the sesame noodles to a serving bowl and garnish with the red pepper strips.

2. Just before serving, squeeze fresh lemon juice over the spinach.

3. When ready for dessert, scoop the lemon ice into dessert bowls, garnish with whole strawberries, and serve.

Sesame Noodles
Single serving is 1/4 of the total recipe
CALORIES 497; PROTEIN 15g; CARBS 62g; TOTAL FAT 22g; SAT FAT 1g; CHOLESTEROL 30mg; SODIUM 188mg; FIBER 0g
Nutrient Analysis does not include a serving of shrimp with soy mayonnaise.

Shrimp and Soy Mayonnaise
Single serving is 1/4 of the total recipe
CALORIES 605; PROTEIN 35g; CARBS 63g; TOTAL FAT 25g; SAT FAT 2g; CHOLESTEROL 225mg; SODIUM 1204mg; FIBER 0g
Nutrient Analysis includes a serving of sesame noodles.

orecchiette
with sausage, tomatoes, and beans

insalata mista

roasted pepper bruschette

biscuit tortoni

shopping list

Orecchiette or similar pasta

Onion slices
(from the salad bar)

Turkey sausage

Dry white wine (optional)

Stewed tomatoes

Cannellini beans

Fresh basil

Grated Parmigiano-Reggiano
cheese

Italian bread

Jarred roasted red peppers

Capers

Prewashed mixed salad
greens

Biscuit tortoni

from your pantry

Salt and pepper

Garlic

Olive oil

Dried fennel seeds

Dried oregano

Balsamic vinegar

serves 4

beforeyoustart

Bring the water to a boil in a large
pot, covered, over high heat to cook
the pasta.

| step | 1 | cook the **orecchiette**; make the **sausage, tomatoes, and beans** |

| step | 2 | make the **bruschette** |

| step | 3 | assemble the **insalata mista** |

| step | 4 | **serve** |

 Bruschette are a great way
to use that half a loaf of
bread that keeps ending up being thrown out. Save that
half loaf. Wrap it well in plastic and freeze. When you go
to make bruschette, all you need to do is defrost it and
assemble the rounds.

"This is an incredibly comforting dish. It fills you up and makes you happy—a perfect dish for a brisk winter night."

—minutemeals' Chef Miriam

step 1

cook the **orecchiette**; make the **sausage, tomatoes, and beans**

For the pasta

4 quarts water

Salt to taste

1 pound orecchiette or similar shaped pasta

For the sauce

1 cup onion slices

3 garlic cloves

1 tablespoon olive oil

8 ounces turkey sausage

1/2 cup dry white wine (optional)

1 can (16 ounces) stewed tomatoes, including the liquid

1/2 teaspoon dried fennel seeds

1/2 teaspoon dried oregano

Salt and pepper to taste

1 can (16 ounces) cannellini beans

3 to 4 tablespoons chopped fresh basil or parsley

Grated Parmigiano-Reggiano cheese for serving

1. Cook the pasta: Pour the water into a large pot, salt slightly, and cover. Bring to a boil over high heat. Add the pasta, stir to separate, and cook 6 to 8 minutes, or until tender. Before draining, reserve 1/2 cup of the pasta cooking water. Drain in a colander. Return the pasta to the pot and keep warm.

2. Make the sauce: Finely chop the sliced onions and garlic.

3. In a large deep nonstick skillet, heat the olive oil over medium-high heat until hot. Slice the sausage lengthwise and remove the casing. Add the sausage to the pan, crumbling it with the side of a spoon, and cook, stirring, until it is no longer pink, about 3 minutes. Add the onions and garlic and cook, stirring, for 1 minute. Add the wine and boil for 1 minute. Add the tomatoes, including the liquid, the fennel seeds, oregano, and salt and pepper and stir to combine. Cover and simmer, stirring once, for 8 minutes.

4. While the sauce simmers, rinse and drain the beans. Chop enough fresh basil or parsley to measure up to 4 tablespoons. Add the beans to the sauce, adjust the seasonings, adding more salt and pepper to taste, and cook, stirring, until the beans are heated through.

5. Pour the sauce over the pasta. Toss to combine, adding enough of reserved cooking liquid to thin the sauce as desired. Add the fresh herbs and toss. Cover and keep warm.

step 2

make the **bruschette**

1/2 loaf crusty Italian bread

Olive oil

1 jar (12 ounces) roasted red peppers

2 tablespoons drained capers

Balsamic vinegar to taste

Salt and pepper to taste

Snipped fresh basil for sprinkling

1. Cut the bread into 4 slices, each 1/2 to 3/4 inch thick. Brush one side of each slice with olive oil. Toast in a toaster oven until lightly browned.

2. Drain the roasted peppers and cut into thin strips. In a bowl, combine the pepper strips, capers, a little olive oil and balsamic vinegar, just to taste, and salt and pepper. Top each slice of bread with the roasted pepper mixture and sprinkle with the basil. Arrange the toasts on a plate and put the plate on the table.

step 3

assemble the **insalata mista**

1 bag (5 ounces) prewashed mixed Italian salad greens

Oil and vinegar to taste

Put the greens in a salad bowl, add the oil and vinegar, and toss. Put the salad on the table.

step 4

serve

1. Divide the pasta among pasta bowls and serve with grated cheese for sprinkling over the top.

2. When ready for dessert, serve the ice cream on each dessert plates.

Orechiette with Sausage, Tomatoes, and Beans
Single serving is 1/4 of the total recipe
CALORIES 687; PROTEIN 32; CARBS 113g; TOTAL FAT 12g; SAT FAT 2g; CHOLESTEROL 30mg; SODIUM 1066mg; FIBER 1g

pasta tuna puttanesca

tomato and mozzarella salad

italian bread

fresh figs with marsala

shopping list

Spaghetti, dried or fresh

Tuna steak

Whole peeled Italian tomatoes

Anchovy fillets

Capers

Fresh parsley

Pitted kalamata olives

Fresh basil leaves

Prewashed arugula, stemmed

Fresh mozzarella

Vine-ripened tomatoes

Italian bread

Fresh figs

Marsala

from your pantry

Salt and pepper

Garlic

Extra virgin olive oil

Dried red pepper flakes

Coarse salt

Freshly ground black pepper

serves 4 generously

beforeyoustart

Bring the water to a boil in a large pot, covered, over high heat to cook the pasta.

step **1** cook the **pasta;** make the **tuna puttanesca**

step **2** assemble the **tomato and mozzarella salad**

step **3** **serve**

You can use canned tuna here, if shopping for fresh isn't possible when you want to make this.

"Tuna, anchovies, olives, tomatoes, olive oil—and this sauce is so easy to prepare; just make and serve. Perfect for summer, especially with the salad."

—minutemeals' Chef Katell

step 1

cook the **pasta;** make the **tuna puttanesca**

For the pasta

4 quarts water

Salt to taste

1 pound spaghetti

For the puttanesca sauce

3/4 pound fresh tuna steak

1 can (35 ounces) whole peeled Italian tomatoes

3 anchovy fillets, or to taste

3 garlic cloves

Olive oil, as needed

Dried red pepper flakes

2 tablespoons drained capers

2 tablespoons minced parsley

1 cup pitted kalamata olives

Salt and pepper to taste

1. Cook the pasta: Pour the water into a large pot, salt lightly, and cover. Bring to a boil over high heat. Add the pasta, stir to separate the strands, and cook according to the directions on the package, until *al dente*. Drain well in a colander. Return to the pot and keep warm, covered.

2. Meanwhile, make the puttanesca sauce: Pat the tuna steak dry with paper towels and cut it into 3/4-inch cubes. Drain the tomatoes in a sieve. Rinse the 3 anchovy fillets; pat them dry with a paper towel. Chop the garlic cloves, if using.

3. In a large nonstick skillet, heat 1 tablespoon of oil over medium heat until hot. Add the cubed tuna and sauté it, turning it gently, until cooked through and slightly colored. Remove to a plate.

4. Add 1 tablespoon more oil to the pan and heat until hot. Add the garlic and cook, stirring, until golden. Add the anchovy fillets and break them up until they form a paste. Add red pepper flakes to taste. Add the drained tomatoes and stir them in, breaking them up. Lower the heat to medium-low and cook, stirring occasionally, for 5 to 7 minutes.

5. Stir in the capers and cook for 3 to 5 minutes.

6. While the sauce simmers, mince 2 tablespoons parsley. Add the tuna and olives to the sauce and stir to combine; cook 2 to 3 minutes, or just until heated through. Remove the pan from the heat, taste for seasoning, and add salt, pepper, and more red pepper flakes, if desired. Pour the sauce over the hot pasta and toss to coat.

step 2

assemble the **tomato and mozzarella salad**

8 to 10 basil leaves

4 ounces prewashed stemmed arugula

8 ounces fresh mozzarella

2 vine-ripened medium tomatoes

Coarse salt

Extra virgin olive oil for drizzling

Freshly ground black pepper

1. Rinse and pat the basil leaves dry.

2. Spread the arugula on a platter. Roll the 8 basil leaves up into a tight cylinder and, with kitchen scissors, cut the cylinder into thin slices over the arugula.

3. With a serrated knife, cut the mozzarella into 8 slices. Core the tomatoes and cut them into even slices. Arrange the tomato and mozzarella slices in a circular pattern on the arugula, alternating the slices. Season with salt.

4. Drizzle the olive oil lightly over the salad and place the platter on the table with the pepper mill.

step 3

serve

1. Divide the pasta among 4 pasta bowls and sprinkle each with chopped parsley. Serve with Italian bread for soaking up the sauce.

2. When ready for dessert, halve the figs and place them in a shallow bowl. Sprinkle with Marsala and place with dessert bowls on the table.

Pasta Tuna Puttanesca
Single serving is 1/4 of the total recipe

CALORIES 662; PROTEIN 36g; CARBS 97g; TOTAL FAT 11g; SAT FAT 0g; CHOLESTEROL 40mg; SODIUM 681mg; FIBER 5g

pasta
with uncooked tomato and balsamic sauce

antipasto platter

herbed italian bread

pistachio ice cream
with assorted biscotti

serves 4 generously

shopping list

Dried spaghetti, perciatelli, or other thick-strand pasta

Firm ripe tomatoes

Fresh basil

Kosher salt

For the antipasto:
sliced Italian cold cuts, such as cappicola, mortadella, and Genoa salami; cheeses, such as sharp Asiago, fresh or smoked mozzarella, and Fontina; marinated vegetables and olives

Flat-leaf parsley

Chives or scallions

Italian bread

Pistachio ice cream

Assorted biscotti

from your pantry

Garlic

Dark brown sugar

Balsamic vinegar

Extra virgin olive oil

Dried red pepper flakes

Butter

beforeyoustart

Bring the water to a boil in a large pot, covered, over high heat to cook the pasta. Preheat the oven to 350°F to heat the bread.

step 1 cook the **pasta;** make the **uncooked tomato and balsamic sauce**

step 2 plate the **antipasto**

step 3 make the **herb butter** and heat the **bread**

step 4 **serve**

headsup

Olive oil is a major flavor component in the pasta dish. Use an extra virgin olive oil, which is oil extracted from the first pressing of the olives. It is lower in acidity than lesser grades, which gives it a light, fruity flavor. Olive oils labeled as "cold-pressed" have better flavor than oils extracted by heat. For everyday cooking, use the less-expensive, more acidic olive oils, labeled "virgin" or "pure."

"Balsamic vinegars from the supermarket will be richer and mellower—more like the expensive kind—if you stir in a little brown sugar."

—minutemeals' Chef Miriam

cook the **pasta;** make the **uncooked tomato and balsamic sauce**

For the pasta

4 quarts water

Salt to taste

1 pound dried spaghetti, perciatelli, or other thick-strand pasta

For the sauce

2 pounds tomatoes, about 4 large

1 cup loosely packed fresh basil leaves

1 tablespoon chopped garlic (3 large garlic cloves)

Pinch of dark brown sugar

1/4 cup balsamic vinegar

1/4 cup extra virgin olive oil

1/4 teaspoon dried red pepper flakes, or to taste

1/2 teaspoon kosher salt

1. Cook the pasta: Pour the water into a large pot, salt lightly, and cover. Bring to a boil over high heat. Add the pasta, stir to separate the strands, and cook according to the package directions until *al dente*. Drain in a colander and return to the pot. Toss for 30 seconds to dry.

2. Make the sauce: Rinse the tomatoes and cut into small cubes. Remove enough leaves from a bunch of basil to measure 1 cup loosely packed. Rinse and pat dry. Finely chop enough garlic to measure up to 1 tablespoon.

3. In a bowl large enough to hold the pasta and sauce, dissolve the brown sugar in the balsamic vinegar.

4. Add the tomatoes, garlic, olive oil, red pepper flakes, and salt. Stir to combine well. Reserve the basil.

step 2

plate the **antipasto**

A selection of sliced Italian cold cuts, such as cappicola, mortadella, and Genoa salami for 4

A selection of cheeses, such as sharp Asiago, fresh or smoked mozzarella, and Fontina for 4

A selection of marinated vegetables and olives, such as mushrooms or artichoke hearts, and kalamata olives for 4

Arrange the cold cuts on a platter with the cheeses. Serve the marinated vegetables and olives in separate bowls. Place on the table with plates for serving salad.

step 3

make the **herb butter** and heat the **bread**

3 tablespoons flat-leaf parsley leaves

3 tablespoons coarsely chopped chives or scallions

4 tablespoons (1/2 stick) butter, in pieces

1 loaf Italian bread

1. Preheat the oven to 350°F.

2. Remove enough parsley leaves from the stems to measure 3 tablespoons. Snip enough chives or

coarsely chop enough green part of scallion to measure 3 tablespoons. Place in a blender and process until roughly chopped. Add the butter and process until well combined.

3. Halve the bread horizontally.

4. Spread the herbed butter on the cut surfaces of the bread, then re-form the loaf. Wrap in foil. Place in the oven and heat until serving time.

step 4

serve

1. Add the pasta to the sauce and toss, distributing the tomatoes throughout. Tear the reserved basil leaves into ragged pieces and add to the pasta. Toss again.

2. Serve the pasta in bowls, making sure with each serving to evenly distribute the tomatoes and dressing that collects in the bottom of the bowl.

3. Serve the herbed bread on a bread board or in a basket.

4. When ready for dessert, scoop the pistachio ice cream into small bowls and serve with the biscotti.

Pasta with Uncooked Tomato and Balsamic Sauce
Single serving is 1/4 of the total recipe
CALORIES 566; PROTEIN 14g; CARBS 87g; TOTAL FAT 16g; SAT FAT 2g; CHOLESTEROL 0mg; SODIUM 315mg; FIBER 1g

pizza-stuffed pitas

marinated mushrooms and artichokes

mixed green salad

butterscotch pudding with whipped cream

menu
gameplan

serves 4

shopping list

Lemon (for juice)

Prewashed Italian blend salad greens

Balsamic vinaigrette dressing, store-bought or homemade

Pita pockets (8-inch diameter)

Sliced pepperoni

Pizza or marinara sauce

Pre-shredded mozzarella

Chopped pitted ripe olives

Butterscotch pudding

Instant whipped cream

from the salad bar

Boston or Bibb lettuce leaves

Marinated mushrooms (or jarred)

Marinated artichokes (or jarred)

Roasted red peppers (or jarred)

from your pantry

Dried oregano

Olive oil

beforeyou**start**

Preheat the oven to 450°F to heat the pitas.

step **1** plate the **marinated mushrooms and artichokes**

step **2** assemble the **mixed green salad**

step **3** make the **pizza-stuffed pitas**

step **4** **serve**

Every ingredient in this menu is easily available in any supermarket.

"These stuffed pita pockets are fun finger food. There's nothing complicated here—they're quick to make and good to eat. They make great snacks, too."

—minutemeals' Chef Miriam

step 1

plate the **marinated mushrooms and artichokes**

2 large Boston or Bibb lettuce leaves, for serving

Marinated mushrooms for 4

Marinated artichokes for 4

Fresh lemon juice to taste

Line 2 small serving bowls with a lettuce leaf. Put the marinated mushrooms in one bowl; the artichokes in the other. Squeeze lemon juice to taste over each, toss, and place the bowls on the table.

step 2

assemble the **mixed green salad**

Roasted red peppers to taste

1 bag (12 ounces) prewashed Italian blend salad greens

1/4 cup balsamic vinaigrette dressing

If using jarred roasted red peppers, drain and cut into strips. Place in a large salad bowl. Add the greens and dressing and toss to coat. Place the bowl on the table.

step 3

make the **pizza-stuffed pitas**

4 pita pockets (8-inch diameter)

1/4 cup chopped sliced pepperoni

1/2 cup prepared pizza or marinara sauce

1/2 teaspoon dried oregano

8 ounces pre-shredded mozzarella

1/4 cup chopped pitted ripe olives

Olive oil for brushing

1. Preheat the oven to 450°F.

2. With a sharp knife, halve the pita pockets horizontally into 2 rounds. Chop enough sliced pepperoni to measure 1/4 cup.

3. On the cut side of 4 of the pita halves, spoon 2 tablespoons sauce; sprinkle with a pinch of the oregano and 1/4 each of the shredded mozzarella, pepperoni, and olives. Top with the remaining pita halves, cut side down.

4. Place the stuffed pitas on a baking sheet and brush with olive oil. Weight with another baking sheet. Place on lowest rack of oven and bake for 5 minutes. Turn, brush with olive oil, and bake for 5 minutes.

step 4

serve

1. Transfer the stuffed pita onto plates, cut into wedges, and serve hot.

2. When ready for dessert, serve the butterscotch pudding in small bowls, garnished with whipped cream.

Pizza-Stuffed Pitas
Single serving is 1/4 of the total recipe
CALORIES 454; PROTEIN 25g; CARBS 36g; TOTAL FAT 24g; SAT FAT 0g; CHOLESTEROL 32mg; SODIUM 1311mg; FIBER 1g

white pizza
with mascarpone and smoked mozzarella

italian greens with salami and olives

orange ice and italian butter cookies

menu
gameplan

serves 4

shopping list

Smoked mozzarella

Fresh thyme

Fresh oregano

Part-skim ricotta cheese

Mascarpone cheese

Boboli pizza shell

Sliced Genoa salami

Prewashed Italian salad
green mix or romaine lettuce

Pitted black olives,
such as Gaeta or kalamata

Italian salad dressing

Croutons

Orange ice

Italian butter cookies

from the salad bar

Red onion slices

Green pepper rings or strips

from your pantry

Garlic

Salt

Freshly ground black pepper

Olive oil

beforeyoustart

Preheat the oven to 450°F to bake
the pizza.

step 1 make the **white pizza with mascarpone and smoked mozzarella**

step 2 assemble the **italian greens with salami and olives**

step 3 serve

luckyforyou

A ready-to-heat pizza shell
is so easy and available.
Without it, a recipe like this is not doable in 20 minutes.
Pizza crust, of course, is made with yeast and yeast
doesn't often rise on schedule!

"I love anchovies, and I add a few to this dish. That's what's so much fun about homemade pizza. You can fashion it as you like."

—minutemeals' Chef Hillary

step 1

make the **white pizza with mascarpone and smoked mozzarella**

8 ounces smoked mozzarella

1 teaspoon chopped fresh thyme or 1/2 teaspoon dried

1 teaspoon chopped fresh oregano or 1/2 teaspoon dried

2 garlic cloves

1/2 cup part-skim ricotta cheese

1/4 cup mascarpone

Salt and freshly ground black pepper to taste

1 large Boboli pizza shell

1 tablespoon olive oil

1. Preheat the oven to 450°F.

2. Grate the smoked mozzarella. If using fresh herbs, chop enough thyme and oregano to measure 1 teaspoon each. Chop the garlic.

3. In a small bowl, blend the ricotta and mascarpone together until well combined and season with salt and plenty of fresh black pepper.

4. Place the pizza shell on a large baking sheet and brush it with the olive oil. Spread the ricotta mixture evenly over the shell. Sprinkle the grated smoked mozzarella over the top, then scatter the 1 teaspoon each of fresh herbs and the chopped garlic over the mozzarella.

5. Bake the pizza for 15 minutes, or until hot and bubbly. Remove the pizza from the oven and let it rest a minute of two before slicing.

step 2

while pizza bakes, assemble the **italian greens with salami and olives**

4 ounces sliced Genoa salami

1 bag (10 ounces) prewashed Italian salad green mix or romaine lettuce

1/2 cup pitted black olives, such as Gaeta or kalamata

1/2 cup thin red onion slices

1/2 cup green pepper rings or strips

1/4 cup Italian salad dressing

1/2 cup prepared croutons

1. Cut the salami into thin strips.

2. In a large salad bowl, combine the salad greens, salami, olives, onion slices, and pepper rings. Add the dressing and toss. Sprinkle the croutons over the top. Place the bowl and 4 salad plates on the table.

step 3

serve

1. At serving time, with a pizza cutter or sharp heavy knife, cut the pizza into 8 slices and place 2 slices on each dinner plate. Serve the salad separately.

2. When ready for dessert, scoop the orange ice into dessert bowls and serve with the butter cookies.

White Pizza with Mascarpone and Smoked Mozzarella
Single serving is 1/4 of the total recipe
CALORIES 626; PROTEIN 33g; CARBS 53g; TOTAL FAT 33g; SAT FAT 17g; CHOLESTEROL 70mg; SODIUM 1230mg; FIBER 2g

⭐ ravioli pie

green salad with cucumber and red pepper
semolina bread
long-stemmed strawberries and meringues

shopping list

Fresh or frozen mini cheese ravioli

Shredded low-fat mozzarella cheese

Semolina bread

Prewashed Italian salad greens

Strawberries

Meringues

from the salad bar

Cucumber slices

Red pepper strips

from your pantry

Salt and pepper

Low-fat (1%) milk

All-purpose flour

Ground nutmeg

Nonstick cooking spray

Grated Parmesan cheese

Seasoned dry bread crumbs

Butter

Olive oil and vinegar

serves 4

beforeyoustart

Preheat the oven to 450°F to finish the ravioli pie. Rinse the strawberries in a colander.

step 1   cook the **ravioli;** make the **cheese sauce**

step 2   heat the **semolina bread**

step 3   assemble the **green salad with cucumber and red pepper**

step 4   **serve**

luckyforyou

You can cook the cheese sauce in the microwave. Place the flour in a 4-cup microwave-safe measure; stir in ½ cup of the milk until smooth. Stir in the remaining 1½ cups milk. Microwave on High for 3 minutes. Stir. Microwave on High 1 to 3 minutes longer, until bubbly and slightly thickened. Stir in the Parmesan, salt, pepper, and nutmeg to taste and set aside.

"Want a variation on this kid-friendly pie? Scatter sliced mushrooms, canned or fresh, between the layers of the pie, and bake as directed."

—minutemeals' Chef Miriam

cook the **ravioli;** make the **cheese sauce**

For the ravioli

4 quarts water

Salt to taste

1 pound fresh or frozen mini cheese ravioli

For the cheese sauce

2 cups low-fat (1%) milk

2 tablespoons all-purpose flour

Salt and pepper to taste

Ground nutmeg to taste

Nonstick cooking spray

1 cup shredded low-fat mozzarella cheese

1/2 cup grated Parmesan cheese

1/4 cup seasoned dry bread crumbs

1 tablespoon butter

1. Preheat the oven to 450°F.

2. Cook the ravioli: Pour the water into a large pot, salt lightly, and cover. Bring to a boil over high heat. Add the ravioli, stir to separate, and cook 7 to 8 minutes, until *al dente*. Drain. Keep warm, if necessary.

3. Make the cheese sauce: In a medium saucepan, bring 1 1/2 cups of the milk to a simmer over medium-high heat. In a small bowl, whisk together the remaining 1/2 cup milk and flour until smooth. Whisk the mixture into the milk and simmer over medium-low heat, whisking occasionally, for 2 to 3 minutes, or until lightly thickened. Season with salt, pepper, and nutmeg.

4. Spray a 9-inch pie plate or shallow baking pan with nonstick cooking spray. Arrange 1/2 the ravioli in the dish, spreading it in one layer; pour 1/2 the sauce over it, and sprinkle with 1/2 the mozzarella. Top with 1/2 the Parmesan. Make a second layer in the same manner with remaining ingredients. Sprinkle the bread crumbs evenly over the top. Dot the top with the butter.

5. Bake for 10 minutes, until heated through.

heat the **semolina bread**

1 loaf semolina bread

Warm the bread in the oven with the ravioli pie; remove the loaf slightly before the pie to prevent the crust from becoming too hard.

assemble the **green salad with cucumber and red pepper**

1 bag (5 ounces) prewashed Italian salad greens

Cucumber slices

Red pepper strips

Olive oil and vinegar to taste

Put the greens in a large salad bowl and add the cucumber slices and red pepper strips. Add the oil and vinegar, and toss. Place the bowl on the table.

serve

1. Bring the ravioli pie to the table with the warm bread. Serve the pie directly from the pie plate.

2. When ready for dessert, arrange the strawberries, just as is with stems, on a platter and serve with the meringues.

Ravioli Pie
Single serving is 1/4 of the total recipe
CALORIES 643; PROTEIN 36g; CARBS 44g;
TOTAL FAT 21g; SAT FAT 14g; CHOLESTEROL 111mg;
SODIUM 831mg; FIBER 0g

rigatoni
with sun-dried
tomato pesto

cold roast chicken

carrot and cucumber salad

coconut cake

serves 6

shopping list

Rigatoni

Sun-dried tomatoes packed in olive oil

Pine nuts *(pignoli)*

Lemon

Whole roast chicken

Coconut cake

from the salad bar

Grated or shredded carrots (or from the produce department)

Cucumber slices

from your pantry

Garlic

Grated Parmesan cheese

Salt

Freshly ground black pepper

Extra virgin olive oil

Cayenne pepper

beforeyoustart

Bring the water to a boil in a large pot, covered, over high heat to cook the rigatoni.

step 1 cook the **rigatoni;** make the **sun-dried tomato pesto**

step 2 assemble the **carrot and cucumber salad**

step 3 plate the **cold roast chicken**

step 4 **serve**

heads up

There are sun-dried tomatoes packed as is in cellophane bags, jarred sun-dried tomatoes packed in oil, and jars of ready-made sun-dried tomato pesto. If time is money, buy the pesto and use it as is. If you want to save money, buy the dry sun-dried tomatoes and rehydrate them in warm water before processing them to a paste with a little olive oil. We've taken the middle road and used sun-dried tomatoes packed in oil. By the way, you will use the oil.

"If you can't stand the heat, don't get out of the kitchen—make this menu! You'll stay cool and the food will be great."

—minutemeals' Chef Hillary

step 1

cook the **rigatoni;** make the **sun-dried tomato pesto**

For the rigatoni

4 quarts water

Salt to taste

1 pound rigatoni

For the pesto

4 garlic cloves

1 jar (8 ounces) sun-dried tomatoes packed in olive oil

$1/4$ cup pine nuts

$1/2$ cup grated Parmesan cheese

Salt and freshly ground black pepper

1. Cook the rigatoni: Pour the water into a large pot, salt lightly, and cover. Bring to a boil over high heat. Add the rigatoni, stir to separate, and cook according to the directions on the package, until *al dente*. Drain in a colander and return to the pot. Keep warm, covered.

2. Make the pesto: Coarsely chop the garlic. In a food processor, combine the sun-dried tomatoes, including the oil, the pine nuts, garlic, and Parmesan and process to a smooth paste, stopping to scrape down the sides of the bowl with a rubber spatula once or twice. Makes about $1^1/2$ cups.

3. Add $1/2$ cup of the pesto, or more to taste, to the rigatoni and toss well to combine. Season with salt and pepper. Transfer any remaining pesto to a plastic container, cover, and store in the refrigerator for up to 2 days. Use in salad dressings, on sandwiches, or on grilled or broiled meat or fish. Cover and keep warm.

step 2

assemble the **carrot and cucumber salad**

1 large garlic clove

2 tablespoons fresh lemon juice ($1/2$ lemon)

$1/3$ cup extra virgin olive oil

Pinch of cayenne pepper

Salt and pepper to taste

1 bag (8 ounces) grated or shredded carrots

$1/2$ cup thin cucumber slices

1. Crush the garlic clove in a garlic press or chop it fine.

2. Squeeze 2 tablespoons lemon juice into a medium bowl. Add the olive oil, garlic, cayenne, and salt and pepper and stir to combine.

3. Add the carrots and stir to coat. Let stand at room temperature until serving time.

step 3

plate the **cold roast chicken**

1 whole roast chicken, about 4 pounds

Cut the chicken into serving pieces and arrange on a platter. Place the platter on the table.

step 4

serve

1. Divide the rigatoni among 6 dinner plates. Serve with the roast chicken.

2. Arrange the cucumber slices on the carrot salad and serve on salad plates or alongside the pasta and chicken.

3. When ready for dessert, cut the coconut cake into slices and serve on dessert plates.

Rigatoni with Sun-Dried Tomato Pesto
Single serving is $1/6$ of the total recipe
CALORIES 530; PROTEIN 12g; CARBS 61g; TOTAL FAT 25g; SAT FAT 4g; CHOLESTEROL 0mg; SODIUM 520mg; FIBER 3g

spaghettini "alla confetti"

zesty watercress winter salad

sesame breadsticks

mango sorbet with
fresh raspberries

shopping list

Belgian endives

Mandarin oranges

Sliced pitted ripe olives

Watercress sprigs
(from the salad bar)

Salad dressing, such as
Catalina, honey-mustard,
or French

Spaghettini or another
thin-strand pasta

Fresh basil or flat-leaf Italian
parsley

Diced tomatoes

Pre-shredded mozzarella

Grated or shredded Swiss
cheese

Grated Parmesan or
Romano cheese

Sesame breadsticks

Mango sorbet

Raspberries

from your pantry

Salt

Freshly ground black pepper

Butter

 A good salad bar will spare
you from having to trim,
rinse, and dry what amounts to 2 bunches of watercress
for the salad here. If watercress isn't available where
you shop, select a ready-to-serve combination of greens.

serves 6

beforeyoustart

Bring the water to a boil in a large pot,
covered, over high heat to cook the pasta.
Place the pasta bowls under hot running
tap water to warm before serving.

step **1** assemble the **zesty watercress winter salad**

step **2** make the **spaghettini "alla confetti"**

step **3** **serve**

"Top this pasta with what's on hand. Try a little shredded roast chicken, slivered ham, or drained canned tuna, warmed in the microwave."

—minutemeals' Chef Ruth

step 1

assemble the **zesty watercress winter salad**

2 Belgian endives

1 can (16 ounces) mandarin oranges

1 can (about 4 ounces) sliced pitted ripe olives

Watercress sprigs to serve 6

1/2 cup store-bought slightly sweet salad dressing

Thinly slice the endives. Drain the mandarin oranges and olives. Place the endives, oranges, and olives in a large salad bowl. Add the watercress, toss to combine, and refrigerate until serving time.

step 2

make the **spaghettini "alla confetti"**

4 quarts water

Salt to taste

1 pound (16 ounces) spaghettini or another thin-strand pasta

1/2 cup shredded fresh basil or coarsely chopped flat-leaf (Italian) parsley

6 tablespoons butter

1 can (about 14 ounces) diced tomatoes

1 cup (4 ounces) pre-shredded mozzarella

1 cup (4 ounces) grated or shredded Swiss cheese

1/2 cup grated Parmesan or Romano cheese

Salt and freshly ground black pepper to taste

1. Pour the water into a large pot, salt lightly, and cover. Bring to a boil over high heat. Add the spaghettini, stir to separate the strands, and cook according to the directions on the package until *al dente*. Reserve about 1 cup of the cooking liquid, then drain.

2. While the pasta cooks, shred enough fresh basil or chop enough parsley to measure 1/2 cup; reserve.

3. Melt the butter in the pasta pot. Add the tomatoes, including the juice, and bring to a boil over medium-high heat. Add the pasta and toss. Remove from the heat.

4. Add the mozzarella, Swiss, and Parmesan to the pasta and toss until just melted. Stir in the basil and salt and pepper and toss lightly to combine. If the mixture seems a little dry, add some of the reserved cooking water and toss gently until the pasta has a creamy look.

step 3

serve

1. Divide the pasta among the 4 warmed pasta bowls and serve at once.

2. Drizzle the dressing over the salad and toss to combine. Place the bowl on the table with 4 individual salad plates.

3. Serve the breadsticks in a basket or stand them in a high-sided narrow container.

4. When ready for dessert, scoop the sorbet into goblets, garnish each with fresh raspberries, and serve.

Spaghettini "alla Confetti"
Single serving is 1/6 of the total recipe
CALORIES 560; PROTEIN 23g; CARBS 59g;
TOTAL FAT 24g; SAT FAT 8g; CHOLESTEROL 69mg;
SODIUM 546mg; FIBER 1g

spaghetti carbonara

arugula with sliced beefsteak tomatoes

crusty italian bread

cappuccino gelato and orange granita coupes

shopping list

Beefsteak tomatoes

Prewashed arugula

Spaghetti

Bacon, preferably thick cut

Grated Parmesan, Romano, or Asiago cheese

Heavy (or whipping) cream

Italian bread

Cappuccino gelato

Orange granita

Bittersweet chocolate (for grating, optional)

from your pantry

Extra virgin olive oil

Salt

Freshly ground black pepper

Eggs

Fat-free reduced-sodium chicken broth

serves 4 to 6

beforeyoustart

Bring the water to a boil in a large pot, covered, over high heat to cook the pasta. Place the bowls in which you plan to serve the pasta in the sink and run hot water over them to warm them for serving.

step 1 assemble the **arugula with sliced beefsteak tomatoes**

step 2 make the **spaghetti carbonara**

step 3 **serve**

 Fresh or dried spaghetti is an option here. Of course, the fresh will cook more quickly than the dried and is always a convenience for the minutemeal cook. If you do use the fresh, coordinate the timing so that the pasta finishes cooking just as you are ready to combine it with the sauce. The pasta should not be finished ahead of time and be allowed to cool.

"This is really a heavenly meal. Spaghetti Carbonara is one of Italy's great pasta dishes and it's so simple."

—minutemeals' Chef Connie

step 1

assemble the **arugula with sliced beefsteak tomatoes**

2 beefsteak tomatoes

2 ounces prewashed arugula, small leaves preferred

Extra virgin olive oil

Salt to taste

1. Slice the 2 tomatoes crosswise into 1/4-inch-thick slices.

2. Rinse the arugula and trim the stems, if necessary. Pat dry. Lay the leaves on a serving platter, and place the tomato slices on top, slightly overlapping. Drizzle with the extra virgin olive oil to taste and salt. Place the platter on the table.

step 2

make the **spaghetti carbonara**

For the pasta

4 quarts water

Salt to taste

1 pound spaghetti

For the sauce

6 ounces bacon, thick cut preferred

2 large eggs

2 egg yolks

1 cup (4 ounces) grated Parmesan, Romano, or Asiago cheese

1 to 2 teaspoons freshly ground black pepper

1 cup fat-free reduced-sodium chicken broth

1/2 cup heavy (or whipping) cream

1. Cook the pasta: Pour the water into a large pot, salt lightly, and cover. Bring to a boil over high heat. Add the spaghetti, stir to separate the strands, and cook, according to the directions on the package until *al dente*. Drain in a colander.

2. Make the sauce: Cut the bacon crosswise into 1/2-inch pieces. Transfer to a large nonstick skillet and turn the heat to medium-low. Cook the bacon, turning it frequently, until nicely browned, but still soft. Remove with a slotted spoon to paper towels to drain. Discard the fat in the skillet, wipe out the pan with paper towels, and set aside to use again.

3. In a medium bowl, with a fork, beat the whole eggs with the egg yolks. Add 1/2 cup of the cheese and 1 teaspoon of pepper and stir to combine.

4. In the large skillet, heat the chicken broth with the cream over medium-low heat until hot. Add the drained cooked spaghetti and the bacon and toss until the pasta is well coated and heated through.

5. Remove the pan from the heat and add the beaten eggs, tossing quickly to coat the strands of spaghetti. Add pepper to taste and salt, if desired. If necessary, return the pan to very low heat just to heat through, being careful not to overheat.

Note: Because of the way the eggs are added to this classic Italian dish, they are not sufficiently heated to be considered "cooked." If, for reasons of food safety you want to cook the eggs longer, be aware that they may solidify, which will alter, undo, in fact, the texture of this renowned sauce.

step 3

serve

1. Serve the pasta immediately in the warmed pasta bowls, with Italian bread. Pass the remaining 1/2 cup grated cheese separately.

2. When ready for dessert, alternate scoops of cappuccino gelato and orange granita in goblets or wine glasses and serve. If desired, sprinkle with a little grated bittersweet chocolate before serving.

Spaghetti Carbonara
Single serving is 1/6 of the total recipe
CALORIES 627; PROTEIN 22g; CARBS 59g; TOTAL FAT 33g; SAT FAT 15g; CHOLESTEROL 212mg; SODIUM 475mg; FIBER 0g

tortellini
with vegetables in basil cream sauce

italian greens vinaigrette

crusty Italian bread

strawberries with balsamic vinegar

menu gameplan

shopping list

Cheese, mushroom, or meat tortellini, fresh or frozen

Frozen peas

Prewashed Italian blend salad greens

White wine vinaigrette dressing

Strawberries

Fresh basil, chives, tarragon, parsley, or a combination

Half-and-half

Crusty Italian bread

from the salad bar

Broccoli florets (or from the produce department)

Cherry tomatoes

from your pantry

Salt

Balsamic vinegar

Butter

Grated Parmesan cheese

Grated nutmeg

serves 4

beforeyoustart

Bring water to a boil in a large pot, covered, over high heat to cook the pasta.

step 1 cook the **tortellini with vegetables**

step 2 assemble the **italian greens vinaigrette**

step 3 prepare the **strawberries with balsamic vinegar**

step 4 make the **basil cream sauce**

step 5 **serve**

luckyforyou
There are a number of ways to use more of the fresh basil you've bought for the cream sauce. Rinse and pat dry a handful of leaves and add them, torn into pieces, to the salad. Or finely chop some, then mash them into softened butter to use on the bread. Or, make Pesto Genovese (page 227).

"Add a few colorful vegetables and an herbed cream sauce and you transform plain tortellini into a delectable dish."

—minutemeals' Chef Anne

step 1
cook the **tortellini with vegetables**

4 quarts water

Salt to taste

1 package (9 ounces) fresh or frozen cheese, mushroom, or meat tortellini

2 cups broccoli florets

1 cup frozen peas

8 cherry tomatoes

1. Pour the water into a large pot, salt lightly, and cover. Bring to a boil over high heat. Add the tortellini, stir to separate, and cook, stirring occasionally, for 3 minutes.

2. Add the broccoli florets and cook, stirring occasionally, for 2 minutes.

3. Add the peas and cook, stirring occasionally, for 1 to 2 minutes, or until the vegetables are just tender. Drain the pasta in a colander and return it to the pot. Cover and keep warm.

4. Rinse the cherry tomatoes, halve, and reserve.

step 2
assemble the **italian greens vinaigrette**

1 bag (10 ounces) prewashed Italian blend salad greens

1/4 cup store-bought white wine vinaigrette dressing

Put the greens in a salad bowl, add the dressing, and toss. Put the bowl on the table with 4 salad plates.

step 3
prepare the **strawberries with balsamic vinegar**

1 pint ripe strawberries

Balsamic vinegar to taste

Rinse and hull the strawberries. Quarter the berries and divide them among 4 dessert bowls or stemmed glasses. Place in the refrigerator until serving time.

step 4
make the **basil cream sauce**

1/4 cup finely chopped fresh basil, tarragon, parsley, or chives, or a combination

2/3 to 1 cup half-and-half

1 tablespoon butter

1/3 cup grated Parmesan cheese, plus additional for serving

Grated nutmeg to taste

1. Remove about 1/2 cup basil leaves from the stems; rinse and pat dry. Finely chop to measure 1/4 cup.

2. In a medium skillet, simmer the half-and-half over medium-high heat for 3 minutes. Add the butter and Parmesan and heat until the butter is melted and the sauce thickens slightly, enough to coat the back of the spoon.

3. Remove the pan from the heat and stir in the fresh herbs and nutmeg to taste.

step 5
serve

1. Add the cherry tomatoes to the tortellini and toss gently to combine. Pour in the cream sauce and toss gently again.

2. Divide the tortellini among 4 large bowls. Serve with additional Parmesan on the table.

3. Put the bread on a bread board and place on the table.

4. When ready for dessert, serve the strawberries with a small cruet of balsamic vinegar. Let each diner add vinegar to his or her berries as desired.

Tortellini with Vegetables in Basil Cream Sauce
Single serving is 1/4 of the total recipe
CALORIES 230; PROTEIN 10g; CARBS 23g; TOTAL FAT 12g; SAT FAT 4g; CHOLESTEROL 32mg; SODIUM 306mg; FIBER 2g

jambalaya
rice salad

romaine and pecan salads
corn muffin toasts
vanilla ice cream with sliced bananas and caramel sauce

shopping list

Frozen baby peas

Salt-free Cajun seasoning

Lemon or citrus vinaigrette

Jumbo shrimp, cooked, peeled, and deveined

Cooked chicken (from the prepared foods section)

Pecan halves

Large corn muffins

Vanilla ice cream

Ripe bananas

Caramel sauce

from the salad bar

Tomato slices or wedges

Chopped red or green pepper

Celery slices

Chopped scallions

Prewashed romaine leaves

from your pantry

Long-grain white rice

Salt

Salad dressing of choice, store-bought or homemade

Butter

serves 4

beforeyoustart

Place the jar of caramel sauce in a pan of very hot tap water to warm before serving.

| step | 1 | make the **jambalaya rice salad** |

| step | 2 | assemble the **romaine and pecan salads** |

| step | 3 | toast the **corn muffins** |

| step | 4 | **serve** |

 Take advantage of the salad bar and prepared foods department in your supermarket to buy as many pre-chopped and precooked ingredients for the salad as you can. They'll make the 20-minute salad possible.

"Turning jambalaya into a salad really works—great taste in so little time."

—minutemeals' Chef Joanne

step 1

make the **jambalaya rice salad**

- 1 cup frozen baby peas
- 2 cups water
- 1 cup long-grain white rice
- 1/2 teaspoon salt-free Cajun seasoning
- 1/4 teaspoon salt
- 1 bottle (8 ounces) prepared lemon or citrus vinaigrette
- 12 cooked, peeled and deveined jumbo shrimp
- 1 cup cooked chicken, leftover or store-bought
- 1 cup tomato slices or wedges
- 1/2 cup chopped red or green pepper
- 1/2 cup celery slices
- 1/4 cup chopped scallions

1. Place the frozen peas in a colander to thaw.

2. Meanwhile, in a 2-quart saucepan, combine the water, the rice, Cajun seasoning, and salt. Cover and bring to a boil over high heat. Reduce the heat to low, and simmer for 15 minutes, or until all the liquid is absorbed. Stir in the thawed peas and 1/3 cup of the prepared vinaigrette.

3. Spread the rice mixture out in a 13- × 9-inch baking pan. Place the pan in the refrigerator or freezer for 5 minutes to cool down quickly.

4. While the salad is chilling, halve the shrimp lengthwise. Cut the chicken into evenly-sized pieces. Coarsely chop the tomato slices.

5. In a wide shallow salad bowl, combine the shrimp, chopped chicken, and tomato with the chopped pepper, celery, and scallions. Taste for seasoning and add salt and pepper, if desired. Drizzle with a little more lemon vinaigrette and toss to combine.

step 2

assemble the **romaine and pecan salads**

- 6 ounces prewashed romaine lettuce
- 1/2 cup pecan halves, toasted, if time allows
- Salad dressing of choice

Divide the romaine lettuce leaves, breaking them into smaller pieces, if necessary, among 4 salad plates. Top each with 1/4 of the pecans. Place the plates on the table, with the dressing of choice for diners to serve themselves.

step 3

toast the **corn muffins**

- 2 large corn muffins
- Softened butter

1. Slice the corn muffins from top to bottom into pieces 1/2-inch-thick slices.

2. In a toaster oven, brown the slices lightly. While the toasts are still hot, butter them. Place in a napkin-lined basket and put the basket on the table.

step 4

serve

1. Spoon the chilled rice mixture into the salad bowl of shrimp, chicken, and vegetables. Toss gently to combine, taste, and adjust seasoning, if desired. Place the bowl on the table. Serve with remaining lemon vinaigrette.

2. When ready for dessert, scoop the ice cream into dessert bowls, slice banana over the ice cream, and top with caramel sauce. Serve.

Jambalaya Rice Salad
Single serving is 1/4 of the total recipe
CALORIES 374; PROTEIN 21g; CARBS 19g;
TOTAL FAT 22g; SAT FAT 0g; CHOLESTEROL 84mg;
SODIUM 977mg; FIBER 3g

polenta
with wild
mushroom stew
spinach salad
rosemary focaccia
flourless chocolate cake

shopping list

Sliced and cleaned mushroom combination, such as white mushrooms, shiitake, portobello, and/or oyster

Fresh rosemary

Onion slices
(from the salad bar)

Dry white wine

Diced canned tomatoes

Fresh parsley

Goat cheese

Rosemary focaccia

Instant polenta

Prewashed baby spinach leaves

Balsamic vinaigrette dressing, store-bought or homemade

Flourless chocolate cake

from your pantry

Garlic

Olive oil

Balsamic vinegar

Bay leaf

Salt and pepper

Butter

luckyforyou

There is a way to use more of the fresh rosemary we've asked you to buy for the mushroom stew. Make your own rosemary focaccia. Buy plain focaccia in the supermarket. Strip some of the leaves from 2 or 3 rosemary branches, add them to flavorful olive oil, and brush it over the surface of the focaccia. Heat as directed.

serves 4

beforeyoustart

Preheat the oven to 350°F to heat the focaccia.

step 1 make the **wild mushroom stew**

step 2 heat the **rosemary focaccia**

step 3 prepare the **polenta**

step 4 assemble the **spinach salad**

step 5 **serve**

"Mushrooms present marvelous possibilities. I use as many types of mushrooms as I can in this stew because each makes a distinct contribution."

—minutemeals' Chef Amanda

step 1

make the **wild mushroom stew**

1 pound sliced and cleaned mushroom combination, such as white mushrooms, shiitake, portobello, and/or oyster

3 large garlic cloves, or 1 tablespoon pre-minced garlic

1 tablespoon minced fresh rosemary or 1 teaspoon dried, crumbled

2 tablespoons olive oil

1/4 cup onion slices

2 tablespoons balsamic vinegar

1/2 cup dry white wine

1/2 cup drained diced canned tomatoes

1 bay leaf

Salt and pepper to taste

1/2 cup chopped fresh parsley

1/3 cup crumbled goat cheese

1. If using portobello mushrooms, cut the slices in half. If using whole garlic, finely chop. Mince enough fresh rosemary to measure 1 table-spoon.

2. Heat the olive oil in a large nonstick skillet over medium heat until hot. Add the onions and garlic and cook, stirring, for 2 minutes, until the onions are softened. Add the mushrooms and cook, stirring, for 2 minutes.

3. Add the balsamic vinegar and wine and cook, stirring, for 4 min-utes. Add the drained tomatoes, bay leaf, and rosemary. Season with salt and pepper. Stir well to combine, cover, lower the heat to maintain a medium simmer, and cook, stirring occasionally, for 10 minutes.

4. Chop enough parsley to measure 1/2 cup; reserve.

step 2

heat the **rosemary focaccia**

1 store-bought rosemary focaccia

Preheat the oven to 350°F. Place the focaccia on a baking sheet and heat until warmed through. Transfer to a bread board and place on the table.

step 3

prepare the **polenta**

4 cups water

1 teaspoon salt

1 cup instant polenta

3 tablespoons butter, softened

Pour the water into a medium sauce-pan, add the salt, and cover. Bring to a boil over high heat. Stir in the polenta. Reduce the heat to a sim-mer and cook, stirring constantly, for 5 minutes. Remove from the heat and beat in the butter until melted and fully combined. Keep warm, covered.

step 4

assemble the **spinach salad**

1 bag (10 ounces) prewashed baby spinach leaves

1/4 cup balsamic vinaigrette dressing

Place the spinach in a salad bowl, add the dressing, and toss. Place the bowl on the table.

step 5

serve

1. Season the mushroom stew with salt and pepper. Stir in the reserved chopped parsley. To serve, ladle some of the hot polenta onto 4 serving bowls. Ladle mushroom stew over the polenta, and sprinkle each serving with some of the goat cheese. Serve immediately.

2. When ready for dessert, cut the cake into slim slices and serve on dessert plates.

Polenta with Wild Mushroom Stew
Single serving is 1/4 of the total recipe
CALORIES 334; PROTEIN 8g; CARBS 20g;
TOTAL FAT 24g; SAT FAT 4g; CHOLESTEROL 29mg;
SODIUM 771mg; FIBER 2g

☆ pork fried rice
chinese egg rolls
melon salad

menu
gameplan

shopping list

Pork loin

Gingerroot

Chile paste

Frozen corn

Frozen peas

Vegetable or shrimp egg rolls
(from Chinese take-out)
or frozen egg rolls

Hot mustard or duck sauce
(optional)

Lime

Mint sprigs (optional)

from the salad bar

Carrot sticks or carrots
(or from the produce
department)

Broccoli florets
(or from the produce
department)

Chopped scallions

Melon chunks
(or from the produce
department)

from your pantry

Canola oil

Lite soy sauce

Leftover cooked rice

Toasted sesame oil

serves 4

step **1** make the **pork fried rice**

step **2** heat the **chinese egg rolls**

step **3** plate the **melon salad**

step **4** **serve**

headsup

The secret to real, authentically textured fried rice is in using day-old cooked rice. This allows the outside of the rice to dry and harden so it doesn't stick when fried.

"Why order out? Look at how easy this fried rice is when you start with ingredients either already chopped or cooked."

—minutemeals' Chef Nancy

step 1

make the **pork fried rice**

1 pound trimmed pork loin

8 to 10 carrot sticks or
2 medium to large carrots

2 cups broccoli florets

3 to 4 tablespoons chopped gingerroot

1/4 cup canola oil

1 to 2 teaspoons prepared chile paste, or less to taste

1/2 cup chopped scallions

2 to 3 tablespoons lite soy sauce

2 tablespoons water

4 to 5 cups leftover cooked rice

2 cups thawed frozen corn

1 cup thawed frozen peas

1 tablespoon toasted sesame oil

1. Dice the pork loin into 1/4-inch cubes. Cut the carrot sticks into 1/4-inch cubes. Cut the broccoli florets into pieces to match the pork and carrots. Chop enough fresh ginger to measure up to 1/4 cup.

2. Line all the foods and condiments up on a tray in the order in which they will be added to the pan. Heat a wok or a heavy 12-inch skillet over high heat. (High heat is very important.) Add 1 tablespoon of the canola oil to the hot pan and heat until hot. Add the pork and cook until no longer pink, about 3 minutes. Stir the meat only occasionally. If you move it too much, it won't caramelize and brown the way it should.

3. Add the ginger and chile paste and cook for 30 seconds. Pour the pork mixture into a bowl; set aside. Wipe out the wok and place it back over high heat.

4. Add 3 more tablespoons oil to the wok and heat until hot. Add the carrots and broccoli and stir-fry until not quite tender, about 1 minute. Add the scallions, 1 tablespoon of the soy sauce, and water and cook until the water almost evaporates, about 1 minute.

5. Add the rice, corn, peas, and pork mixture to the wok, toss to mix, and cook until heated through, about 2 minutes. Season with more soy sauce to taste. (If the rice sticks, add more oil or a little water around the edges, and toss.) When the rice is hot, add the sesame oil and toss to combine. Mound the fried rice on a platter.

step 2

heat the **chinese egg rolls**

4 vegetable or shrimp egg rolls or frozen egg rolls

Hot mustard or duck sauce for serving (optional)

Reheat the take-out egg rolls, if necessary, in a toaster oven or heat frozen egg rolls according to the directions on the package. Keep warm until serving time.

step 3

plate the **melon salad**

4 cups melon chunks

1 lime

Mint sprigs (optional)

Place the melon chunks in a serving bowl. Quarter the lime and set the quarters around the edge of the bowl. Garnish with mint sprigs, if desired. Place the bowl in the refrigerator until serving time.

step 4

serve

1. Place the fried rice on the table, with chopsticks, if desired.

2. Place the egg rolls on a platter and serve with the hot mustard sauce or duck sauce for dipping.

3. When ready for dessert, serve the melon in dessert bowls with fresh lime juice squeezed over the top.

Pork Fried Rice
Single serving is 1/4 of the total recipe
CALORIES 693; PROTEIN 37g; CARBS 83g; TOTAL FAT 27g; SAT FAT 4g; CHOLESTEROL 67mg; SODIUM 395mg; FIBER 6g

lentil salad
with goat cheese, olives, and oranges
herbed garlic yogurt dip with pita bread
strawberry shortcakes

menu
gameplan

serves 4

step	1	make the **lentil salad with goat cheese, olives, and oranges**
step	2	make the **herbed garlic yogurt dip**
step	3	prepare the **strawberry shortcake**
step	4	**serve**

shopping list

Lentils

Mandarin oranges

Red onion

Fresh parsley

Pitted ripe olives

Lemon (for juice)

Goat cheese

Lettuce leaves for cups
(from the salad bar)

Plain low-fat yogurt

Scallions

Chives

Fresh mint

Pita pockets
(8-inch diameter)

Strawberries

Prebaked Buttermilk biscuits

Instant whipped cream

from your pantry

Garlic

Extra virgin olive oil

Ground cumin

Salt

Freshly ground black pepper

Sugar

lucky for you

The health-food section in many supermarkets is a fascinating place to get to know. Begin by looking for the canned lentils we call for in this salad; then move on to all the beans and legumes you can stock as pantry items.

"This salad is a great choice when you want something a little more substantial than a green salad but not as filling as pasta salad."

—minutemeals' Chef Hillary

step 1

make the **lentil salad with goat cheese, olives, and oranges**

2 cans (15 ounces each) lentils

1 can (11 ounces) mandarin oranges

1 small red onion

1/2 cup chopped parsley

1/2 cup chopped pitted ripe olives

2 garlic cloves

1/3 cup extra virgin olive oil

2 tablespoons fresh lemon juice (1/2 large lemon)

1/2 to 1 teaspoon ground cumin

1 teaspoon salt

Freshly ground black pepper to taste

1 log (8 ounces) goat cheese

4 lettuce leaf cups, for serving

1. Rinse and drain the lentils. Drain the mandarin oranges. Mince the onion. Chop enough parsley to measure 1/2 cup. Chop enough olives to measure 1/2 cup.

2. Finely chop the garlic cloves. In a medium bowl, combine the garlic, olive oil, lemon juice, cumin to taste, salt, and pepper until well blended.

3. Gently fold in the lentils and oranges, onion, parsley, and olives and combine well.

4. Slice the goat cheese into 1/2-inch-thick rounds.

step 2

make the **herbed garlic yogurt dip**

1 pint plain low-fat yogurt

1 scallion

1 garlic clove

2 tablespoons snipped chives

1 tablespoon minced fresh mint

4 pita pockets (8-inch diameter), for serving

1. Drain the yogurt in a colander lined with dampened cheesecloth or paper towels 5 minutes.

2. Meanwhile, finely chop the scallion and garlic. Snip enough chives to measure 2 tablespoons. Mince enough mint to measure 1 tablespoon. Combine all in a medium bowl.

3. Add the drained yogurt and blend well. Transfer the dip to a wide shallow bowl and place in middle of a serving platter.

4. Cut the pita pockets into triangles and arrange around the edge of the platter. Place the platter on the table.

step 3

prepare the **strawberry shortcakes**

1 pint ripe strawberries

Sugar to taste

4 prebaked buttermilk biscuits

Instant whipped cream

Rinse the strawberries, slice, and place in a bowl. Sprinkle with sugar to taste, toss, and let stand at room temperature.

step 4

serve

1. Place 1 lettuce leaf on each serving plate. Spoon lentil salad over each leaf and top with 2 rounds of the goat cheese.

2. When ready for dessert, split each buttermilk biscuit in half horizontally and place on a dessert plate. Spoon some of the strawberries and juice over the bottom half of each biscuit. Add whipped cream to taste and place the biscuit top on the cream. Pass any remaining strawberries and additional whipped cream at the table. Serve.

Lentil Salad with Goat Cheese, Olives, and Oranges
Single serving is 1/4 of the total recipe
CALORIES 631; PROTEIN 31g; CARBS 54g; TOTAL FAT 34g; SAT FAT 8g; CHOLESTEROL 26mg; SODIUM 916mg; FIBER 19g

black beans and rice

sliced cucumbers and tomatoes vinaigrette

babas au rhum or rum raisin ice cream

serves 4

shopping list

Black beans

Salsa flavored with chipotle chiles

No-salt-added tomatoes

Lemon (optional)

Cilantro (optional)

Balsamic vinaigrette dressing or other dressing

Babas au rhum or rum raisin ice cream

from the salad bar

Cucumber slices

Tomato wedges

Prewashed romaine leaves

from your pantry

Boil-in-bag white rice

Onion

Garlic

Vegetable cooking spray

Ground cumin

step 1 prepare the **rice;** make the **black beans**

step 2 assemble the **sliced cucumbers and tomatoes vinaigrette**

step 3 **serve**

luckyforyou The main ingredients for this healthful rice dish—the rice, beans, tomatoes, and salsa—are all nonperishable items that can be stocked ahead of time. In that event, shopping for this menu entails only a quick trip at the salad bar.

*"There's a reason rice and beans, whether they're black or red,
is a staple food in parts of in the world. It's filling and satisfying."*

—minutemeals' Chef Hillary

step 1

prepare the **rice; make the black beans**

For the rice

2 bags boil-in-bag white rice

For the black beans

1 1/2 cups chopped onion
(1 medium-large onion)

2 garlic cloves

1 can (16 ounces) black beans,
rinsed and drained

Vegetable cooking spray

1/2 teaspoon cumin

1/3 cup salsa flavored with
chipotle chiles

1/2 cup water

1 can (14 1/2 ounces)
no-salt-added tomatoes,
including the liquid

1 teaspoon grated lemon zest
(optional)

1 teaspoon lemon juice
(optional)

2 tablespoons chopped cilantro,
or to taste (optional)

Cilantro sprigs

1. Prepare the rice: Microwave 1 bag of rice at a time according to the directions on the package. Repeat with the remaining bag. Transfer the rice to a bowl and keep warm, covered with plastic wrap.

2. Prepare the black beans: Finely chop the onion to measure about 1 1/2 cups. Finely chop the garlic. Rinse and drain the beans; reserve.

3. Coat a large nonstick skillet with vegetable cooking spray and heat over medium-high heat just until hot. Add onions and cook, stirring, for 4 minutes, or until slightly translucent. Add the garlic and cumin and cook, stirring, for 1 minute longer. Add the salsa, water, and tomatoes with the liquid. Bring to a boil, reduce the heat to medium, and simmer, stirring occasionally, for 5 minutes.

4. While the bean mixture cooks, zest and juice the lemon, and chop enough cilantro to measure 2 tablespoons, if using.

5. Remove the pan from the heat. Stir in the beans, lemon zest and juice, and optional cilantro. Keep warm, covered.

step 2

assemble the **sliced cucumbers and tomatoes vinaigrette**

1 cup cucumber slices

2 cups tomato wedges

2 tablespoons store-bought
balsamic vinaigrette or other
dressing

12 prewashed romaine leaves

In a salad bowl, combine the cucumbers, tomatoes, and vinaigrette and toss to coat. Line 4 salad plates with the romaine lettuce and top with the salad, dividing it evenly. Place the plates on the table.

step 3

serve

1. Place 1 cup of the rice in the center of each dinner place and top with 1 cup of the bean mixture. Garnish with a sprig of cilantro, if desired.

2. When ready for dessert, serve the pastries on dessert plates or the ice cream in small dessert bowls.

Black Beans and Rice
Single serving is 1/4 of the total recipe
CALORIES 362; PROTEIN 13g; CARBS 72g;
TOTAL FAT 2g; SAT FAT 0g; CHOLESTEROL 0mg;
SODIUM 397mg; FIBER 7g

spanish rice

romaine with hearts of palm
fruited "sangria"
crusty rolls
flan with fresh raspberries

shopping list

Reduced-sodium boiled ham

Green pepper

Onion slices
(from the salad bar)

Chopped tomatoes

Grated Cheddar cheese
(optional)

Orange

Cranberry juice

Grape juice

Lemons (for juice)

Lime (for juice)

Prewashed hearts of romaine

Hearts of palm

Crusty rolls

Prepared flan

Raspberries

from your pantry

Garlic

Olive oil

Paprika

Chili powder

Instant white rice

White wine vinegar

serves 4

| step | 1 | make the **spanish rice** |

| step | 2 | prepare the **fruited "sangria"** |

| step | 3 | assemble the **romaine with hearts of palm** |

| step | 4 | **serve** |

This is a one-dish meal—
our favorite kind from a
clean-up point of view.

"This is a good menu for a weeknight and if you omit the chili powder, kids love Spanish Rice, too."

—minutemeals' Chef Hillary

make the **spanish rice**

4 ounces reduced-sodium boiled ham

1 medium green pepper

1 garlic clove

2 teaspoons olive oil

1/2 cup onion slices

1 teaspoon paprika

1/2 to 1 teaspoon chili powder

1 can (14 1/2 ounces) chopped tomatoes, including liquid

1 1/2 cups water

2 cups instant white rice

2 tablespoons grated Cheddar cheese (optional)

1. Dice the boiled ham. Dice the pepper (you should have about 1 cup). Finely chop the garlic.

2. In a 12-inch nonstick skillet, heat the olive oil over medium-high heat until hot. Add the onions and pepper and cook, stirring constantly, for 4 minutes, or until softened. Add the garlic, paprika, chili powder, and ham. Cover the pan and cook over medium heat, stirring once, for 3 minutes.

3. Add the tomatoes, including the liquid, and water and bring the mixture to a boil over high heat. Add the rice, stir, sprinkle the top with Cheddar, if using, and cover. Remove from the heat and allow to stand for 5 to 7 minutes, or until most of the liquid has been absorbed.

prepare the **fruited "sangria"**

1 orange

1 quart cranberry juice

2 cups grape juice

Juice of 2 lemons

Juice of 1 lime

2 cups ice

Cut the orange into 8 wedges. Place in a large pitcher and add the remaining ingredients. Stir to combine and place the pitcher on the table with tall glasses.

assemble the **romaine with hearts of palm**

5 to 6 ounces prewashed hearts of romaine

1 can (16 ounces) hearts of palm

Olive oil and white wine vinegar to taste

1. Tear the romaine into pieces and place in a large bowl.

2. Drain the hearts of palm and place on the lettuce.

3. Drizzle with olive oil and vinegar to taste, toss, and place the bowl on the table.

serve

1. Place 1 cup Spanish rice in each serving bowl or plate. Serve with crusty rolls and the salads.

2. When ready for dessert, place a flan on each dessert plate and top with fresh raspberries. Serve the remaining raspberries on the side.

Spanish Rice
Single serving is 1/4 of the total recipe
CALORIES 378; PROTEIN 12g; CARBS 72g; TOTAL FAT 3g; SAT FAT 1g; CHOLESTEROL 13mg; SODIUM 376mg; FIBER 1g

These menus use the dietary guidelines from the United States Department of Agriculture and its food pyramid as well as the American Heart Association and American Cancer Society:

30% or less of calories from fat

Salt use was based on the American Heart Association recommendation of less than 6 grams of salt per day (2400 milligrams of sodium). Based on a 2000-calorie-a-day intake, the Healthy Menus in this chapter are just what they say they are: quick to make—20 minutes quick, that is—and better for you.

There is one more very important change in this chapter.

- The Nutrient Analyses in Chapters 1 through 5 were for the main dish in a menu; the analyses in this chapter include all the components of an entire menu, including dessert.

minute

20-minute gourmet

healthy menus

20 healthy **minutemeals**
that are quick to make
and good for you, too

meals

menus

lemon-pepper cod
on lightly dressed greens
cumin-scented rice
ginger-poached pears

menu
gameplan

serves 4

shopping list

Gingerroot
Bosc pears
Lemon (for juice)
Salad greens
(from the salad bar)
Cod fillets
Dry white wine

from your pantry

Sugar
Onion
Olive oil
Ground cumin
Long-grain rice
Low-fat vinaigrette dressing
Lemon pepper

step **1** poach the **pears**

step **2** cook the **cumin-scented rice**

step **3** dress the **greens**

step **4** cook the **lemon-pepper cod**

step **5** **serve**

headsup For most people, fish is cooked through when it flakes in the thickest part when tested with a fork. If you like fish a bit more moist, remove it from the pan a minute before the suggested cooling time.

"If you use the freshest fish you can and fresh lemon juice, you can't go wrong here. The delicious sauce seeps down into the salad."

—minutemeals' Chef Marge

step 1

poach the **pears**

3 tablespoons chopped gingerroot

2 ripe Bosc pears

3/4 cup water

1/3 cup sugar

1 tablespoon fresh lemon juice (1/2 lemon)

1. Chop enough ginger to measure 3 tablespoons. Peel, halve, and core the pears.

2. In a medium saucepan, combine the water, sugar, ginger, and lemon juice and bring to a boil over high heat, stirring to dissolve the sugar. Add the pears. Cover and simmer over low heat, turning occasionally, until the pears are tender, about 15 minutes. Let stand in the syrup until serving time.

step 2

cook the **cumin-scented rice**

1 small onion

1 tablespoon olive oil

1 tablespoon ground cumin

1 1/2 cups long-grain rice

2 1/2 cups water

1. Finely chop the onion.

2. Combine the onion and olive oil in a medium saucepan and sauté, stirring, for 3 minutes, until softened. Stir in the cumin and cook for 30 seconds.

3. Add the rice and water, stir, and reduce the heat to low. Cover and simmer for 15 minutes, until the liquid is absorbed.

step 3

dress the **greens**

2 cups salad greens

2 tablespoons low-fat vinaigrette dressing

Place the salad greens in a bowl, add the vinaigrette, and toss. Dividing the greens equally, place a serving on each of 4 dessert plates.

step 4

cook the **lemon-pepper cod**

4 cod fillets, each 3/4 to 1 inch thick (1 1/4 pounds total weight)

1 teaspoon lemon pepper

1 teaspoon olive oil

1/3 cup dry white wine

1 tablespoon fresh lemon juice (1/2 lemon)

1. Rinse the cod fillets and pat dry. Sprinkle the lemon pepper on both sides of the fillets and pat it on.

2. In a large nonstick skillet, heat the olive oil over medium-high heat until hot. Add the cod fillets in one layer and cook about 4 minutes per side, or until golden and cooked through when tested with a fork. Remove to a plate and keep warm.

3. Increase the heat to high and add the wine and lemon juice to the skillet. Cook for 3 or 4 minutes, until slightly thickened.

step 5

serve

1. Top the greens on each plate with a cod fillet and drizzle some of the lemon sauce over each serving.

2. Fluff the rice with a fork. Add a serving of rice to each plate and serve.

3. When ready for dessert, spoon a pear half into each dessert bowl, being sure to include some of the cooking syrup and ginger.

Lemon-Pepper Cod on Lightly Dressed Greens Menu
Single serving is 1/4 of the total menu, including dessert

CALORIES 440; PROTEIN 30g; CARBS 64g; TOTAL FAT 5g; SAT FAT 1g; CHOLESTEROL 61mg; SODIUM 91mg; FIBER 2g

11% of calories from fat

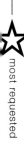

crispy oven-fried flounder
with tomato vinaigrette

new potatoes with butter and parsley

sautéed zucchini

chocolate pudding

menu
gameplan

shopping list

New potatoes

Fresh parsley

Flounder fillets

Zucchini slices
(from the salad bar)

Tomato

Fresh basil

Fat-free chocolate pudding
cups (4), such as Swiss Miss

from your pantry

Butter

Salt

Freshly ground black pepper

Vegetable cooking spray

Yellow cornmeal

Cayenne pepper

Milk

Olive oil

Vinaigrette dressing,
store-bought

Cornstarch

serves 4

beforeyoustart

Preheat the oven to 450°F to oven-fry the flounder fillets.

| step | 1 | microwave the **new potatoes** |

| step | 2 | oven-fry the **fish fillets**; make the **tomato vinaigrette** |

| step | 3 | sauté the **zucchini** |

| step | 4 | **serve** |

luckyforyou We suggested buying sliced zucchini from the salad bar as a way of saving on prep time. If your market doesn't sell it, buy 1½ pounds zucchini, trim them, and slice a scant ¼ inch thick. The thinner the rounds, the shorter the cooking time.

"I especially like this tomato vinaigrette. You can use it on all types of fish. It's wonderful on grilled or pan-fried swordfish or tuna."

—minutemeals' Chef Hillary

step 1

microwave the **new potatoes**

1 pound very small new potatoes, each one pierced with fork

2 tablespoons water

1/4 cup chopped fresh parsley

1 tablespoon butter

1/4 teaspoon salt

Pinch of freshly ground black pepper

1. Pierce each potato with a fork.

2. Arrange the potatoes in a circle on a microwave-safe plate, sprinkle with the water. Cover tightly, microwave on High for 10 minutes.

3. Meanwhile, chop enough fresh parsley to measure 1/4 cup; reserve.

4. Add the butter and salt and pepper to the potatoes, toss to coat, and keep warm, covered.

step 2

oven-fry the **fish fillets;** make the **tomato vinaigrette**

For the fish fillets

Vegetable cooking spray

4 flounder fillets, each about 1/2 inch thick (1 1/4 pounds total weight)

3/4 cup yellow cornmeal

1/4 teaspoon salt

Pinch of fresh pepper

Pinch of cayenne pepper

1/2 cup milk

1 tablespoon olive oil

For the vinaigrette

1 1/2 tablespoons store-bought vinaigrette dressing

1 large tomato

1 tablespoon chopped fresh basil, dill, or parsley

1. Preheat the oven to 450°F. Line a baking sheet with foil and coat the foil with nonstick vegetable cooking spray. Rinse the flounder fillets and pat dry.

2. Cook the fish fillets: In a shallow dish, stir together the cornmeal, salt, and black and cayenne peppers. Pour the milk into another shallow dish.

3. Dip each flounder fillet in the milk, making sure both sides are well moistened, then dredge in the cornmeal mixture, pressing the coating on both sides. Place in 1 layer on the prepared baking sheet. Drizzle with the olive oil. Bake 8 to 10 minutes, until the fish just flakes when tested with a fork and coating on the fillets is crispy. Remove from the oven.

4. While the fillets are cooking, make the vinaigrette: Rinse and chop the tomato. Chop enough basil, dill, or parsley to measure 1 tablespoon.

5. In a small serving bowl, combine the vinaigrette, tomato, and herbs. Season with salt and pepper. Place the vinaigrette on the table.

step 3

sauté the **zucchini**

1 tablespoon olive oil

1 1/2 pounds zucchini slices

Salt and pepper to taste

In a 12-inch nonstick skillet, heat the olive oil over medium-high heat until hot. Add the zucchini and sauté, tossing frequently, about 4 minutes, until crisp-tender. Season with salt and pepper. Transfer to a serving bowl and place on the table.

step 4

serve

1. Place the potatoes in a serving bowl, add the chopped parsley, and toss. Place on the table.

2. With a spatula, transfer each flounder fillet to a dinner plate. Pass the tomato vinaigrette at the table as a sauce for spooning over the fillets.

3. When ready for dessert, serve the chocolate puddings.

Crispy Oven-Fried Flounder with Tomato Vinaigrette Menu
Single serving is 1/4 of the total menu, including dessert

CALORIES 576; PROTEIN 41g; CARBS 67g; TOTAL FAT 17g; SAT FAT 5g; CHOLESTEROL 89mg; SODIUM 816mg; FIBER 8g

26% of calories from fat

flounder fillets
with mustard, capers, and fennel seed
baby carrots with fresh dill
quick slaw
caramel pudding

menu gameplan

shopping list

Baby carrots

Fresh dill

Flounder fillets

Capers

Fennel seeds

Dry white wine

Pre-shredded green cabbage or coleslaw mix

from your pantry

Olive oil

Salt

Freshly ground black pepper

Country-style Dijon mustard

Dark brown sugar

Cornstarch

Low-fat (2%) milk

Rice vinegar

Sugar

serves 4

beforeyoustart
Preheat the oven to 425°F to roast the carrots and bake the fish.

step **1** roast the **baby carrots with fresh dill**

step **2** bake the **flounder fillets**

step **3** make the **caramel pudding**

step **4** prepare the **quick slaw**

step **5** **serve**

headsup
When the oven is set at 400°F or above, pay attention to whatever it is that you are cooking in the oven. Even a few extra minutes can mean the difference between done and overcooked.

"You do so little to the flounder here, but it ends up so flavorful. You don't feel as if you're eating 'low-fat' at all."

—minutemeals' Chef Marge

step 1

roast the **baby carrots with fresh dill**

1 package (1 pound) baby carrots

1 tablespoon olive oil

$1/2$ teaspoon salt

2 tablespoons snipped fresh dill

1. Preheat the oven to 425°F.

2. In a small casserole, toss the carrots with the olive oil and salt. Cover tightly and bake for 15 minutes, until tender.

step 2

bake the **flounder fillets**

4 fresh flounder fillets ($1^1/4$ pounds total weight)

2 tablespoons country-style Dijon mustard

$1/2$ teaspoon salt

Freshly ground black pepper to taste

1 tablespoon drained capers

1 teaspoon fennel seeds

$1/4$ cup dry white wine

1. Rinse the flounder fillets and pat dry. Arrange them in a shallow baking dish large enough to hold them in 1 layer without overlapping. Spread some of the mustard on each fillet and sprinkle the salt, pepper, capers, and fennel seeds over all. Pour the wine around the fillets. Cover the dish with foil and bake for 8 minutes.

2. Remove the foil carefully and bake the fillets another 3 to 4 minutes, just until cooked through.

step 3

make the **caramel pudding**

$1/3$ cup dark brown sugar

$1/4$ cup cornstarch

$1/8$ teaspoon salt

$2^1/2$ cups low-fat (2%) milk

In a medium saucepan, stir together the brown sugar, cornstarch, and salt, crushing any lumps in the brown sugar and cornstarch with the back of the spoon. Gradually stir in the milk until smooth. Place the pan over medium heat and, stirring constantly, bring to a boil. Boil, stirring, until thickened, about 1 minute. Remove from the heat. Pour into serving bowls and chill until serving time, if desired. The pudding can also be served warm.

step 4

prepare the **quick slaw**

2 tablespoons rice vinegar

1 teaspoon sugar

1 package (1 pound) pre-shredded cabbage or coleslaw mix

In a serving bowl, stir together the rice vinegar and sugar until the sugar is dissolved. Add the shredded cabbage and toss well to combine. Place on the table.

step 5

serve

1. Snip 2 tablespoons fresh dill directly over the carrots, toss, and place the casserole on the table.

2. Place 1 flounder fillet on each of 4 dinner plates. Serve immediately with the slaw as an accompaniment.

3. When ready for dessert, serve the pudding.

Flounder Fillets with Mustard, Capers, and Fennel Seeds Menu
Single serving is $1/4$ of the total menu, including dessert

CALORIES 404; PROTEIN 33g; CARBS 50g; TOTAL FAT 9g; SAT FAT 3g; CHOLESTEROL 79mg; SODIUM 958mg; FIBER 5g

25% of calories from fat

☆ roasted red snapper
with olive and tomato sauce

orzo with feta
steamed baby spinach
fresh berries with ladyfingers

menu gameplan

shopping list

Diced garlic-flavored tomatoes

Chopped green olives with pimientos

Lemon (for juice)

Fresh herbs, such as oregano, thyme, rosemary, basil, cilantro, chives, or parsley

Red snapper fillets

Orzo

Feta cheese

Prewashed baby spinach leaves

Fresh seasonal berries (such as blackberries, blueberries, and raspberries, 3 cups total)

Ladyfingers (4)

Lite Cool Whip

from your pantry

Salt

Onion

Garlic

Olive oil

Freshly ground black pepper

serves 4

beforeyoustart

Preheat the oven to 450°F. Bring a saucepan of water to a boil, covered. Rinse the berries.

step 1 cook the **tomato sauce;** roast the **snapper**

step 2 while the snapper roasts, cook the **orzo**

step 3 steam the **spinach**

step 4 **serve**

headsup
You will have at least 1, if not 2, partial bunches of fresh herbs left after making this meal. To store: Don't wash them. Put each bunch in a plastic bag, seal tightly, and place in the refrigerator. Basil, cilantro, and mint are especially perishable, so it is best to use those sooner rather than later. To use fresh basil, see Pesto Genovese on page 227.

"All this great food and just a little over 500 calories total. It goes to show just how good healthful cooking can be."

—minutemeals' Chef Miriam

step 1

make the **tomato sauce;** roast the **snapper**

For the tomato sauce

1 onion

2 garlic cloves

1 tablespoon olive oil

1 can (14 ounces) diced garlic-flavored tomatoes

1/4 cup chopped green olives with pimientos

2 tablespoons fresh lemon juice (1/2 large lemon)

1/2 teaspoon sugar

2 tablespoons chopped fresh herbs

For the fish fillets

4 red snapper fillets (1 1/4 pounds total weight)

1. Preheat the oven to 450°F.

2. Make the tomato sauce: Chop the onion; finely chop the garlic.

3. In a medium nonstick skillet, heat the olive oil over medium-high heat until hot. Add the onion and garlic and cook, stirring, until slightly softened, 2 to 3 minutes.

4. Add the tomatoes, olives, lemon juice, and sugar. Bring the mixture to a simmer and cook, stirring occasionally, for 5 minutes.

5. Chop the fresh herbs to equal 2 tablespoons. (If you want to add fresh herbs to the orzo as well, chop an additional 2 tablespoons at this time; reserve.)

6. Make the fish fillets: Rinse the snapper fillets and pat dry. Arrange them in a baking dish large enough to hold them in 1 layer without overlapping. Pour the tomato sauce over the fillets, making sure to cover each one. Roast for 8 to 10 minutes. Start checking for doneness around 7 minutes to avoid overcooking. Prod one of the fillets at its thickest point with a fork. It should be opaque, just beginning to flake, and release milky white, not clear or watery, juices. Remove from the oven.

step 2

while the snapper roasts, cook the **orzo**

Salt to taste

1 cup orzo

1 teaspoon olive oil

2 tablespoons feta cheese

Freshly ground black pepper to taste

1 tablespoon chopped fresh herbs, such as chives or parsley, or a mix

Fill a 2-quart saucepan with water, salt lightly, and cover. Bring to a boil over high heat. Add the orzo and cook 5 to 7 minutes, or until *al dente*. Drain, transfer to a serving bowl, and toss with the olive oil. Add the feta and freshly ground black pepper and toss again. Keep warm, covered.

step 3

steam the **spinach**

2 bags (10 ounces each) prewashed baby spinach leaves

Put the spinach in a large colander and run under cold water. Do not shake the water off the leaves. Tip the spinach into a large pot. Cover and place pot over high heat. Steam for 2 minutes, or just until spinach is wilted. Remove from the heat.

step 4

serve

1. If using fresh herbs with the orzo, add them and toss to combine. Spoon a serving of orzo onto each of 4 dinner plates.

2. Place a snapper fillet on each plate. Spoon the sauce over the fillets and the orzo. Divide the spinach among the plates and serve immediately.

3. When ready for dessert, place a ladyfinger in each dessert bowl and top with 3/4 cup of fresh berries and 1 tablespoon Cool Whip. Serve.

Roasted Red Snapper with Olive and Tomato Sauce Menu
Single serving is 1/4 of the total menu, including dessert

CALORIES 514; PROTEIN 33g; CARBS 70g; TOTAL FAT 11g; SAT FAT 3g; CHOLESTEROL 79mg; SODIUM 693mg; FIBER 11g

20% of calories from fat

salmon teriyaki
on gingered spinach

miso soup

cellophane noodles

mandarin oranges
with grand marnier

shopping list

Cellophane noodles

Mandarin oranges

Grand Marnier

Mint leaves (optional)

Instant miso soup

Firm tofu (optional)

Nori (optional)

Skinned salmon fillets

Low-sodium teriyaki basting
and glazing sauce

Prewashed baby spinach
leaves

Gingerroot

from your pantry

Salt and pepper

Vegetable cooking spray

Canola oil

Lite soy sauce

serves 4

beforeyoustart

Bring water to a boil in a large pot, covered, over high heat to cook the noodles.

step 1 cook the **cellophane noodles**; prepare the **mandarin oranges**

step 2 make the **miso soup**

step 3 cook the **salmon teriyaki**

step 4 wilt the **gingered spinach**

step 5 **serve**

 Even though there are
4 courses in this meal, 2 of
them—the soup and dessert—take only minutes to make.
Do take the time at the fish market or supermarket,
however, to have the salmon fillets skinned. It can be tricky
if you've never done it, and quite time-consuming, too.

"This meal is particularly pretty—with the pink of the salmon, the green of the spinach. Then you taste it, and it tastes lovely, too."

—minutemeals' Chef Hillary

step 1

cook the **cellophane noodles**; prepare the **mandarin oranges**

3 quarts water

Salt to taste (optional)

8 ounces cellophane noodles

2 cans (11 ounces each) mandarin oranges

2 tablespoons Grand Marnier

Mint leaves, for garnish (optional)

1. Pour the water into a large pot, salt lightly if desired, and cover. Bring to a boil over high heat. Add the cellophane noodles, stir to separate, and simmer until just tender, about 3 minutes. Drain.

2. Drain the oranges. Place in a serving bowl, drizzle with the Grand Marnier, and toss. Chill until serving time.

step 2

make the **miso soup**

4 packages instant miso soup

$1/2$ cup diced firm tofu (optional)

1 sheet nori (dried seaweed), cut into strips (optional)

1. In a large saucepan, make the soup according to the directions on the package. Keep warm until serving time.

2. If using the tofu and nori, dice enough tofu to measure $1/2$ cup; cut the sheet of nori into strips; reserve.

step 3

cook the **salmon teriyaki**

4 skinned salmon fillets (5 ounces each)

Salt and pepper to taste

Vegetable cooking spray

$1/4$ cup low-sodium teriyaki basting and glazing sauce

1. Rinse the salmon fillets and pat dry. Season on both sides with salt and pepper.

2. Spray a 12-inch nonstick skillet with vegetable cooking spray. Heat over medium heat until hot. Add the salmon fillets and cook for 2 to 3 minutes on each side, until opaque. Transfer the salmon to a platter, pour the teriyaki glaze over the fillets, and keep warm, covered.

step 4

wilt the **gingered spinach**

2 bags (10 ounces each) prewashed baby spinach leaves

2 tablespoons grated ginger (small knob fresh gingerroot)

2 teaspoons canola oil

2 tablespoons lite soy sauce

1. Stem the spinach, if necessary. Grate enough ginger to measure 2 tablespoons; reserve.

2. In a large nonstick saucepan, heat the canola oil over high heat until hot. Add the ginger and cook, stirring, for 1 minute. Add the spinach and cook, tossing constantly, until wilted, about 3 minutes.

Add the soy sauce and toss to coat spinach. Remove the pan from the heat.

step 5

serve

1. Add the tofu and nori to the miso soup, if using. Divide the soup evenly among 4 soup bowls and serve.

2. Divide the cellophane noodles evenly among 4 dinner plates. Top with a serving of the gingered spinach and a salmon fillet. Spoon some of the teriyaki glaze over all. Serve at once.

3. When ready for dessert, serve the chilled oranges in cups with some of the juice in the bowl spooned over the top. Garnish with fresh mint, if desired.

Salmon Teriyaki on Gingered Spinach Menu
Single serving is $1/4$ of the total menu, including dessert

CALORIES 500; PROTEIN 34g; CARBS 96g; TOTAL FAT 16g; SAT FAT 5g; CHOLESTEROL 94mg; SODIUM 1245mg; FIBER 7g

28% of calories from fat

spice-rubbed roasted tuna

white rice with cilantro, pimientos, and capers

steamed broccoli

pan-roasted pineapple with nonfat vanilla ice cream

shopping list

Cilantro

Chopped pimientos

Capers

Tuna steaks

Lemon

Broccoli florets
(pretrimmed, from the
salad bar or the produce
department)

Pineapple slices
(from the produce
department, or canned)

Nonfat vanilla ice cream

from your pantry

Long-grain rice

Sweet paprika

Dried oregano

Garlic powder

Cayenne pepper

Salt

Freshly ground black pepper

Canola oil

Sugar or honey

serves 4

beforeyoustart

Preheat the oven to 400°F to roast the salmon and dessert.

step	1	cook the **white rice**
step	2	prepare the **spice-rubbed roasted tuna**
step	3	steam the **broccoli**
step	4	pan-roast the **pineapple**
step	5	**serve**

luckyforyou If you make the spice rub
ahead, you'll save yourself
considerable prep time. And, if you'd prefer not to grind
1/2 teaspoon fresh pepper for the rub, use cracked pepper, which you can buy in a jar.

"The tuna is just spicy enough, but you can tame it if you like by cutting back on the peppers. The rice and pineapple balance the rub wonderfully."

—minutemeals' Chef Marge

step 1

cook the **white rice**

2 cups water

1 cup long-grain rice

1/3 cup chopped cilantro

2 tablespoons chopped jarred pimientos

1 tablespoon drained capers

1. Pour the water into a medium saucepan, cover, and bring to a boil over high heat. Add the rice, stir, and cover. Lower the heat and simmer for 15 minutes, or until the water has been absorbed. Remove from the heat and keep warm, covered.

2. While the rice cooks, chop enough cilantro to measure 1/3 cup; reserve.

step 2

prepare the **spice-rubbed roasted tuna**

For the spice rub

2 teaspoons sweet paprika

2 teaspoons dried oregano

1 teaspoon garlic powder

1 teaspoon cayenne pepper

1 teaspoon salt

1/2 teaspoon freshly ground black pepper

2 teaspoons water

For the tuna

4 tuna steaks, each 1/2 to 2/3 inch thick (1 pound total weight)

2 teaspoons canola oil

Lemon wedges, for serving

1. Preheat the oven to 400°F.

2. In a small bowl, stir together all the spice rub ingredients until smooth.

3. Rinse the tuna steaks and pat dry. Brush both sides of the tuna with 1 teaspoon canola oil. Smear the spice rub onto both sides of the tuna.

4. Brush a large, heavy ovenproof skillet (such as cast iron) with the remaining 1 teaspoon oil. Heat the skillet over high heat until it smokes. Add the tuna steaks in 1 layer and cook for 1 minute per side. Transfer the skillet to the oven and roast the tuna 6 to 8 minutes for medium-rare to medium, or until the fish is cooked to desired degree of doneness. Remove from the oven.

step 3

steam the **broccoli**

About 1 pound bright-green broccoli florets

Fit a large saucepan with a vegetable steamer basket, then add about 1 inch of water. Cover and bring to a boil over high heat. Carefully place the broccoli florets in the basket, cover the pan, and steam for 5 to 7 minutes, until crisp-tender. Transfer the broccoli to a bowl and place the bowl on the table.

step 4

pan-roast the **pineapple**

2 teaspoons sugar or honey

8 fresh pineapple slices or canned sliced pineapple rings, drained

1 cup nonfat vanilla ice cream, for serving

Sprinkle the sugar or drizzle the honey over the surface of a large nonstick skillet. Place the pineapple rings in a single layer in the pan and turn the heat to medium. Cook for 3 minutes per side. Remove the pan from the heat and keep warm.

step 5

serve

1. Add the cilantro, pimientos, and capers to the rice and toss.

2. Place 1 tuna steak on each of 4 dinner plates and garnish with a lemon wedge. Spoon a portion of the rice alongside. Serve with the steamed broccoli.

3. When ready for dessert, divide the pineapple rings among 4 dessert plates. Top with 1/4 cup nonfat ice cream and serve at once.

Spice-Rubbed Roasted Tuna Menu
Single serving is 1/4 of the total menu, including dessert

CALORIES 595; PROTEIN 43g; CARBS 85g; TOTAL FAT 11g; SAT FAT 2g; CHOLESTEROL 46mg; SODIUM 787mg; FIBER 5g

21% of calories from fat

pan-seared sea scallops

couscous with herbs

spinach, radicchio, and orange salad

warm sliced peaches with peach sorbet

serves 4

shopping list

Ripe peaches

Peach sorbet

Radicchio

Fennel seeds

Prewashed baby or flat-leaf spinach

Flavored or plain couscous

Fresh parsley, cilantro, or mint

Sea scallops

Fresh thyme

Dry white wine

from the salad bar

Orange slices

Red onion slices

from your pantry

Butter

Brown sugar

Extra virgin olive oil

Sherry or red wine vinegar

Salt

All-purpose flour

Ground cumin

Cayenne pepper

Freshly ground black pepper

menu gameplan

step **1** pan-roast the **peaches**

step **2** assemble the **spinach, radicchio, and orange salad**

step **3** prepare the **couscous with herbs**

step **4** cook the **pan-seared sea scallops**

step **5** **serve**

luckyforyou There are any number of ready-to-serve salad blends available. Use an Italian or European blend here if time runs short.

"Because they are special and often pricey, sea scallops make a wonderful party dish or special-occasion dinner."

—minutemeals' Chef **Marge**

step 1

pan-roast the **peaches**

2 large ripe peaches

1 tablespoon butter

2 tablespoons brown sugar

1 cup peach sorbet, for serving

1. Peel and slice the peaches.

2. Melt the butter in a medium saucepan. Add the sliced peaches and sprinkle with the brown sugar. Pan-roast, tossing gently until they begin to caramelize, about 6 minutes. Remove the pan from the heat and keep warm, partially covered.

step 2

assemble the **spinach, radicchio, and orange salad**

1 small head radicchio

1 teaspoon fennel seeds

2 tablespoons extra virgin olive oil

1 tablespoon sherry or red wine vinegar

1/4 teaspoon salt

5 ounces prewashed baby or flat-leaf spinach

1 cup orange slices

1/2 cup thin red onion slices

1. Tear the radicchio into bite-sized pieces. Crush the fennel seeds.

2. In a serving bowl, combine the olive oil, vinegar, fennel seeds, and salt. Add the spinach, radicchio, orange slices, and onion and toss. Refrigerate until serving time.

step 3

prepare the **couscous with herbs**

2 cups water

1 box (5.7 ounces) flavored or plain couscous

2 tablespoons chopped fresh parsley, cilantro, or mint

1. Pour the water into a 1- to 2-quart saucepan, cover, and bring to a boil over high heat. Stir in the couscous. Cover and remove from the heat. Let stand for 5 minutes, until the water is absorbed.

2. Chop enough fresh parsley, cilantro, or mint to measure 2 tablespoons; reserve until just before serving.

step 4

cook the **pan-seared sea scallops**

3 tablespoons all-purpose flour

1 teaspoon ground cumin

1 teaspoon chopped fresh thyme

1/2 teaspoon salt

1/4 teaspoon cayenne pepper, or to taste

1 pound sea scallops

1 tablespoon extra virgin olive oil

1/2 cup dry white wine

1. In a medium bowl, combine the flour, cumin, thyme, salt, and cayenne. Add the sea scallops and toss to coat.

2. In a nonstick skillet large enough to hold the scallops in a single layer without crowding, heat the olive oil and butter over medium-high heat. (If your skillet is not large enough to hold the scallops without crowding, use 2 skillets.) Add the scallops in a single layer and cook until golden brown and cooked through, about 3 minutes per side. Remove from the skillet and divide among 4 serving plates; keep warm.

3. Add the wine to the skillet, increase the heat to high, and boil until reduced by half, about 3 minutes. Spoon the pan sauce over the scallops.

step 5

serve

1. Divide the scallops among 4 plates.

2. Fluff the couscous with a fork, add the chopped herbs, and toss to combine. Add a serving of couscous to each of the dinner plates. Serve.

3. Grind fresh black pepper over the salad and place the bowl on the table.

4. When ready for dessert, divide the peach slices among 4 dessert bowls and top each serving with 1/4 cup of the peach sorbet. Serve immediately.

Pan-Seared Sea Scallops Menu
Single serving is 1/4 of the total menu, including dessert

CALORIES 503; PROTEIN 27g; CARBS 61g; TOTAL FAT 15g; SAT FAT 4g; CHOLESTEROL 47mg; SODIUM 758mg; FIBER 6g

26% of calories from fat

shrimp and green bean stir-fry

parsleyed vermicelli

blackberry and blueberry parfaits with lemon yogurt

menu gameplan

shopping list

Vermicelli or another thin-strand pasta

Fresh parsley

Blueberries, fresh or frozen

Blackberries, fresh or frozen

Nonfat lemon yogurt

Lemon juice

Gingerroot

Green beans

Medium shrimp, peeled and deveined

from your pantry

Olive oil

Cornstarch

Worcestershire sauce

Tomato paste

Hoisin sauce

Garlic

Toasted sesame oil

serves 4

beforeyoustart

Bring a large pot of water to a boil, covered, over high heat to cook the pasta.

step 1 cook the **vermicelli with chopped parsley**

step 2 prepare the **blackberry and blueberry parfaits with lemon yogurt**

step 3 cook the **shrimp and green bean stir-fry**

step 4 **serve**

luckyforyou You can skip chopping of any kind at all in the stir-fry: Buy pre-chopped garlic and ginger, available in jars in the produce department of many supermarkets.

"Chinese cooking often calls for a lot of oil. Not here—you use only 1 tablespoon and it is fragrant sesame oil."

—minutemeals' Chef Marge

step 1

cook the **vermicelli with chopped parsley**

4 quarts water

8 ounces vermicelli or
another thin-strand pasta

2 teaspoons olive oil

1/4 cup chopped fresh parsley

1. Pour the water into a large pot, cover, and bring to a boil over high heat. Add the pasta, stir to separate the strands, and cook according to the directions on the package, until *al dente*. Drain, transfer to a serving bowl, and add the olive oil. Toss to coat.

2. While the pasta is cooking, finely chop enough parsley to measure 1/4 cup.

3. Add the parsley to the pasta and toss well. Keep warm, covered.

step 2

prepare the **blackberry and blueberry parfaits with lemon yogurt**

1 cup fresh blueberries or
frozen, thawed

1 cup fresh blackberries
or frozen, thawed

2 containers (8 ounces each)
nonfat lemon yogurt

2 teaspoons fresh lemon juice

If using fresh berries, rinse each separately in a colander and gently shake dry. Place 1/4 cup blueberries in the bottom of each of 4 clear wine glasses. Top each serving with 1/2 container lemon yogurt. Sprinkle each with 1/2 teaspoon lemon juice. Divide the blackberries equally among the parfaits. Refrigerate until serving time.

step 3

cook the **shrimp and green bean stir-fry**

1 tablespoon cornstarch

1 teaspoon Worcestershire
sauce

1 tablespoon tomato paste

1 tablespoon hoisin sauce

1/2 cup water

2 garlic cloves

2 teaspoons minced ginger

12 ounces pre-trimmed
green beans

1 tablespoon toasted sesame oil

1 pound peeled and deveined
medium shrimp

1. Make the sauce: Place the cornstarch in a small cup and add the Worcestershire. Stir until blended. Stir in the tomato paste, hoisin sauce, and water until combined.

2. Finely chop the garlic and enough ginger to measure 2 teaspoons. Combine the garlic, ginger, and green beans in a bowl.

3. In a large nonstick skillet, heat the sesame oil over medium-high heat until hot. Add the seasoned green beans and stir-fry for 15 seconds. Add the shrimp and stir-fry for 30 seconds.

4. Stir the sauce, add it to the wok, and cook for about 4 minutes, stirring, until the shrimp turn pink and the sauce thickens slightly. Transfer the stir-fry to a serving dish.

step 4

serve

1. Place a serving of the pasta on each of 4 dinner plates.

2. Place the shrimp stir-fry on the table and serve at once over or alongside the pasta.

3. When ready for dessert, serve the parfaits.

Shrimp and Green Bean Stir-fry Menu
Single serving is 1/4 of the total menu,
including dessert

CALORIES 552; PROTEIN 33g; CARBS 87g;
TOTAL FAT 9g; SAT FAT 1g; CHOLESTEROL 163mg;
SODIUM 387mg; FIBER 8g

14% of calories from fat

quick-marinated beef kabobs

brown rice
peach chutney
strawberry slush

serves 4

shopping list

Strawberry sorbet

Frozen sliced strawberries

Lite frozen whipped cream/topping

Beef tenderloin

Red pepper

Mushrooms

Peach or mango chutney

Instant brown rice

from your pantry

Garlic

Olive oil

Balsamic vinegar

Onion

Salt and pepper

beforeyoustart

Preheat the broiler, or preheat the barbecue grill. Bring a 4-quart saucepan of water to a boil, covered, over high heat.

step **1** prepare the **strawberry slush**

step **2** assemble and grill the **quick-marinated beef kabobs**

step **3** prepare the **brown rice**

step **4** **serve**

luckyforyou Some supermarkets and specialty markets sell ready-to-cook beef (or chicken) and vegetable kabobs. Invest in those, and you've banked yourself valuable prep time.

"Kabobs make fun dinner-party fare, especially if you grill them on the barbecue."

—minutemeals' Chef Hillary

step 1

prepare the **strawberry slush**

3/4 cup strawberry sorbet

2 cups frozen sliced strawberries

1/2 cup lite frozen whipped cream/topping for serving

Place the sorbet in a microwave-safe dish and microwave on Medium-high to soften slightly, about 20 to 30 seconds. Stir in the sliced strawberries. Pour into a pie plate and freeze until serving time. (The slush will be only partially frozen when you serve it.)

step 2

assemble and grill the **quick-marinated beef kabobs**

1 pound beef tenderloin

2 garlic cloves

1 tablespoon olive oil

2 teaspoons balsamic vinegar

1 large onion

1 red pepper

8 medium mushrooms

1/2 cup peach or mango chutney, for serving

1. Preheat the broiler or barbecue grill. Bring a covered 4-quart sauce-pan of water to a boil, covered, over high heat.

2. Meanwhile, cut the beef tenderloin into 1-inch cubes. Finely chop the garlic. Place the tenderloin and garlic in a resealable plastic bag with the olive oil and balsamic vinegar. Let marinate at room temperature while you prepare the vegetables.

3. Cut the onion into 8 wedges. Cut the pepper into 8 squares. Stem the mushrooms, then wipe the caps clean. Blanch the onions and pepper in the saucepan of boiling water for 2 minutes; drain.

4. Thread the onion wedges, pepper squares, mushroom caps, and beef cubes onto 4 metal skewers, beginning and ending with an onion wedge. Broil or grill the kabobs, for about 5 minutes on each side or until cooked to desired doneness.

step 3

prepare the **brown rice**

2 cups water

Salt to taste

2 cups instant brown rice

Pour the water into a medium sauce-pan, salt lightly, and cover. Bring to a to boil over high heat. Stir in the rice, remove the pan from the heat, and let stand for 5 minutes, until the water is absorbed.

step 4

serve

1. Fluff the rice with a fork. Spoon a serving of rice onto each of 4 dinner plates, place a kabob on top, and serve with the peach chutney.

2. When ready for dessert, divide the strawberry slush among 4 dessert bowls. Top each serving with 2 tablespoons of the whipped topping and serve.

Quick-Marinated Beef Kabobs Menu
Single serving is 1/4 of the total menu, including dessert
CALORIES 566; PROTEIN 31g; CARBS 83g; TOTAL FAT 13g; SAT FAT 4g; CHOLESTEROL 71mg; SODIUM 215mg; FIBER 7g

20% of calories from fat

☆

molasses and black pepper pork tenderloin

smashed creamers

spinach salad with beets and pickled ginger vinaigrette

orange sorbet with fruit

menu gameplan

serves 4

beforeyoustart

Preheat the oven to 425°F to roast the pork tenderloin.

shopping list

Pork tenderloin

Creamers or small Yukon gold potatoes

Low-fat plain yogurt

Mandarin oranges

Frozen sliced peaches

Frozen berries

Orange sorbet

Pickled ginger

from the salad bar

Roasted beets (or jarred)

Baby or flat-leaf spinach

Red onion slices

from your pantry

Vegetable cooking spray

Molasses

Cracked black pepper

Ground cumin

Coarse salt

Fat-free reduced-sodium chicken broth

Salt and pepper

Canola oil

Rice vinegar

step 1 roast the **molasses and black pepper pork tenderloin**

step 2 while the tenderloin roasts, cook the **smashed creamers**

step 3 prepare the **dessert**

step 4 assemble the **spinach salad**

step 5 **serve**

headsup

Although the brief cooking time needed by the pork tenderloin is a boon to busy cooks, it also is not quite enough to impart a crispy, brown exterior to the meat. The molasses helps a bit. Here is a solution: If you can tolerate a bit more fat in the meal, try lightly browning the tenderloin first in a hot pan filmed with canola oil. Reduce the roasting very slightly if you sear the pork before roasting.

"This is a meat-and-potatoes dinner. Only this one, unlike so many others, is fairly low cal."

—minutemeals' Chef Marge

roast the **molasses and black pepper pork tenderloin**

Vegetable cooking spray

1 tablespoon molasses

2 teaspoons cracked black pepper

1/2 teaspoon ground cumin

1/2 teaspoon coarse salt

1 pound pork tenderloin

1. Preheat the oven to 425°F. Coat a small roasting pan or shallow baking dish with vegetable cooking spray.

2. In a small bowl, combine the molasses, pepper, cumin, and salt. Rub the mixture over the pork tenderloin.

3. Place the tenderloin in the prepared pan and roast in the center of the oven until a meat thermometer registers 155°F, 12 to 15 minutes. Remove the tenderloin to a cutting board.

step 2

while the tenderloin roasts, cook the **smashed creamers**

1 pound creamers or small Yukon gold potatoes

1/2 cup fat-free reduced-sodium chicken broth

1/4 cup low-fat plain yogurt

1/2 teaspoon salt

Pepper to taste

1. If the potatoes are very small, halve them; if larger, quarter them.

2. Put the potatoes in a medium saucepan and add water to cover. Bring to a boil over high heat. Simmer until tender when tested with a fork, 10 to 15 minutes.

3. Meanwhile, in a small saucepan, bring the chicken broth to a boil. Cover.

4. Drain the potatoes and return to the pan. Add the hot broth, and using a potato masher, smash them into pieces. (Do not "mash" them.) Beat in the yogurt, salt, and pepper, if desired. Keep warm, covered.

step 3

prepare the **dessert**

1 can (6 ounces) mandarin oranges

1/2 cup frozen sliced peaches

1/2 cup frozen berries

1 cup orange sorbet

1. Drain the mandarin oranges.

2. Thaw the sliced peaches and berries, if necessary in the microwave according to the directions on the packages.

3. In a bowl, combine the fruits and chill until serving time.

step 4

assemble the **spinach salad**

2 tablespoons canola oil

1 tablespoon rice vinegar

1 tablespoon thinly sliced pickled ginger

1/4 teaspoon salt

1 cup roasted beets, preferably in chunks, drained if from a jar

1 bag (5 ounces) baby or flat-leaf spinach

1/2 cup thin red onion slices

In a serving bowl, combine the canola oil, vinegar, pickled ginger, salt, and beets and toss to combine. Add the spinach and onion slices, toss well, and place the bowl on the table.

step 5

serve

1. Slice the pork tenderloin and arrange the slices on a serving platter. Place on the table.

2. Spoon a serving of the potatoes on each of 4 dinner plates. Serve at once, with the pork and salad alongside, or the salad on separate salad plates.

3. When ready for dessert, scoop 1/4 cup orange sorbet into 4 small bowls and top each serving with 1/4 cup of the fruit.

Molasses and Black Pepper Pork Tenderloin Menu
Single serving is 1/4 of the total menu, including dessert
CALORIES 596; PROTEIN 31g; CARBS 71g; TOTAL FAT 12g; SAT FAT 3g; CHOLESTEROL 67mg; SODIUM 970mg; FIBER 13g
20% of calories from fat

barbecued pork sandwiches

potato and green
bean salad

applesauce and cookies

menu
gameplan

serves 4

| step | 1 | cook the **barbecued pork sandwiches** |

| step | 2 | make the **potato and green bean salad** |

| step | 3 | **serve** |

shopping list

Pork tenderloin

Hard rolls, such as kaiser

Precut potatoes

Pre-trimmed green beans

Red onion slices
(from the salad bar)

Low-fat buttermilk

Caraway seeds

Applesauce
(no sugar added,
16-ounce jar)

Oatmeal raisin cookies,
such as Archway brand
(1 per person)

from your pantry

Ketchup

Spicy brown mustard

Molasses

Worcestershire sauce

Garlic powder

Onion powder

Ground ginger

Light mayonnaise

Red wine vinegar

Ground cumin

Light brown sugar

Ground cinnamon

headsup
You will have a considerable amount of buttermilk left over if you have had to buy it in a quart container. It is sometimes sold in pints, but may be difficult to find. Use what's left over as a substitute for regular milk in baking or for drinking.

"Go ahead, enjoy the potato salad. We've combined buttermilk with light mayonnaise for a wonderful low-cal 'take' on mayo."

—minutemeals' Chef Marge

step 1

cook the **barbecued pork sandwiches**

- 1 pound pork tenderloin
- 1 cup ketchup
- 2 tablespoons spicy brown mustard
- 1 tablespoon molasses
- 2 teaspoons Worcestershire sauce
- 1 teaspoon garlic powder
- 1 teaspoon onion powder
- 1/2 teaspoon ground ginger
- 2 hard rolls, such as kaiser rolls

1. Cut the pork tenderloin in half lengthwise and place 1/2 on your work surface; place a piece of plastic wrap over the top. With the bottom of a heavy skillet, lightly pound the tenderloin until 1/2 inch thick. Repeat with the remaining half, then cut the tenderloins crosswise into 1/2-inch-wide strips.

2. In a medium skillet, combine the ketchup, mustard, molasses, Worcestershire sauce, garlic powder, onion powder, and ginger and bring to a boil over medium-high heat. Immediately reduce the heat and simmer for 5 minutes.

3. Add the pork strips to the skillet and cook, stirring occasionally, for 10 minutes.

4. Meanwhile, split the 2 hard rolls in half horizontally. Place the halves in a toaster oven and toast until lightly colored.

step 2

make the **potato and green bean salad**

- 1 bag (16 ounces) precut potatoes
- 1/4 pound pre-trimmed fresh green beans
- 1/2 cup red onion slices
- 1/4 cup low-fat buttermilk
- 2 tablespoons light mayonnaise
- 1 to 2 tablespoons red wine vinegar
- 1 1/2 teaspoons caraway seeds
- 1/2 teaspoon ground cumin

1. Place the potatoes in a large saucepan, add enough cold water to cover them by 1 inch, and bring to a boil over high heat. Boil until tender when tested with a fork, 8 to 10 minutes.

2. Add the green beans to the pan for the last 2 minutes of cooking time. Drain immediately. Transfer the vegetables to a medium shallow salad bowl and add the onion slices.

3. While the potatoes are cooking, whisk together the buttermilk, mayonnaise, vinegar, caraway seeds, and cumin until combined. Pour the dressing over the still-warm vegetables and toss gently to combine. Let stand at room temperature.

step 3

serve

1. Place a kaiser roll half on each of 4 dinner plates. Spoon pork and barbecue sauce over each halved roll, and serve immediately with the potato and green bean salad.

2. When ready for dessert, spoon 1/2 cup applesauce into each dessert bowl and garnish each with an oatmeal raisin cookie. Serve.

Barbecued Pork Sandwiches Menu
Single serving is 1/4 of the total menu, including dessert

CALORIES 515; PROTEIN 33g; CARBS 77g; TOTAL FAT 9g; SAT FAT 2g; CHOLESTEROL 70g; SODIUM 1182mg; FIBER 7g

16% of calories from fat

lentil, sausage, and spinach stew
couscous with raisins
ambrosia

shopping list

Smoked turkey kielbasa

Lentil soup

Frozen chopped spinach

Frozen sliced carrots

Tomato juice

Fresh parsley

Plain couscous

Mandarin oranges

Ripe bananas

Shredded coconut

Fresh mint leaves (optional)

from your pantry

Vegetable cooking spray

Dijon mustard

Raisins

Cinnamon

serves 4

step **1** cook the **lentil, sausage, and spinach stew**

step **2** prepare the **couscous with raisins**

step **3** assemble the **ambrosia**

step **4** **serve**

headsup If you omit the sausage from the stew, this becomes a vegetarian meal. "Bulk" the stew back up with garbanzo beans or soy crumbles, if desired.

"Comfort food can also be good for you. This stew is a nice example of that . . . and so easy to make."

—minutemeals' Chef Marge

step 1

cook the **lentil, sausage, and spinach stew**

8 ounces smoked turkey kielbasa

Vegetable cooking spray

2 cans (19 ounces each) lentil soup

1 package (10 ounces) frozen chopped spinach

1 cup frozen sliced carrots

3/4 cup tomato juice

2 tablespoons Dijon mustard

1. Slice the kielbasa into generous 1/4-inch-thick slices.

2. Coat a medium nonstick skillet with cooking spray and heat over medium-high heat just until hot. Add the sausage slices and cook about 2 minutes, turn, and cook 2 minutes longer, until browned on both sides.

3. In a large saucepan, combine the lentil soup, spinach, carrots, and tomato juice. Bring to a boil over medium-high heat. Add the sausage and mustard and cook for about 8 minutes, until well combined and heated through.

step 2

prepare the **couscous with raisins**

2 tablespoons chopped fresh parsley

1 cup water

1/3 cup raisins

1/2 teaspoon ground cinnamon

1 cup plain couscous

1. Chop enough parsley to measure 2 tablespoons and place in a medium saucepan.

2. Add the water, raisins, and cinnamon. Cover and bring to a boil over medium-high heat. Stir in the couscous and remove the pan from the heat. Cover and let stand until the water is absorbed, about 7 minutes.

step 3

assemble the **ambrosia**

2 cans (11 ounces each) mandarin oranges

2 ripe large bananas

1/4 cup shredded coconut

Fresh mint leaves (optional)

1. Drain the oranges and place in a serving bowl.

2. Slice the bananas into the bowl and toss gently. Sprinkle the coconut over all. If using fresh mint, rinse and pat dry several large leaves. Tear into pieces and scatter over the fruit. Chill until serving time.

step 4

serve

1. Fluff the couscous with a fork, then ladle a serving into 4 large soup bowls. Top with lentil and sausage stew. Serve.

2. When ready for dessert, divide the ambrosia among 4 dessert bowls and serve.

Lentil, Sausage, and Spinach Stew Menu
Single serving is 1/4 of the total menu, including dessert

CALORIES 554; PROTEIN 26g; CARBS 68g; TOTAL FAT 7g; SAT FAT 2g; CHOLESTEROL 18mg; SODIUM 607mg; FIBER 26g

11% of calories from fat

☆ caribbean chicken

sweet potato puree with orange
chopped collard greens
coconut rice pudding

menu
gameplan

shopping list

Orange (for zest)

Canned sweet potatoes

Frozen chopped collard greens or kale

Lemon juice

Lite coconut milk

Lime (for juice)

Thin-sliced skinless boneless chicken breasts

from your pantry

Fat-free reduced-sodium chicken broth

Freshly ground black pepper

Sugar

Ground cinnamon or cardamon

Instant rice

Cider vinegar

Brown sugar

Garlic powder

Ground ginger

Ground allspice

Cayenne pepper

Canola oil

serves 4

step **1** make the **sweet potato puree with orange**

step **2** prepare the **chopped collard greens**

step **3** make the **coconut rice pudding**

step **4** cook the **caribbean chicken**

step **5** **serve**

lucky for you With the single exception of the lime, all the ingredients needed for the sauce on the chicken are standard pantry items.

"Thin-sliced skinless boneless chicken breasts are one of the best quick-cook items of all. They've even been trimmed!"

—minutemeals' Chef Marge

step 1

make the sweet potato puree with orange

1 teaspoon orange zest
(1 orange)

2 cans (15 ounces each)
sweet potatoes, drained

1/2 cup fat-free reduced-sodium
chicken broth

1. Grate enough orange zest to measure 1 teaspoon.

2. Place the drained sweet potatoes and chicken broth in a food processor and process until smooth.

3. Transfer the puree to a large microwave-safe bowl and stir in the orange zest. Microwave on High for 2 minutes. Stir and microwave for another 1 1/2 minutes. Keep warm.

step 2

prepare the chopped collard greens

2 packages (10 ounces each)
chopped frozen collard greens
or kale

Fresh lemon juice to taste

Freshly ground black pepper
to taste

Cook the collard greens or kale according to the directions on the package. Season with lemon juice and fresh pepper. Drain well and keep warm.

step 3

make the coconut rice pudding

2 cups lite coconut milk

1/2 cup sugar

2 teaspoons ground cinnamon
or cardamom

1 cup instant rice

In a medium saucepan, bring the coconut milk, sugar, and spices to a boil over medium-high heat, stirring to dissolve the sugar. Stir in the rice. Cover, remove the pan from the heat, and let stand for 5 minutes, or until the milk is absorbed. Divide the pudding among 4 custard cups and chill until serving time.

step 4

cook the caribbean chicken

For the sauce

2 tablespoons fresh lime juice
(1 large lime)

1 tablespoon cider vinegar

1 tablespoon brown sugar

1 teaspoon garlic powder

1 teaspoon ground ginger

1/2 teaspoon ground cinnamon

1/2 teaspoon ground allspice

1/8 to 1/4 teaspoon cayenne
pepper, or to taste

For the chicken

1 tablespoon canola oil

1 pound thin-sliced skinless
boneless chicken breasts

1. Combine the sauce: Squeeze 2 tablespoons fresh lime juice into a small bowl. Stir in the vinegar, brown sugar, garlic powder, ginger, cinnamon, allspice, and cayenne.

2. Cook the chicken: In a large nonstick skillet, heat the canola oil over medium heat. Add the chicken and cook for 2 minutes per side, until golden brown and the chicken lifts easily off the surface of the pan without sticking. Transfer to a platter and keep warm.

3. Pour the sauce mixture into the pan and cook, stirring, about 2 minutes. Return the chicken to the pan and heat it briefly. Remove the pan from the heat.

step 5

serve

1. Spoon a serving of sweet potato puree onto each of 4 dinner plates.

2. Toss the collard greens with lemon juice and add fresh pepper to taste. Add a serving to each plate.

3. Add a serving of chicken to each plate. Spoon sauce over both the chicken and the puree. Serve.

4. When ready for dessert, serve the rice puddings.

Caribbean Chicken Menu
Single serving is 1/4 of the total menu,
including dessert

CALORIES 503; PROTEIN 26g; CARBS 69g;
TOTAL FAT 13g; SAT FAT 6g; CHOLESTEROL 56mg;
SODIUM 221mg; FIBER 8g

22% of calories from fat

stir-fried chicken
with red pepper and snow peas

jasmine rice

cucumber and carrots vinaigrette

gingery lemon pudding

shopping list

Jasmine rice

Lemon juice

Gingerroot

Lemon pudding mix

Kirby cucumbers

Bean sprouts

Skinless boneless chicken breast cut for stir-fry

Stringed snow peas

from the salad bar

Shredded carrots
(or from the produce department)

Red pepper slices

Chopped scallions

from your pantry

Light corn syrup

Lite soy sauce

Rice vinegar

Toasted sesame oil

Garlic

Cornstarch

Fat-free reduced-sodium chicken broth

Canola oil

menu gameplan

serves 4

step **1** cook the **jasmine rice**

step **2** make the **gingery lemon pudding**

step **3** assemble the **cucumber and carrot vinaigrette**

step **4** make the **stir-fried chicken**

step **5** **serve**

luckyforyou Chicken is now available in packages already cut for stir-fry. Add it to your list of items tailor-made for the minute chef.

"This colorful easy stir-fry has all the appeal of a far more complicated dish. And it can be prepared in minutes."

—minutemeals' Chef Marge

step 1

cook the **jasmine rice**

1 1/2 cups jasmine rice

In a medium saucepan, cook the rice as suggested on the package. Keep warm, covered.

step 2

make the **gingery lemon pudding**

1/4 cup fresh lemon juice

2 quarter-size ginger slices

1 package 4-serving size cook-and-serve lemon pudding mix

1. Smash the slices of ginger with a large knife. Place the ginger slices in a medium saucepan.

2. Prepare the pudding in the saucepan as directed on the package but reduce the amount of water by 1/4 cup. Stir in the lemon juice once the pudding begins to thicken slightly. Cook to the desired consistency.

3. Remove the ginger slices, divide the pudding among 4 custard cups, and refrigerate until serving time.

step 3

assemble the **cucumber and carrots vinaigrette**

For the vinaigrette

1/4 cup light corn syrup

2 tablespoons lite soy sauce

2 tablespoons rice vinegar

1 teaspoon toasted sesame oil

For the salad

3 Kirby cucumbers

1/2 cup fresh bean sprouts

1/2 cup shredded carrots

1. Make the vinaigrette: In a glass measuring cup, combine the corn syrup, soy sauce, rice vinegar, and sesame oil. Stir well to combine.

2. Prepare the salad: Slice the cucumbers as thinly as possible on the diagonal. Rinse the bean sprouts.

3. In a bowl, combine the cucumber slices, bean sprouts and carrots. Add the vinaigrette and toss to combine. Refrigerate until serving time.

step 4

make the **stir-fried chicken**

2 garlic cloves

1 piece (a 1-inch knob) gingerroot

3 tablespoons lite soy sauce

2 tablespoons cornstarch

1 pound skinless boneless chicken breast cut for stir-fry

1 cup fat-free reduced-sodium chicken broth

1 teaspoon canola oil

1 cup red pepper slices

8 ounces stringed snow peas

1/4 cup chopped scallions

1. Mince the garlic. Peel and grate the ginger.

2. In a medium bowl, combine 2 tablespoons of the soy sauce, 1 tablespoon of the cornstarch, the garlic, and ginger and stir to combine. Add the chicken strips and toss to coat.

3. Put the remaining 1 tablespoon cornstarch in a small bowl and whisk in the remaining 1 table-spoon soy sauce and chicken broth.

4. In a large nonstick skillet, heat the oil over medium-high heat. Add the chicken and stir-fry until no longer pink, 4 to 5 minutes. Add the pepper slices, snow peas, and scallions, and stir-fry for 2 minutes.

5. Stir the broth mixture, add it to the skillet, and cook, stirring, until the sauce is thickened, 1 to 2 minutes.

step 5

serve

1. Place the salad on the table.

2. Fluff the rice with a fork. Divide the rice among 4 dinner plates and top with the chicken stir-fry.

3. When ready for dessert, serve the lemon puddings.

Stir-Fried Chicken with Red Pepper and Snow Peas Menu
Single serving is 1/4 of the total menu, including dessert

CALORIES 519; PROTEIN 27g; CARBS 92g; TOTAL FAT 5g; SAT FAT 1g; CHOLESTEROL 51mg; SODIUM 911mg; FIBER 4g

9% of calories from fat

golden chicken nuggets

boiled new potatoes
with garlic and parsley

mixed green salad

peaches with
raspberry sauce

menu gameplan

shopping list

Chicken tenders

Pre-trimmed and scrubbed
new potatoes

Grape tomatoes

Fresh parsley

Prewashed spring or
baby greens

Raspberries

Frozen sliced peaches

from your pantry

Vegetable cooking spray

All-purpose flour

Cornstarch

Cornflake crumbs

Eggs

Garlic

Olive oil

Salt

Low-fat vinaigrette dressing,
store-bought

Honey

serves 4

beforeyoustart

Preheat the oven to 375°F to cook
the chicken.

step	1	cook the **golden chicken nuggets**
step	2	cook the **boiled new potatoes with garlic and parsley**
step	3	assemble the **mixed green salad**
step	4	prepare the **peaches with raspberry sauce**
step	5	**serve**

luckyforyou

Chicken tenders give you
a big jump-start on the
preparation here.

"Wouldn't you rather decide what goes into the chicken nuggets you give your family? I would, which is why I created the recipe."

—minutemeals' Chef Marge

step 1

cook the **golden chicken nuggets**

Vegetable cooking spray

1 pound chicken tenders

2 tablespoons all-purpose flour

2 tablespoons cornstarch

2 large egg whites

3/4 cup cornflake crumbs

1. Preheat the oven to 375°F. Coat a baking sheet with cooking spray. Cut the chicken tenders in half crosswise.

2. Mix the flour and cornstarch together in a shallow bowl. In another bowl, beat the egg whites together lightly. Spread the cornflakes out on a plate.

3. Working with 1 piece of chicken at a time, dredge the chicken in the flour mixture. Dip it next into the egg whites, then roll in the cornflakes crumbs coating all sides.

4. Place the chicken pieces in 1 layer on the prepared baking sheet. Bake for 10 minutes, or until the pieces are cooked through.

step 2

cook the **boiled new potatoes with garlic and parsley**

1 pound pre-trimmed and scrubbed new potatoes

1 cup grape tomatoes

1/4 cup chopped fresh parsley

2 garlic cloves

1 tablespoon olive oil

Salt to taste (optional)

1. Place the potatoes in a medium saucepan, add water to cover, and bring to a boil over high heat. Simmer for 12 to 15 minutes, or until tender when tested with a fork.

2. While the potatoes cook, chop enough parsley to measure 1/4 cup; finely chop the garlic.

3. Drain the potatoes, place in a bowl, and add the grape tomatoes, parsley, garlic, and olive oil. Toss to combine. Sprinkle with salt, if desired, and place the bowl on the table.

step 3

assemble the **mixed green salad**

1 bag (5 ounces) prewashed spring or baby greens

2 tablespoons store-bought low-fat vinaigrette dressing

Place the greens in a salad bowl, add the vinaigrette, and toss to coat. Place the bowl on the table.

step 4

prepare the **peaches with raspberry sauce**

1 pint fresh raspberries

1 tablespoon honey

2 cups frozen sliced peaches

1. Rinse the raspberries in a colander and shake dry. Place in a food processor or blender. Add the honey and puree. Pour the sauce into a serving bowl.

2. Thaw the sliced peaches in a microwave oven according to the directions on the package.

step 5

serve

1. Divide the chicken nuggets among 4 dinner plates and serve immediately with the potatoes and salad.

2. When ready for dessert, divide the peaches among 4 dessert bowls. Serve with the raspberry sauce for spooning over the top.

Golden Chicken Nuggets Menu
Single serving is 1/4 of the total menu, including dessert

CALORIES 480; PROTEIN 33g; CARBS 65g; TOTAL FAT 10g; SAT FAT 2g; CHOLESTEROL 63mg; SODIUM 335mg; FIBER 8g

19% of calories from fat

turkey picadillo
mock guacamole
baked tortilla chips
sliced mango with mango sorbet

menu gameplan

shopping list

Corn tortillas
Green bell pepper
Raisins
Ground turkey breast
Black beans
Chili-style stewed tomatoes
Frozen peas
Chopped chiles
Cilantro or fresh parsley
Ripe avocado
Nonfat sour cream
Lime (for juice)
Medium mango
Mango sorbet

from your pantry

Vegetable cooking spray
Salt
Garlic cloves
Onion
Olive oil
Chili powder
Raisins
Garlic
Salt and pepper
Hot red pepper sauce (optional)

serves 4

beforeyoustart
Preheat the oven to 400°F to bake the tortilla chips.

step	1	bake the **baked tortilla chips**
step	2	make the **turkey picadillo**
step	3	prepare the **mock guacamole**
step	4	prepare the **sliced mango with mango sorbet**
step	5	**serve**

luckyforyou Dishes like picadillo (and chili) actually develop flavor if made in advance. Take a few minutes the day before you plan to serve the picadillo to whip up the batch. You'll be glad you did. All the flavors will have mellowed, and you'll have completed half of the menu.

"There's just enough avocado in the guacamole to make it work. But it's the smooth and creamy texture that keeps people coming back for more."

—minutemeals' Chef Hillary

step 1

prepare the **baked tortilla chips**

1 package (6 ounces) corn tortillas

Vegetable cooking spray

Salt (optional)

1. Preheat the oven to 400°F.

2. Meanwhile, stack the tortillas and cut them into quarters. Spread the tortilla quarters in a single layer on baking sheets, spray with vegetable cooking spray, and sprinkle with salt, if desired.

3. Bake until crisp and slightly golden, about 10 minutes. Transfer the chips to a large serving basket lined with paper napkins.

step 2

make the **turkey picadillo**

2 garlic cloves

1 small onion

1 small green bell pepper

2 teaspoons olive oil

2 teaspoons chili powder

3 tablespoons raisins

8 ounces ground turkey breast

1 can (15 ounces) black beans, drained

1 can (15 ounces) chili-style stewed tomatoes

1. Crush the garlic cloves through a press. Coarsely chop the onion and bell pepper.

2. In a large nonstick skillet, heat the olive oil over medium heat.

Add the chopped onion and bell pepper, the garlic cloves, and the chili powder and cook, stirring, 4 minutes or until softened. Add the raisins and cook for 1 for minute, stirring.

3. Add the turkey, and cook, breaking it up with a fork, for 5 minutes. Add the beans and tomatoes and simmer 5 minutes.

step 3

prepare the **mock guacamole**

1 cup frozen peas

1/4 cup water

1 can (4 1/2 ounces) chopped chiles

2 tablespoons chopped cilantro or fresh parsley

1 medium ripe avocado

1/4 cup nonfat sour cream

2 garlic cloves

1 tablespoon fresh lime juice

Salt and pepper to taste

Hot red pepper sauce (optional)

1. In a small saucepan, combine the frozen peas with the water, cover, and bring to the boil over medium heat. Cook for 2 minutes, drain, and rinse under cold water to stop the cooking process. Drain again and place in a food processor.

2. Drain the chiles. Chop enough cilantro or parsley to measure 2 tablespoons.

3. Peel the avocado. Roughly chop the flesh. Add to the food processor

with the sour cream, chiles, garlic, cilantro or parsley, and lime juice and process until smooth. Taste and season with salt and pepper and hot red pepper sauce, if desired.

step 4

prepare the **sliced mango with mango sorbet**

1 ripe medium mango

2 cups mango sorbet

With a vegetable peeler, remove the skin on the mango. With a sharp knife, cut the flesh off the pit. Cut into spears or coarsely chop. Reserve at room temperature.

step 5

serve

1. Scrape the guacamole into a wide shallow bowl and place on the table alongside the tortilla chips.

2. Ladle the picadillo into soup bowls and serve, with additional hot sauce on the table, if desired.

3. When ready for dessert, scoop 1/2 cup mango sorbet into each dessert bowl. Top or surround with the fresh mango.

Turkey Picadillo Menu
Single serving is 1/4 of the total menu, including dessert

CALORIES 569; PROTEIN 26g; CARBS 96g; TOTAL FAT 11g; SAT FAT 2g; CHOLESTEROL 41mg; SODIUM 912mg; FIBER 17g

17% of calories from fat

pasta with three mushroom sauce

arugula and spring green salad

seeded semolina bread

orange-scented stewed plums

shopping list

Rotini or other short pasta

Shiitake mushrooms

Portobello mushrooms (stemmed and presliced, if available)

Cremini mushrooms (stemmed and presliced, if available)

Tomatoes

Dry red wine

Canned purple plums, packed in water

Orange slices (from the salad bar)

Prewashed arugula, stemmed

Prewashed spring or baby greens

Seeded semolina bread

from your pantry

Onion

Garlic

Extra virgin olive oil

Dried marjoram

Salt and pepper

Grated Parmesan cheese (optional)

Sugar

Cinnamon stick

Low-fat salad dressing, preferably balsamic dressing

serves 4

beforeyoustart

Bring the water in a large pot, covered, to a boil over high heat to cook the pasta.

step 1 make the **pasta with three mushroom sauce**

step 2 make the **orange-scented stewed plums**

step 3 assemble the **arugula and spring green salad**

step 4 serve

headsup

Arugula is a peppery green that adds a lot to a simple salad. Unless you can purchase it prewashed and ready to use, however, it will have to be rinsed and spun dry because it can be very gritty. If you haven't the time, omit it from the salad.

"I used a small amount of red wine in the mushroom sauce. If you don't cook with wine, use ¹/₂ cup reduced-sodium chicken broth."

—minutemeals' Chef Marge

step 1

make the **pasta with three mushroom sauce**

For the pasta

3 quarts water

8 ounces rotini or other short pasta

For the sauce

1 small onion

4 garlic cloves

1 box (3¹/₂ ounces) shiitake mushrooms

³/₄ pound portobello mushrooms

1 box (10 ounces) cremini mushrooms

2 cups chopped ripe tomatoes (4 medium tomatoes)

2 tablespoons extra virgin olive oil

¹/₂ cup dry red wine

¹/₂ teaspoon dried marjoram

¹/₂ teaspoon salt

¹/₄ teaspoon pepper

¹/₄ cup grated Parmesan cheese, for serving (optional)

1. Cook the pasta: Pour the water into a large pot, cover, and bring to a boil over high heat. Add the rotini, stir to separate, and cook according to the directions on the package, until *al dente*. Drain, return to the pot, and keep warm, covered.

2. Prepare the sauce: Chop the onion and finely chop the garlic. Stem the shiitakes, then clean and quarter the caps. Cut the portobello mushroom caps into ¹/₄- by 2-inch slices.

Stem the cremini mushrooms, and slice the caps. Chop the tomatoes to measure 2 cups.

3. In a large nonstick skillet, heat 1 tablespoon of the olive oil over medium heat until hot. Add the onion and garlic and cook, stirring, for 2 minutes, or until softened. Add all the mushrooms and cook, stirring, for 1 minute. Add the tomatoes and stir to combine. Add the red wine and cook, stirring, for 5 minutes.

4. Stir in the remaining tablespoon olive oil, the marjoram, salt, and pepper, and cook for 3 to 4 minutes. Add the cooked rotini to the mushroom sauce and toss to combine and heat through, if necessary.

step 2

prepare the **orange-scented stewed plums**

¹/₄ cup sugar

¹/₄ cup water

2 cups pitted canned purple plums packed in water

2 orange slices

1 cinnamon stick, about 1 inch long

In a medium saucepan, combine the sugar and water over medium heat, stirring until the sugar is dissolved. Add the remaining ingredients and bring to a boil. Simmer, stirring occasionally, for 5 minutes.

step 3

assemble the **arugula and spring green salad**

2 ounces prewashed stemmed arugula

6 ounces prewashed spring or baby greens

3 tablespoons low-fat salad dressing, preferably balsamic dressing

1. Drain the plums.

2. In a salad bowl, combine the arugula with the baby greens. Add the dressing and toss to coat. Place the bowl on the table.

step 4

serve

1. Serve the pasta in 4 bowls with the Parmesan for sprinkling over the top, if desired. Serve with the semolina bread and the mixed green salad.

2. When ready for dessert, divide the plums among dessert bowls and serve with the cooking syrup spooned over the top.

Pasta with Three Mushroom Sauce Menu
Single serving is ¹/₄ of the total menu, including dessert

CALORIES 497; PROTEIN 11g; CARBS 108g; TOTAL FAT 2g; SAT FAT 0g; CHOLESTEROL 0mg; SODIUM 273mg; FIBER 11g

4% of calories from fat

penne in cream sauce
with vegetables

greens with fresh fruit and balsamic vinegar

strawberry, kiwi, and banana frappes

menu
gameplan

shopping list

Penne

Green beans

Broccoli florets
(from the salad bar or
produce department)

Whole tomatoes

Fresh basil

Fat-free sour cream

Kiwi

Strawberries

Banana

Fat-free frozen ice cream,
yogurt, or sorbet

Prewashed arugula

Peaches, nectarines,
or raspberries

from your pantry

Onion

Garlic

Olive oil

Skim milk

Grated Parmesan cheese

Ground nutmeg

Fat-free milk

Extra virgin olive oil

Balsamic vinegar

Freshly ground black pepper

serves 4

beforeyoustart

Bring the water in a large pot, covered,
to a boil over high heat to cook
the pasta.

step **1** cook the **penne in cream sauce with vegetables**

step **2** Make the **strawberry, kiwi, and banana frappes**

step **3** assemble the **greens**

step **4** **serve**

luckyforyou Broccoli florets are sold pre-trimmed and ready to use, which saves on prep and clean-up time, too.

"This homey menu fills me up and makes me happy. And the really good news is that my weight's the same the next day!"

—minutemeals' Chef Marge

step 1

cook the **penne in cream sauce with vegetables**

For the pasta

3 quarts water

8 ounces penne

For the sauce

1 pound fresh green beans

8 ounces broccoli florets

1 small onion

2 garlic cloves

1 can (28 ounces) whole tomatoes, drained

2 tablespoons fresh basil

2 teaspoons olive oil

1/2 cup fat-free sour cream

2 tablespoons skim milk

1/4 cup grated Parmesan cheese

Pinch ground nutmeg

1. Cook the pasta: Pour the water into a large pot, cover, and bring to a boil over high heat. Add the penne, stir to separate, and cook according to the directions on the package until barely *al dente*.

2. Meanwhile, slice the green beans in half. Add the beans and the broccoli florets to the pasta for the last 3 minutes of cooking time. Drain the pasta and vegetables and return to the pot.

3. Make the sauce: Chop the onion and the garlic. Drain the tomatoes and chop coarsely. Slice or tear enough fresh basil to equal 2 tablespoons.

4. In a large nonstick skillet, heat the olive oil over medium heat until hot. Add the onion and garlic and cook, stirring, until softened, about 3 minutes. Add the tomatoes and cook, stirring occasionally, until hot, about 4 minutes.

5. Remove the skillet from the heat and stir in the basil, sour cream, skim milk, Parmesan, and nutmeg until combined. Pour the cream sauce over the pasta and toss thoroughly to coat and combine. Keep warm, covered.

step 2

make the **strawberry, kiwi, and banana frappes**

1 ripe peeled kiwi fruit

10 strawberries

1 medium banana

1 1/2 cups fat-free milk

2 scoops fat-free ice cream, yogurt, or sorbet

1. Peel the kiwi. Rinse and hull the strawberries. Chop the banana into chunks.

2. Combine all the ingredients in a blender and mix until just combined. Chill in the blender container until serving time.

step 3

assemble the **greens**

8 ounces prewashed arugula

2 teaspoons extra virgin olive oil

2 ripe peaches or nectarines, or 1/2 pint fresh raspberries

Balsamic vinegar, for serving

Freshly ground black pepper to taste

1. Wash and dry the arugula leaves.

2. In a large bowl, toss the arugula with the olive oil. Divide the greens among 4 salad plates.

3. If using peaches or nectarines, slice each into 8 pieces. Arrange the slices or raspberries on the arugula.

step 4

serve

1. Divide the pasta among 4 pasta bowls.

2. Place the salads on the table. Pass balsamic vinegar and a pepper mill at the table for the salad.

3. When ready for dessert, serve the frappes in tall glasses or mugs.

Penne in Cream Sauce with Vegetables Menu
Single serving is 1/4 of the total menu, including dessert

CALORIES 505; PROTEIN 21g; CARBS 91g; TOTAL FAT 9g; SAT FAT 2g; CHOLESTEROL 7mg; SODIUM 449mg; FIBER 13g

15% of calories from fat

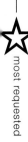

☆ salad pizza
roasted bananas with low-fat vanilla frozen yogurt

menu
gameplan

serves 6

beforeyoustart

Preheat the oven to 450°F to bake the pizza.

step **1** make the **salad pizza**

step **2** prepare the **roasted bananas with low-fat vanilla frozen yogurt**

step **3** **serve**

shopping list

Prebaked pizza crust
(12-inch diameter)

White beans

Prewashed spring or
baby salad greens

Cherry tomatoes
(from the salad bar)

Roasted peppers

Capers

Grated lite mozzarella

Bananas

Low-fat vanilla frozen yogurt

from your pantry

Extra virgin olive oil

Balsamic vinegar

Dijon mustard

Salt and pepper

Vegetable cooking spray

 Don't confuse light mozzarella
with part-skim mozzarella.
Part-skim is somewhat higher in both fat and calories.
You want light mozzarella here.

"People love this pizza. Here is a way to have pizza and still be watching your weight. And on this pizza you get salad, too!"

—minutemeals' Chef Marge

step 1

make the **salad pizza**

1 12-inch prebaked pizza crust (16 ounces)

1 can (15 ounces) white beans, drained

8 cups prewashed spring or baby greens

1 cup cherry tomatoes (about 8 large)

1 jar (7 ounces) roasted peppers

2 tablespoons drained capers

2 tablespoons extra virgin olive oil

1 tablespoon balsamic vinegar

1/2 teaspoon Dijon mustard

Salt and pepper to taste

1/2 cup grated lite mozzarella

1. Preheat the oven to 450°F. Place the pizza crust on a large side-less baking sheet.

2. While the oven heats, prepare the topping: Drain and rinse the white beans. Cut the salad greens into 1-inch pieces. Lightly mash about half the beans with the back of a fork. In a bowl, toss the greens and beans together.

3. Cut the tomatoes into quarters. Drain the jar of roasted peppers and cut the peppers into 1/2-inch pieces. Add the peppers, tomatoes, capers, and remaining beans to the salad mixture.

4. In a small bowl, combine the olive oil, balsamic vinegar, mustard, and salt and pepper to taste. Add the dressing to the salad mixture and toss to combine.

5. Top the pizza crust with the salad mixture, then scatter the grated mozzarella over the top. Bake for 10 minutes.

step 2

prepare the **roasted bananas with low-fat vanilla frozen yogurt**

Vegetable cooking spray

3 large firm-but-ripe bananas

1 1/2 cups low-fat vanilla frozen yogurt, softened

1. Do not turn the oven off after baking the pizza. Spray a large baking sheet with sides lightly with vegetable cooking spray.

2. Peel the bananas, then halve them crosswise and lengthwise to make 12 spears. Arrange the banana pieces in a single layer on the baking sheet. Roast the bananas for 5 to 7 minutes, or until lightly golden and hot.

step 3

serve

1. With a pizza cutter or sharp knife, cut the pizza into wedges and serve at once. (Forks and knives are recommended.)

2. When ready for dessert, serve the roasted bananas while still hot, each serving of 2 pieces topped with 1/4 cup of the frozen yogurt.

Salad Pizza Menu
Single serving is 1/6 of the total menu, including dessert

CALORIES 435; PROTEIN 17g; CARBS 72g; TOTAL FAT 11g; SAT FAT 3g; CHOLESTEROL 4mg; SODIUM 887mg; FIBER 7g

21% of calories from fat

creamy pumpkin soup

corn bread

mixed greens vinaigrette

pears poached in red wine

shopping list

Corn bread mix

Frozen corn

Bosc pears

Dry red wine

Lemon

Canned pumpkin

Plain soy milk

Pumpkin seeds (optional)

Prewashed mixed lettuces

from your pantry

Egg

Low-fat (1%) milk

Sugar

Cinnamon stick

Onion

Olive oil

Ground cumin

Ground ginger

Fat-free low-sodium chicken broth or vegetable broth

Salt and pepper

Cayenne pepper (optional)

Low-fat vinaigrette dressing, store-bought

serves 4

beforeyoustart

Preheat the oven to 400°F.

step	1	bake the **corn bread**
step	2	prepare the **pears poached in red wine**
step	3	make the **creamy pumpkin soup**
step	4	assemble the **mixed greens vinaigrette**
step	5	**serve**

headsup

Soy milk is available plain or flavored. For this recipe it is best to use plain soy milk. Look for soy milk in the dairy section of most supermarkets. It is also sold in boxes on the shelf. One important point when cooking with soy milk: Do not allow it to boil.

"This soup is creamy, but does not contain cream. It has a lovely seasonal quality about it. You smell the soup cooking and you know it's fall."

—minutemeals' Chef Linda

bake the **corn bread**

1 large egg

1/3 cup low-fat (1%) milk

1 box (8 1/2 ounces) corn bread or muffin mix

1 box (10 ounces) frozen corn

1. Preheat the oven to 400°F. Grease a 10-inch cast-iron skillet.

2. Combine the egg, milk, and muffin mix in a bowl, and stir just until combined. Stir in the frozen corn.

3. Spread the batter in the prepared skillet, and bake until firm and golden, about 10 minutes.

step 2

prepare the **pears poached in red wine**

2 ripe Bosc pears

3/4 cup water

3/4 cup dry red wine

1/4 cup sugar

1/2 lemon

1 cinnamon stick, 1 inch long

1. Peel, halve, and core the pears. Cut in half.

2. In a small saucepan, combine the water, wine, sugar, lemon, and cinnamon stick. Heat over medium heat, stirring, until the sugar is dissolved. Add the pears and turn to coat them in the syrup. Cover and simmer for 15 minutes.

3. Remove the pan from the heat.

step 3

make the **creamy pumpkin soup**

1 small onion

1 tablespoon olive oil

1 teaspoon ground cumin

1/2 teaspoon ground ginger

1 can (29 ounces) pumpkin (puree, not pie filling)

2 cups fat-free reduced-sodium chicken or vegetable broth

Salt and pepper to taste

1/4 teaspoon cayenne pepper (optional)

1 1/2 cups plain soy milk

3 tablespoons pumpkin seeds, toasted, for garnish (optional)

1. Dice the onion.

2. In a large saucepan, heat the olive oil over medium heat. Add the onion and cook, stirring, until softened, about 3 minutes.

3. Add the cumin and ginger and cook, stirring, for 1 minute. Whisk in the pumpkin and chicken or vegetable broth until combined. Bring the soup to a boil, cover, lower the heat, and simmer, stirring occasionally, for 5 to 7 minutes.

4. Add salt, pepper, and a pinch of cayenne, if desired. Stir in the soy milk and bring the soup to a low simmer. Do not allow it to come to a full boil. Remove the pan from the heat.

step 4

assemble the **mixed greens vinaigrette**

1 bag (10 ounces) prewashed mixed lettuces

3 tablespoons store-bought low-fat vinaigrette dressing

Place the lettuce in a large salad bowl, add the vinaigrette, and toss. Place the bowl on the table, with 4 salad plates.

step 5

serve

1. Place the skillet of corn bread on the table and cut into wedges.

2. Ladle the soup into individual serving bowls. Serve immediately with the salads.

3. When ready for dessert, serve the poached pears in small dessert bowls with some of the poaching syrup spooned over each serving.

Creamy Pumpkin Soup Menu
Single serving is 1/4 of the total menu, including dessert

CALORIES 507; PROTEIN 22g; CARBS 63g; TOTAL FAT 9g; SAT FAT 0g; CHOLESTEROL 51mg; SODIUM 750mg; FIBER 20g

15% calories from fat

a

Almond macaroons, store-bought, 42–43

Almonds, smoked, broccoli with, 94–95

Amaretto Ice Cream with Amaretti Cookies, store-bought, 218–19

Ambrosia, 294–95

Antipasto Platter, 242–43

Apple Berry Salad, 14–15

Apple Crumb Cake, store-bought, 126–27

Apple Pie with Cinnamon Ice Cream, store-bought, 66–67

Applesauce, store-bought

    and cookies, 292–93

    with heavy cream and gingersnaps, 2–3

Apple Wedges and Orange Sections, store-bought, 78–79

Apricot sauce, pork medallions in, 150–51

Apricots, chilled, 92–93

Artichokes

    broiled sole with potatoes and, 184–85

    greens with cherry tomatoes and, 194–95

    marinated, roasted peppers, and olives, 220–21

    mushrooms and, marinated, 244–45

Arugula

    bocconcini with, 228–29

    sautéed, 178–79

    with Sliced Beefsteak Tomatoes, 254–55

    and Spring Green Salad, 304–5

Asian sauce, microwave pork and broccoli with, 144–45

Asian Turkey Pot Stickers, 92–93

Asparagus

    beef and, stir-fry, 110–11

    capellini with ham and, 218–19

    steamed, 186–87

    tip about, 110

b

Avocado

    and olive salad, 196–97

    tomato, and cucumber salad, 86–87

    yellow tomato and, salad, 90–91

Babas au Rhum or Rum Raisin Ice Cream, store-bought, 266–67

Baby carrots. *See* Carrots, baby

Baby Lettuce and Black Olive Salads, 6–7

Baby Peas with Endive, 182–83

Bacon, Canadian, and Monterey Jack cheese sandwiches, 160–61

Baguette, store-bought

    French, 36–37

    sourdough, 222–23

Baked Tortilla Chips, 302–3

Baklava, store-bought, 138–39

Balsamic-honey glaze, roasted pork medallions with, 152–53

Balsamic-orange sauce, salmon with, 180–81

Balsamic vinegar

    greens with fresh fruit and, 306–7

    vinegar, strawberries with, 256–57

Banana(s)

    in Ambrosia, 294–95

    chilled plums and, with vanilla yogurt, 28–29

    chutney, gingery, 70–71

    kiwi, and strawberry frappes, 306–7

    roasted, with low-fat vanilla frozen yogurt, 308–9

    splits à la minute, 208–9

Barbecued Flank Steak, 114–15

Barbecued Pork Sandwiches, 292–93

Basil, tip about, 40, 256

Basil cream sauce, tortellini with vegetables in, 256–57

Basmati Rice, 70–71, 88–89

Bean sprout(s)

    with Snow Peas, 170–71

    watercress and, salad, 118–19

Bean(s). *See also* Chili

    black, refried, 90–91

    black, and rice, 266–67

    black, soup, with smoked ham, microwave, 2–3

    cannellini, orecchiette with sausage, tomatoes, and, 238–39

    green, couscous with chickpeas and, 142–43

    green, potato and, salad, 292–93

    green, salad, 100–101

    green, shrimp and, stir-fry, 286–87

    green, steamed, 60–61

    green, with almonds, 66–67

    green, with browned-in-butter pine nuts, 174–75

    three-, greens and, salad, 130–31

    tip about, 2

    white, and pasta soup, 4–5

    white, shrimp and, salad, 48–49

    white, tortellini in broth with baby spinach and, 12–13

Beef

    and asparagus stir-fry, 110–11

    and brown rice salad with roasted vegetables, 34–35

    Chicken Fried Steak, 116–17

    Hamburger Pie, 128–29

    Hamburger Stroganoff, 126–27

    kabobs, quick-marinated, 288–89

    Meatball and Pepper Subs, 130–31

    Microwave Southwestern Chili with All the Fixin's, 136–37

    Roquefort Burgers, 122–23

    salad, Southeast Asian, 36–37

    Saucy Mini Meat Cakes, 124–25

    Sliced Steak with Asian Vegetables, 118–19

    Stroganoff, 120–21

    and vegetable soup, 16–17

Beets, spinach salad with pickled ginger vinaigrette and, 290–91

Beets Vinaigrette on Mixed Greens, 22–23

f

t

Tangerines and Almond Cookies, store-bought, 60–61

Tapenade, olive-caper, flounder with, 164–65

Tarragon Chicken with Mushrooms and Onions, 88–89

Tart, fruit, store-bought, 112–13

Tartar Sauce, store-bought, 172–73

Tartlettes, fruit, store-bought, 226–27

Teriyaki, salmon, on gingered spinach, 280–81

Thai Chicken Curry, 82–83

Tiramisù, store-bought, 134–35

Toasted sesame oil, tip about, 144

Toasts

    garlic, 194–95

    Parmesan, 100–101

    sesame cheese, 14–15

Toasty Olive Bread, 50–51

Tofu, gingery chicken vegetable soup with, 18–19

Tomato(es)

    and balsamic sauce, uncooked, pasta with, 242–43

    and basil focaccia, 40–41

    beefsteak, sliced, arugula with, 254–55

    cherry, sautéed, turkey meatballs, Italian, with, 102–3

    cherry, snow peas and, sautéed, with garlic, 68–69

    cucumber, and chickpea salad, 172–73

    juice with lemon, 200–201

    and mozzarella salad, 240–41

    olive and, sauce, roasted red snapper with, 278–79

    olive, and feta salsa, 138–39

    orecchiette with sausage, beans, and, 238–39

    and pepper toss, 122–23

    and red onion salad, 212–13

    and romaine salad, 76–77

    sauce, 164–65

    and scallion salad, 226–227

    sliced, and red onion with olive oil and basil, 46–47

    sliced, with basil, 134–35

    sun-dried, butter, sole fillets with, 182–83

    sun-dried, pesto, rigatoni with, 250–51

    vine-ripened, sliced, 222–23

    vine-ripened, tip about, 46

Tonnato, turkey cutlets, 100–101

Topping

    biscuit, microwave turkey pot pie with, 104–5

    blueberry, cheesecake with, store-bought, 84–85

Tortellini

    in broth with baby spinach and beans, 12–13

    cooking tip about, 12

    with vegetables in basil cream sauce, 256–57

Tortilla(s)

    casserole, 90–91

    chips, baked, 302–3

    flour, store-bought, 136–37

Toss, tomato and pepper, 122–23

Tossed Salad with Cherry Tomatoes, 24–25

Tostadas, vegetable, 106–7

Tuna

    puttanesca, pasta, 240–41

    roasted, spice-rubbed, 282–83

    salad niçoise, 52–53

    sauce, 100–101

    steaks, spicy grilled, 190–91

    steaks with green peppercorn vinaigrette, 188–89

    tip about, 188

Turkey

    burgers, spicy, on whole-grain buns, 96–97

    chili, white, 106–7

    chowder, 22–23

    cutlets in mustard cream sauce, 98–99

    cutlets tonnato, 100–101

    and fettuccine with mushroom garlic cream sauce, 94–95

    meatballs, Italian, with sautéed cherry tomatoes, 102–3

    picadillo, 302–3

    pot pie, microwave, with biscuit topping, 104–5

    pot stickers, Asian, 92–93

    sausages, grilled, 158–59

    smoked, with couscous salad on arugula, 42–43

    and walnut salad, 40–41

v

Vanilla frozen yogurt, store-bought

    with fresh strawberries, 140–41

    with gingersnap crumble, 118–19

Vanilla ice cream, store-bought

    with candied ginger, 110–11

    with dark cherries and chocolate sauce, 190–91

    with maple syrup and sliced peaches, 176–77

    with sliced bananas and caramel sauce, 258–59

    with sliced bananas and chocolate sauce, 58–59

Veal Marsala (Veal in Wine Sauce), 134–35

Vegetable(s). See also specific names

    Asian, sliced steak with, 118–19

    beef and, soup, 16–17

    chicken and, baked in foil, 64–65

    and chicken soup, gingery, with tofu, 18–19

    packages, red snapper with, 168–69

    roasted, beef and brown rice salad with, 34–35

    salad, marinated, 8–9

    soup, fresh, 14–15

    sticks, 2–3

    tortellini with, in basil cream sauce, 256–57

    tostadas, 106–7

W

Y

Z